Secrets Of Cruising: *The N*

D1553960

British Columbia Coast
&
Undiscovered Inlets

By Hugo Anderson

Dedication

To my wife, Rachel, who has been my constant travelling companion and mate, and who has contributed to and worked on this book with me; and to my editors, and good friends, Gwen and Phil Cole, for their assistance and direction.

Also to the thousands of boaters we hope will enjoy visiting the memorable passages, inlets, bays, and anchorages described in this book, as we have enjoyed them. This book can serve as a guide for those who take their maiden voyages to these wonderful waters, or to introduce new waterways to more seasoned boaters.

First Edition: 1995. Printed in U.S.A. ISBN 0-945989-25-3

1

Editor's Preface

Hugo Anderson is the most modest and unassuming man we have ever met. It requires spending more than a casual amount of time with him to find out just how deep his still waters run. When we first proposed the title "Secrets of Cruising" for this series, Hugo objected, saying, "I don't know any secrets". As we edited the first book, *North To Alaska,* we noted the wealth of useful and hard-to-come-by information. He finally relented in regard to the title.

This second book is packed full of such information, and includes hundreds of revelations of NEW SECRETS about the undiscovered inlets of the Northern British Columbia Coast.

If you have a sense of, and desire for, adventure; if you ever expect to go beyond the crowded waters teeming with boats, people, pollution, and noise, this book is must reading for you. Not only is it packed with useful information, you can also use it to enjoy the adventures of Hugo and Rachel from the comfort of your easy chair or boat cabin, without even making the trip in person. Through their eyes, you will see and enjoy a new frontier for boaters, described in vivid, meticulous, and informative detail.

If, after you share the excitement of the author's adventures, you decide to make the trip yourself, you will want this book on board as your constant guide to where and how to go, what to see, and how to do it safely and enjoyably.

Phil & Gwen Cole
Editors, *Northwest Boat Travel*

Library of Congress Cataloging In Publication Data:
Anderson, Hugo 1915-
     Secrets of Cruising, The New Frontier, British Columbia Coast & Undiscovered Inlets / Hugo Anderson.

     Includes bibliographical references and index.

ISBN 0-945989-25-3
[Published 1995]

Table of Contents

Parry Bay, Observatory Inlett

Canadian Sunset

The New Frontier: British Columbia Coast & Undiscovered Inlets

Foreword

The British Columbia mainland coast stretches, by airline distance, 640 statute miles, or 1,024 kilometers from White Rock, at the United States border, to Stewart at the head of Portland Canal. The shortest distance by water isn't much longer, 691 statute miles, or 600 nautical miles. The province's coast is dotted with hundreds of islands and mountainous fjords, creating an irregular coastline that stretches more than 4,350 miles, or 7,000 kilometers on the mainland alone, not including the shores of the countless islands.

In our opinion, **these are the best cruising waters** on this continent, if not in the entire world. What makes them unique is the presence of the offshore islands that, with the exception of the 40-mile gap in Queen Charlotte Sound north of Vancouver Island, give protection from the seas and winds coming off the Pacific Ocean. In addition, the majority of the channels along this British Columbia section of the Inside Passage are narrow enough, and the mountains tall enough, to afford relatively protected cruising waters.

Our favorite coastal waters lie along the **Northern British Columbia Coast**, from Cape Caution to Dixon Entrance at the Alaskan border, a distance of 275 miles. It is these seldom visited, and often overlooked, waters suitable for today's (and tomorrow's) exploration, that comprise the **major emphasis of this book and the reason for writing it**.

Many pleasure boaters who cruise to Alaska are so drawn by the lure of "heading north to Alaska" that they rush along the periphery of this northern coast, and miss much that it has to offer. Even though we have made five trips to Alaska on board the *Sea Otter*, our 34-foot CHB trawler, my wife, Rachel, and I have cruised this region for three to four months every year, for the past 14 years. We have cruised in every inlet, enjoying the beauty and grandeur of this impressive area.

Unlike Alaska, British Columbia does not have tidewater glaciers which calve icebergs into the inlets, instead, it does have hundreds of magnificent glaciers, high up on the mountain sides. One advantage of cruising the northern British Columbia coast, versus Alaska, is its closer proximity to moorages in Washington and southwestern British Columbia.

Also, the channels and passages are not as wide and long as those in Alaska, offering more protection, a much greater number of anchorages, and shorter cruising distances from one anchorage to the next.

Before heading to the Northern British Columbia's coastal waters, it is advisable to check with your **boat insurance** company or broker. Many policies require a waiver to permit you to travel in the waters north of a line that is at the approximate location of Minstrel Island. Other policies specify that you may only pass *through* the waterways of northern British Columbia twice each year, traversing them for the purpose of passaging to and from Alaska. We have had no trouble, and very little expense, getting permission to linger in these waters between June 1 and September 1 each year, but insurance is a detail that needs to be attended to annually.

Today, fewer people are living along the non-urban British Columbia coast than at any time since shortly after the retreat of the glaciers, some 10,000 years ago. The Northern British Columbia coast is particularly sparsely populated. By land, there are only four roads leading to the salt water. These roads are at Bella Coola, Kitimat, Prince Rupert, and Stewart. If you eliminate the urban areas of Vancouver, Powell River and Prince Rupert, you could call it the "Deserted Coast". The native population was very large before the arrival of the white man, but 70% to 80% of them were wiped out by a series of smallpox epidemics that began in the late 18th century and culminated in the great epidemic of 1862. Many of the remaining natives abandoned their traditional villages and have migrated to large urban centers such as Vancouver, Victoria, and Prince Rupert as well as smaller communities like Campbell River, Port Hardy, and Bella Bella.

The northwest coast had five principal resources that were exploited by the arriving Europeans. These were furs, whales, fish, minerals, and timber. The most important fur bearing mammal was the sea otter, and it was their presence that brought the first Europeans. Over-hunting soon drove the sea otter to near extinction. The same thing happened to the whales. The result was the eventual abandonment of the fur trading posts and whaling stations.

At one time there were over 80 salmon canneries scattered along the British Columbia coast. Today, commercial canning operations are concentrated in Prince Rupert and Vancouver. The rest have been abandoned. Originally, fishing was done from row boats or small sailboats; today it is done from large power boats. This has resulted in fewer commercial fishermen and cannery employees living along the coast.

The mining industry, once active, is now shut down, except for some small operations in the Stewart area. The once thriving mining towns of Anyox and Alice Arm, in Observatory Inlet, each with over 2,000 inhabitants in the early years of this century, have been abandoned, except for a handful of residents at Alice Arm. Anyox had a copper mine and the largest copper smelter in the world. Alice Arm was a silver mining town with an 18-mile-long narrow gauge railway from the mine to salt water. Another, more recent venture in Alice Arm, was the molybdenum mine at Kitsault. It came and went in the 1970's and 1980's. This settlement is now reduced to a caretaker and his wife. Lastly, the big gold mine at Port Belmont, in Surf Inlet on Princess Royal Island, once had 600 inhabitants. Now there are none.

The timber industry is still strong, witness the big clear-cuts all along the coast, but mechanization has drastically reduced the number of loggers required. The last big reduction of work force in the timber industry population was the shut-down of the pulp mill at Ocean Falls in the 1970's. Its population, which was once over 2,000, is now about 50.

Farmers and ranchers also settled along the coast in the 19th and early 20th centuries and, for some time, succeeded. As their local markets dried up and the means of transportation disappeared, they abandoned their farms and ranches, and moved back to the cities.

All of the these factors have caused the drastic reduction of the coastal population. The low point may have been in the 1970's and 1980's with the closing of the operations at Ocean Falls and Kitsault.

In the last few years, especially since 1990, we have seen a proliferation of aquaculture operations, or "fish farms", and sports fishing camps. New resorts, and some marinas, are being established. Every year new homes are visible along the shoreline. The British Columbia non-urban coast now seems to be in the process of re-population, but it has a long way to go.

Since 1983, we have published the cruising guide, *Northwest Boat Travel*, constantly gathering information to expand the coverage of that publication. In December, 1993 *Secrets of Cruising: North to Alaska* was released as the first book in this series. That book described the length of the *Inside Passage* from Olympia, Washington to Skagway and Glacier Bay,

Inner Harbour, Victoria

Canada Place, Vancouver

Howe Sound

Alaska. In it, coverage of British Columbia waters primarily dealt with the "mainline" route to Alaska. In this book, coverage is expanded to include, what we refer to as, "The New Frontier", the extensive number of inlets which indent deep into the mainland of British Columbia and are yet to be discovered by most pleasure boaters.

Published charts that readers use for navigation vary in showing the depths in feet, fathoms, or meters. For the sake of consistency, I have used fathoms throughout this book. The reader will need to convert to meters when using one of the new metric charts.

I hope that readers will be encouraged to explore these new areas, and enjoy more of the great variety of wonders that nature has bestowed on the beautiful coast of British Columbia.

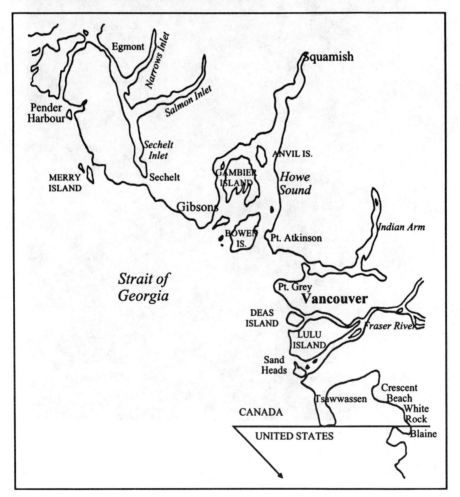

Chapter 1: Boundary Bay to Pender Harbour

The British Columbia coastline begins at the United States border in Boundary Bay, just south of White Rock, British Columbia. For information regarding clearing customs and immigration, see Appendix A. **White Rock**, a community of 16,000 population, received its name from a prominent white boulder on the shoreline. Two sets of floats are at the end of the 1,500 foot wharf. The eastern floats are for transient moorage, and the western floats for permanent moorage. Transient moorage is limited to two hours. Several restaurants and cafes are along the waterfront, as well as a large public park. Shopping facilities are in town, quite a distance up a hill. White Rock has been a resort community for 100 years.

Departing White Rock, it is necessary to traverse United States waters to get around Point Roberts, before heading north in the Strait of Georgia. Be sure to keep the red buoy, marking the shoal off Point Roberts, to starboard. Use Metric Chart #3463, scale 1:80,000. Point Roberts is a peninsula projecting south of the 49th parallel, the International Border, and thus part of the United States. (To reach Point Roberts by land from the mainland United States, it is necessary to cross the border, proceed west towards Tsawwassen, British Columbia, and then head south.) The Point Roberts Marina is a United States customs check-in port, by telephone.

It is 23 miles northwest, up the Strait of Georgia, from the west point of Point Roberts to Point Grey, the entrance to English Bay, which leads to Vancouver Harbour. This route skirts the **Fraser River** delta for this entire distance, and close attention to numerous navigation aids is necessary, to stay off the shallows. The Fraser River is the largest river in British Columbia. Over 1,500,000 people live in close proximity to the river, as it flows past Vancouver and other communities.

Continuing north in the Strait of Georgia, The B.C. Ferry Terminal and the big terminal for loading ships with coal are located at Tsawwassen, about three miles northwest of Point Roberts.

Next is the South Arm, the main channel of the Fraser River. It is entered at Sand Heads, identified by its strange looking lighthouse sitting on stilts. Many facilities for pleasure boaters are located along the South Arm. The town of Steveston on the north side of the main channel, is a

Chatterbox Falls, Princess Louisa Inlet

Burke Channel, near Bella Coola

Alexander Mackenzie Monument, Dean Channel

Ocean Falls

salmon processing center. A public wharf, with several floats equipped with power and water, is in the northwest part of Cannery Channel. Metric Chart #3490, scale 1:20,000 should be used.

The North Arm of the Fraser is entered just south of Point Grey. Use Metric Chart #3491, scale 1:20,000. There are marine related activities and business located along the river, including several that cater to pleasure boaters.

Vancouver Vicinity

The Port of Vancouver offers a Small Craft Guide that illustrates navigational paths and speed limits when cruising the waterways of Vancouver. To obtain the free, 11" X 17" diagram, call 604-666-2405. The Vancouver area has numerous marine facilities that cater to pleasure boaters. See the Appendix in this book.

English Bay is located northeast of Point Grey. There are usually several large freighters anchored in the bay, waiting for moorage space in Vancouver Harbour. The skyline of downtown Vancouver is clearly visible on the east side of the bay.

False Creek, off the southeast end of English Bay, is entered by cruising under the Burrard Street and Granville Street bridges. These have clearances of 90 feet and 92 feet respectively. Tidal streams run to three knots, the traffic can be heavy, and there is a speed limit of five knots. Only a few places offer transient moorage and reservations are definitely needed. No anchoring is permitted. Use Metric Chart #3493, scale 1:10,000.

Vancouver Harbour is entered at Prospect Point, through First Narrows, with the Lion's Gate Bridge overhead. Currents in the narrows can run to six knots, and there is usually very heavy traffic. Incoming vessels must stay close to the Stanley Park side. No fishing, sailing, or cross traffic is allowed. Listen to VHF Channel 12 to hear commercial traffic information. Boats must be under power between the entry to First Narrows and mid-harbor in Vancouver Harbour. Times of current changes and velocities are listed in Volume 5 of the Canadian Tide and Current Tables. Metric Chart #3493 should be used.

Coal Harbour is south and west of Brockton Point. This is the site of marina and float facilities, fuel floats and the Royal Vancouver Yacht Club. On the North Vancouver side of Vancouver Harbor is Mosquito Creek Marine Basin, a full service marina. Private yacht clubs are nearby.

Four miles east of First Narrows is Second Narrows, with its landmark bridge. Lynnwood Marina, located under the north end of the bridge, has moorage as well as repair facilities.

Port Moody lies east of Second Narrows, and Indian Arm to the north. Use Metric Charts #3494 and #3595, both on a scale of 1:10,000. Port Moody ends in drying flats. There is a marina at Reed Point that has moorage and gas and diesel fuels.

Three-mile-wide, ten-mile-long **Indian Arm** has mountains on both sides, some as high as 5,000 feet. There are numerous waterfalls in the spring and summer. Speed limits of five knots are in effect in several sections of the arm, including Belcarra Bay, Deep Cove and Bedwell Bay. The best anchorage is at the head of Bedwell Bay in four to five fathoms. It is exposed to down-inlet winds from the northeast. Deep Cove, on the west side of the arm has a small public float, with moorage for loading and unloading only. Seycove Marina, on the north shore of Deep Cove, has moorage, gas and diesel fuels, water and limited power. A yacht club is located at the west end of the bay.

Howe Sound

Howe Sound, just north of Vancouver, is about 20 miles long and eight miles wide. Its southern-most entrance, at Point Atkinson, is only five miles west of Stanley Park and the First Narrows in Vancouver. There are four entrances into Howe Sound. From east to west, these are Queen Charlotte Channel, Collingwood Channel, Barfleur Passage, and Shoal Channel. These entrances are subject to very rough conditions when strong west or southeast winds meet an opposing tide. Rough conditions may also be encountered in the vicinity of Point Atkinson when tides from Howe Sound and Burrard Inlet meet.

Rugged mountains, as high as 5,000 feet rise directly from the water edge. Several islands cover a good bit of the sound. Bowen, Gambier, and Anvil are the largest, each having mountains 2,500 feet high. Bowen is connected to the mainland by a ferry from Horseshoe Bay, and is the only island which is populated to any extent. This may seem strange in light of the island's close proximity to Vancouver. Chart #3526 (Metric), scale 1:40,000 covers all of Howe Sound, and Chart #3534, Plans, Howe Sound, with its harbor charts, is helpful.

Because of extreme depths throughout the sound, anchorages are few, and many are encumbered by log storage rafts. Long time storage of logs has also resulted in a great deal of debris. Logs, chains and cables are on the bottoms of some of the anchorages. Marina facilities are at Horseshoe Bay, Snug Cove, Lions Bay, Sunset Beach, Squamish and Gibsons, and there are marine parks at Porteau Cove and Plumper Cove.

Heavy ferry traffic can be expected in Queen Charlotte Channel in the vicinity of Horseshoe Bay. Large ferries bound for Nanaimo on Vancouver Island, and Langdale, serving the Sunshine Coast, enter and depart from Horseshoe Bay. These are in addition to the previously

Wreck of the Ohio, Carter Bay

Anyox Ruins, Observatory Inlet

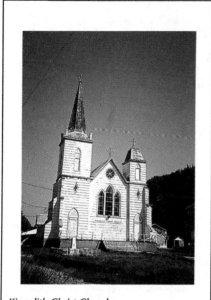

Kincolith Christ Church

Gillies Bay, Texada Island

Kincolith, Nass Bay

mentioned Bowen Island Ferry. Southern Howe Sound also has considerable pleasure boat traffic. Because of its relatively sheltered waters and reliable winds, Howe Sound is a favorite area for sailors.

Strong winds, typical of all British Columbia inlets, can be encountered, especially in the upper sound in the afternoon. Caused by the warming of the land, strong inflow winds result. In the winter strong "Squamish" outflow winds occur frequently. A separate weather forecast is made for Howe Sound on WX-3 Bowen Island and WX-4 Vancouver. An automated weather reporting station is located at Pam Rocks, on the east side of Gambier Island, about ten miles north of Horseshoe Bay, giving conditions for Howe Sound.

Snug Cove, Bowen Island, is the site of the Bowen Island ferry landing and the Union Steamship Company Marina. This relatively new development is very nice, run by friendly people. Doc Morgan's Inn, is a popular spot, with good food. Snug Cove has a very interesting history. One of its earliest developers, the Union Steamship Company, operated the ships that carried passengers from Vancouver to Bowen Island, as well as all along the entire British Columbia coast. The current developers have tried to retain as much of the original flavor as possible. The book, "Whistle Up the Inlet", by Gerald Rushton, is the fascinating history of the Union Steamship Company, which ceased operating in 1958, after 66 years of service.

Porteau Cove Marine Park, on the east side of Howe Sound, across from the north end of Anvil Island, has mooring buoys and anchorage for small craft. Shelter appears to be very limited, however. This is an ideal spot for divers because several shipwrecks have been placed under water here. Large launch ramps, restrooms, sani-station, trailer parking and campsites are provided.

Scenery in Howe Sound, with its steep mountain sides, is truly spectacular. Anvil Island, the outstanding landmark, was given its name because of its shape, by Captain George Vancouver in 1792. Highway 99, the road to Squamish and the skiing resort of Whistler, and a railroad line run along the eastern shore of the sound. At Britannia Beach the mill of the old Britannia Mine can be seen. The mine operated for 75 years, starting in 1889, and was once the largest copper mine in Canada. The B. C. Museum of Mining took over the old buildings and mine when it was shut down, due to depressed copper prices. It is now a popular tourist attraction. In May, 1994, the old Canadian National ship, the *Prince George*, was moored at the wharf.

There are two large paper pulp mills on the west side of the sound, one at Port Mellon, north of Gibsons and the other at Woodfibre, near Squamish, at the head of the inlet.

Squamish, with a population of 12,000, lies at the head of Howe

Sound. The economy is centered around the shipment of salt and inorganic chemicals, and forest products. The dredged boat harbor, with public floats and launching ramp, is on the west bank of the east arm of the Squamish River. The entry channel is dredged and has a five-foot minimum depth. When entering, put the FCC plant to port, then line up the amber range lights. Chart #3534 is very helpful. There is overnight moorage at the public floats, but they are usually very crowded. Do not raft to any of the tugs because they are likely to depart in the middle of the night, or at some other inconvenient time. Diesel, gas and fresh water are available, and a liquor store, provisions, and public phone are nearby. The floats of the Squamish Yacht Club are immediately north of the public floats. Two thousand foot Stawamus Chief Mountain is a notable landmark on the east side of the valley.

Gibsons, a town of 3,500 population, is located on the mainland across from Keats Island. There are two marinas and many shopping facilities in this interesting and picturesque town.

Gibsons Marina is a 400 berth marina with several spots for transient boaters on "A" dock. Call on VHF Channel 68. Water and power are available and there is a small shop with fishing supplies and clothing at the head of the ramp. Hyak Marine, adjacent to Gibsons Marina, has fuel, propane, showers and laundry, as well as some moorage.

All shopping facilities are nearby. There are several cafes and restaurants, as well as other shops along the main lower street, Gower Point Road. These include a supermarket. On top of the hill is a large, modern shopping mall.

Plumper Cove Marine Park, on Keats Island across Shoal Channel from Gibsons, has mooring buoys and floats in the bay to the east of the Shelter Islets. Anchorage is also possible. Enter north of the islets. There is exposure to winds from the north and southwest.

Strait of Georgia to Welcome Pass

Leaving Howe Sound to proceed north up the coast, Gower Point is the point of departure. Departing Gibsons via Shoal Channel, we showed a least depth of 15 feet on the fathometer at mid-tide. It is about 7-½ miles up the Strait of Georgia to the light on the White Islets. The village of Sechelt is on the shore to starboard. Trail Bay, in front of the town is too exposed for anchoring and there are no good mooring facilities on this, the Georgia Strait side of Sechelt. Sechelt's moorage area is in Porpoise Bay in Sechelt Inlet, but it is a distance of about 45 miles all the way around the Sechelt Peninsula to reach it.

Continuing northwest past the Trail Islands, it is about eight miles to the Merry Island Lighthouse which marks the southern end of Welcome

Shoal Bay, East Thurlow Island

Seymour River, Seymour Inlet

South Bentinck Arm Falls

Red Snapper

Kitlope Anchorage, Gardner Canal

Pass. It is then another 3-½ miles through Welcome Pass to the light on Grant Island at the northwest end of the passage. Currents can run 2-½ to three knots, flooding northwest and ebbing southeast. There are two unmarked rocks in the pass. Fraser Rock, near Lemberg Point, has about seven feet of water covering it at low tide. Edgerton Rock lies south of Lemberg Point. Pirate Rock is marked by a day beacon. Metric Chart #3535, Plans in Malaspina Strait, will be helpful in navigating Welcome Passage.

There are moorages and anchorages in the vicinity of Welcome Pass. The first is Halfmoon Bay, on the south side of the pass. There is a public wharf at the head of Halfmoon Bay with a float attached to it. A store is one block from the wharf. Frenchman's Cove, with anchorage, is nearly hidden in a niche along the northwest shore of Halfmoon Bay.

Malaspina Strait to Pender Harbour

Smuggler Cove Marine Park and Secret Cove are on the north side of Welcome Pass. Chart #3535 will help when entering either of them. A narrow entrance with reefs on both sides leads into Smuggler Cove. Favor the Isle Capri side when entering. There is extensive anchorage with fair to good holding bottom in the two main bays. On the south side of the first bay there is an uncharted rock about 50 feet out from the house on the shore. This rock is covered about five feet at high tide. When entering the inner bay, the reef in the passage, extends farther into the passage than you might think; beware.

Secret Cove is the site of marinas, fuel and a repair facility, a hotel, and offers anchorage as well. There is a light on a drying rock in the entrance that should be kept to starboard. Reduce speed when entering the cove. There are three arms in Secret Cove. The southeast arm has a narrow entrance with rocks to starboard, a day beacon should be kept to port. All floats in this arm are private, but limited anchorage may be possible.

Buccaneer Marina is in the northeast arm, just past the Jolly Roger floats, and offers complete marine repair services as well as fuel, propane, fishing supplies, postal outlet and groceries. Moorage is on an annual basis, but spots are available for those seeking repairs.

The Jolly Roger Marina is located on the north shore, between Buccaneer and Secret Cove Marinas. It has moorage, power, water, showers, and laundry. Hotel accommodations, restaurant, pub and lounge are on the hillside overlooking the marina.

Secret Cove Marina is in the northwest arm, to port when entering. It offers transient moorage, power, water, fuel, showers and garbage disposal. A store containing groceries, charts, liquor and fishing supplies is conveniently located.

Courtesy pick-up service transports those who moor at Secret Cove Marina and wish to dine at Lord Jim's Lodge. Located in a small niche on the Strait of Georgia shoreline north of Secret Cove, this waterfront resort does not have space for transient moorage. Lord Jim's has cottages, lodge rooms, restaurant and licensed lounge.

Across from Secret Cove and Smuggler Cove are North and South Thormanby Islands. Buccaneer Bay separates the two islands. At the southwest end of the bay the islands are joined by a drying flat. When entering Buccaneer Bay, avoid Tottenham Ledge and the shoal extending north from North Thormanby Island. There is good anchorage near Water Bay at the head of the bay, and Gill Beach has a temporary anchorage, unprotected from north winds.

Continuing northwest from Welcome Passage, Malaspina Strait lies between Texada Island and the mainland. It is 6-½ miles northwest to the light on Francis Point, and a mile and a half more to the entrance to Pender Harbour. Use Chart #3512, scale 1:80,000, Strait of Georgia, Central Portion, Chart #3535 is a big help in approaching Pender Harbour and navigating inside it.

Pender Harbour is a large, well-protected harbor with numerous marinas and shopping facilities. During summer months moorages may be crowded, so it may be wise to call and reserve space if cruising at that time of the year.

This area was first settled about 1880 by Charlie Irvine, who gave his name to the first landing. Madeira Park was named by a later arrival, Joe Gonsales, a Portuguese native of the Madeira Islands. Pender Harbour was, at first, a logging center, and later an important fishing center. Today, its economy is based on tourism.

The main entrance to Pender Harbour is between Williams Island and Henry Point, but it is also possible to pass between Williams Island and Charles Island to the south. The reef at the east end of this passage is marked by a day beacon. Passage between Charles Island and the mainland via "The Gap" is not recommended because it is obstructed by drying reefs. A speed limit of seven knots is enforced in the harbor.

There is bus service to Vancouver and Powell River from Madeira Park in Pender Harbour, as well as float plane service to Seattle.

Irvines Landing, in Joe Bay just east of Henry Point, is the first marina encountered when entering Pender Harbour. It offers moorage, water, fuel and showers. The next facilities on the north shore are in **Hospital Bay.** Fisherman's Resort and Marina, owned by Wally and Susan Nowik, offers moorage, with power, water, laundry, showers, lodging, fishing tackle and marine charts. Just past Fisherman's is John Henry's Marina and store, with moorage, water, fuel, propane, and a complete

Hartley Bay Church, Douglas Channel

Alison Sound Coho

Bella Coola

Alice Arm, Observatory Inlet

Big Bay, Stuart Island

grocery store and liquor agency. A large set of public floats is just north, or to port, of John Henry's.

The building on the hillside behind the public floats is the former hospital, from which the bay received its name. It is now the Sundowner, a newly remodeled, ten room inn which also serves meals.

The next facilities are in **Garden Bay**. To port, when entering, is a yacht club out-station, open to members only. Garden Bay Hotel and Marina, owned by Ron Johnston and Marita Jonkela, is located at the head of the bay. In addition to moorage with water and power, there is an excellent restaurant and pub. This site is only a short walk from Fisherman's Resort, John Henry's, or the public floats in Hospital Bay, if you are moored there. Garden Bay Marine Park has dinghy floats, launching ramp and anchorage.

Madeira Park, in Welbourn Cove on the south side of Pender Harbour, is the largest community. It has a large set of public floats, a supermarket, pharmacy, banks, post office, liquor store, restaurant and beauty shop. Madeira Marina, to port of the public floats, does repairs and has moorage for lodging guests only. The floats and boat houses to starboard of the public floats are for permanent moorage only. Nearby, in the bay near the entrance to Gunboat Bay, Sunshine Coast Resort Marina and RV Park has moorage with power and water, camping, laundry and showers.

Pender Harbour

Chatterbox Falls, Princess Louisa Inlet

Oatswish Falls, Mussel Inlet

Kemano, Gardner Canal

Canadian Sunrise

Codville Lagoon Marine Park

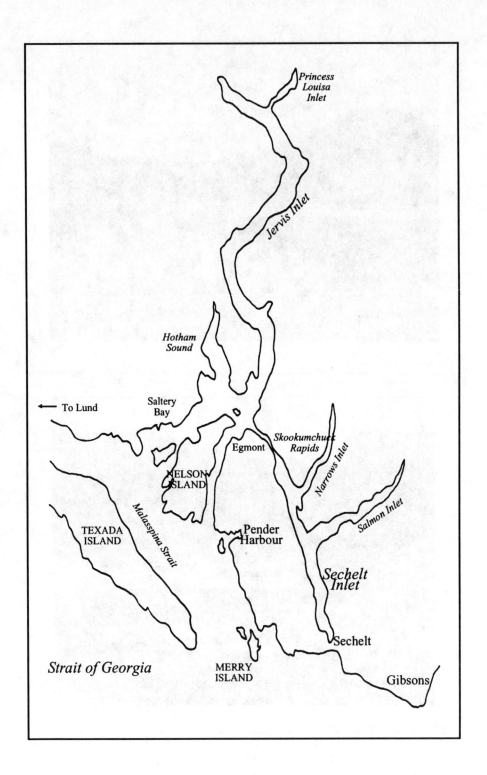

Princess
Louisa
Inlet

Jervis Inlet

Hotham
Sound

Saltery
Bay

← To Lund

Skookumchuck
Rapids

Egmont

Narrows Inlet

NELSON
ISLAND

Malaspina Strait

Salmon Inlet

TEXADA
ISLAND

Pender
Harbour

*Sechelt
Inlet*

Sechelt

Strait of Georgia

MERRY
ISLAND

Gibsons

Chapter 2: Jervis Inlet, Sechelt Inlet, Malaspina Strait

Before continuing north along Malaspina Strait to Westview, Powell River, and Lund, we will digress to venture into two local attractions. These are **Jervis Inlet**, with famed Princess Louisa Inlet, and **Sechelt Inlet** and its Skookumchuck Narrows and Rapids. Metric Chart 3514, scale 1:50,000 should be used.

Agamemnon Channel

From the entrance to Pender Harbour, it is about 12 miles up Agamemnon Channel to Egmont, the jumping-off place for Sechelt Inlet and upper Jervis Inlet. This channel was named for "HMS Agamemnon" a 64-gun ship commanded by Lord Horatio Nelson, the English Naval hero. The island to port is Nelson Island and, directly northwest of it, is Hardy Island, named for Nelson's second in command. Green Bay, on Nelson Island off Agamemnon Channel, has anchorage in five to seven fathoms. As you pass Earl's Cove to starboard you will notice the terminal for the ferry which runs to Saltery Bay, on the north side of Jervis Inlet. From that point, Highway 101 runs to Westview, Powell River and eventually Lund, the northern terminus of the Pacific Coast Highway.

Jervis Inlet

Jervis Inlet is entered off Malaspina Strait between Scotch Fir Point and Ball Point. Nelson Island, wedged between Agamemnon Channel and Jervis Inlet, has several anchorages. These include Quarry Bay on the south side and Ballet Bay, off Blind Bay, on the northwest side of the island. Recommended entry into Ballet Bay is from the west. Watch for uncharted rocks. There is good anchorage in the outer bay in five to seven fathoms, and a more protected anchorage in the inner bay in four to five fathoms at high tide. Good holding mud is in the center of the bay.

Vanguard Bay, on Nelson Island's northern shore, also offers shelter. Limited anchorage is found north of the islets off the east shore.

Hardy Island, adjacent to Nelson Island, has several niches on its south side which offer anchorages, close in, with a shore tie. The bay between Fox and Hardy Islands has an anchorage, but the bottom is rocky, making shore ties necessary in order to keep the anchor set.

Continuing up Jervis Inlet, **Saltery Bay**, on the mainland, has public floats adjacent to the ferry landing, as well as a boat launching ramp, camp and picnic sites. A nine foot bronze statue of a mermaid is underwater, marking this popular Scuba diving spot.

Prince Rupert, Kaien Island

Sea Otter at Port Hardy

Hotham Sound, a deep, six-mile-long inlet surrounded by mountains, extends off Jervis Inlet. Temporary anchorages are in a niche on the west shore and in Grenville Bay off the flats. The head of the sound has anchorages in Baker Bay, close to shore, and in the niche to the southeast.

Harmony Islands Marine Park is a favorite of boaters. The bottom is rocky and anchoring can be difficult. Shore ties are usually necessary. Mosquitoes can be a problem. Just southeast of the islands, beautiful Friel Falls cascades into the sound.

Jervis Inlet-Egmont Vicinity

Agamemnon Channel and Jervis Inlet meet at Captain Island. Facilities located at nearby **Egmont** offer the last chance to get fuel, water, and supplies if going to Princess Louisa or through the Skookumchuck Narrows into Sechelt Inlet. Egmont Marina is located to starboard near Skookumchuck Narrows. Bathgate General Store and Marina is located about one mile southeast in Secret Bay. Both offer fuel, water, moorage, power, and provisions. Bathgate also has a government liquor store. If fueling at Egmont Marina, be aware that currents can be very strong at the fuel float.

If going to Princess Louisa Inlet, the distance to Malibu Rapids is 30 miles. There are no suitable anchorages in this stretch, due to the extreme depths and steep shore lines. Heading up Prince of Wales Reach, using Chart #3514, scale l:50,000, Jervis Inlet, you will notice several prominent mountains directly ahead, their names all connected with Winston Churchill. The sharp peak to the right, 6,300 feet tall, is Mt. Spencer, which is Mr. Churchill's middle name, as well as his mother's family name. The two blocky peaks to the left are Marlborough Heights, named for Marlborough Castle, the Churchill family estate. The very sharp peak between, and behind them, is Mt. Churchill, 6,500 feet. You will notice that the inlet is very deep here, 662 meters or about 2,200 feet in some places.

At the head of Prince of Wales Reach, the inlet turns to starboard into Princess Royal Reach, and finally, at Patrick Point, to port, up Queens Reach. Beautiful mountains continue on both sides.

Princess Louisa Inlet

The entrance to Princess Louisa Inlet is through **Malibu Rapids**, which can run up to nine knots, with overfalls, or white water. Passage should be made at or near slack water, either high or low, because there is plenty of depth. On small tides we have gone through as much as an hour early, with a following current, and had no trouble. Don't try this if it is a large tide, or if you see any white water. Under these conditions, passage should only be at slack. Slack water occurs about 30 minutes after high or low water at Point Atkinson, listed in Volume 5, Canadian Tide and Current Tables. The buildings to port at Malibu Rapids were originally built as a private lodge by a wealthy individual in the 1940's, and are now being used by a religious organization as a summer camp. There are no facilities for boaters.

Known to some as the "Eighth Wonder of the World", or the "Yosemite of the North", this four-mile-long inlet has 5,000 to 8,000 foot mountains around it, and numerous waterfalls, especially after some rain. Huge Chatterbox Falls is at the head of the inlet. There is room for 15 to 20 boats on new floats to the right of the falls. The floats are provided and maintained by the Princess Louisa Society through membership and donations. Anchorage is possible directly in front of the falls in 30-60 feet, soft bottom. The current should keep you facing the falls, unless a strong up-inlet wind occurs, when you may be forced to move if you swing into shallow water. Some rings are also placed in the rock shoreline along this anchorage basin.

There are hiking trails on shore, and fresh water is available. A trail leads to a viewing platform near the falls, and a blazed trail leads up the valley to the Trapper's Cabin, a climb of about two hours. Hikers are rewarded with views of Jervis and Princess Louisa Inlets and Mount Albert.

Additional moorage is found at mooring buoys located about halfway up the inlet between McDonald Island and the shore. It is best to approach them from the west, because of foul ground on the east side of the island. There is a dinghy float and ramp to shore. Tent sites, and picnic tables are available. Rings installed in rocks on shore are available for shore ties.

Princess Louisa Inlet is truly a wonderful place, well deserving its reputation, and is always popular with boaters in spite of, or perhaps because of, its remote location. There is no radio reception, and WX-1 Comox weather can be heard only to the head of Prince of Wales Reach.

Sechelt Inlet

Sechelt Inlet, often coined "The Inland Sea", is entered near Egmont, through the Skookumchuck Narrows and Sechelt Rapids. Use Metric Charts #3512, scale 1:80,000, and #3514, scale 1:50,000. Rapids at the entrance can run to 15 or 16 knots at large spring tides, and I'm sure have deterred many boaters from passing through them, thereby missing one of the most enjoyable experiences on the British Columbia south coast. We believe that Sechelt Inlet has been, to use an old phrase, "a well kept secret". We encourage other boaters to visit. Cruising Sechelt Inlet, one weekend in early June, 1992, we saw practically no pleasure boats, except for several local outboard skiffs buzzing around. If you consult Volume 5 of the Canadian Tide and Current Tables, you can determine the times of tide changes. Passage at or near either a high or low slack is very easy. The preferred route is west of Boom Islet, and Sechelt Islets light. Give Roland Point a wide berth, especially on a flood tide.

Narrows Inlet, about eight miles long lies off the east side of Sechelt Inlet, four miles south of the rapids. This inlet is very scenic, especially the area around Tzoonie Narrows, three miles from the entrance. Currents can run to three to four knots, but present no problems because it is quite deep. There are, what appear to be, summer homes in the area near Ramona Creek, with its big waterfall. A large logging camp and booming ground are at the head of the inlet. Depths appear to be too deep for anchoring in the inlet, but Storm Bay, on the south side of the entrance to Narrows Inlet, offers the best anchorage in Sechelt Inlet in seven fathoms, soft bottom, and decent protection. Even better protection can be found in the little bight on the west side of Storm Bay, just south of the small island. We anchored in 3-½ fathoms at low tide. It is a well protected and scenic anchorage.

Salmon Inlet, about 12 miles in length, has some very nice scenery, and several possible anchorages. Entrance is between Kunechin Islets and Nine Mile Point. The first possible anchorage is in the nook on the east side of Kunechin Point, but it is open to south and east winds, as we found out when we investigated it. Misery Bay, about three miles from the head of Salmon Inlet, offers excellent, protected anchorage in five to 11 fathoms at the far west end. There was a large logging camp in the bay in 1992, and log rafts were present. Another anchorage, though not as well protected, is in the bight on the northeast side of the spit at Sechelt Creek. Anchorage is also possible at the very head of the inlet in four to five fathoms, with adequate shelter. All of the floats appear to be private or designated "Aircraft Only". I would be a bit hesitant to try the bottom, as it may be foul, the result of what appears to be years of logging activity. If you go to the very end of the inlet, you can see the small powerhouse, and the outlines of the dam above it. There is a large logging camp here, and some private homes.

Proceeding south down the inlet towards the town of Sechelt, Tillicum Bay Marina lies on the east side, about 3-½ miles south of Nine Mile Point. It offers moorage and water. Another 3-½ miles brings you to the town of **Sechelt** at the head of Porpoise Bay.

The mooring facilities consist of a public float, which is usually very crowded, and, to port, the Royal Reach Marina. Beware of shoaling to port of the marina. The mooring facilities at the marina are a bit rudimentary;

the floats were originally part of a fish farm, and some of the railings still remain. The marina manager says that there is always six to seven feet of water at the outer end of the floats, even on the lowest tides. The marina office is in the brown building to the left at the top of the ramp. From this location it is about a 15 minute walk to the center of town, and cab service is available. There are stores, shops, restaurants, and other services in Sechelt. There is no fuel available in Sechelt Inlet. The Blue Heron Inn, about one mile north of the head of Porpoise Bay, is about a 20 minute walk from the marina. The food, decor, view and service are all excellent. Closed Mondays and Tuesdays.

Malaspina Strait to Westview/Powell River

Heading northwest from either Pender Harbour or Jervis Inlet, you will be traversing Malaspina Strait, named for an early Spanish explorer, until you reach Westview/Powell River. It is 22 miles from Pender Harbour to Westview. Use Metric Charts #L/C 3512 and #3513, both at scales of 1:80,000.

To the west, the huge bulk of Texada Island provides some shelter from westerly winds. Malaspina Strait is not as big as Georgia Strait, but it is still large enough to be very rough under windy conditions, especially at the entrance to Jervis Inlet. There aren't many places to seek shelter, so check the weather reports from Comox Coast Guard, WX-1; or Vancouver, WX-2 or WX-4 (Channel 21-B). There is always quite a bit of traffic in Malaspina Strait because it is the main coastal route north from Vancouver.

At Northeast Point on Texada Island you are eight miles from Grief Point where Beach Gardens Resort Hotel and Marina offers breakwater-protected moorage with water, power, and fuel available. The restaurant in the large hotel on the hillside has a view of Malaspina Strait. For overnight guests, a laundromat, swimming pool and showers are available.

This part of the coast is known as the Sunshine Coast because of the estimated 2,400 hours of annual sunshine.

Westview is two miles north of Grief Point, and Powell River is another three miles. Westview, where there are two large public boat basins, has the only facilities for pleasure craft. The northern basin is for permanent moorage, and the southern for transients, though it is usually very crowded, even with mandatory rafting. The terminus of the Powell River-Texada and Powell River-Little River (Comox) ferries is between the two boat basins. A fuel facility is adjacent to the southern basin. Some provisions are available near the marina, and there are three shopping malls in the upper part of town, which is up a steep hill. The provincial liquor store is there also. A courtesy bus makes runs every day except Sunday, and taxi service is available. Powell River/Westview also has bus and airline service to Vancouver.

Proceeding three miles north from Westview, you pass the huge paper pulp mill at Powell River. There are no facilities for pleasure craft. You might notice the novel breakwater in front of the mill, several World War II "Liberty Ships" in a row. Continuing northwest along the coast, you pass Harwood Island and Savary Island to port. Both are surrounded by shoals, so don't go in too close. Savary has beautiful sand beaches, and some people think that it resembles a South Seas island.

About two miles north of Savary Island, you come to the small village of **Lund**, the north end of the Pacific Coast Highway 101. A sign post opposite the hotel points to the southern terminus, in Chile, South America. By way of interest, the next location on this coast that is reachable by road is Prince Rupert, 450 miles northwest, unless you count Bella Coola, which is 50 miles up Burke Channel, and that is accessible only by a 300 mile long road, mostly unpaved, from Williams Lake.

Lund has a public wharf and floats, protected by a floating concrete breakwater. Entry can be made around either end of the breakwater. If the floats are full, you can moor to the inside of the breakwater and go ashore in a dinghy. Use Metric Chart #3538, scale 1:40,000.

The Thulin brothers built a hotel here in 1899, and, later, another in Campbell River on Vancouver Island. Lund is named after their home town in Sweden. On shore is a hotel, with a pub, coffee shop, restaurant, grocery and liquor agency. They also sell fishing licenses, if you forgot to get one earlier on the trip. We often stop in Lund for a sweet roll and a cup of tea, or lunch. A fuel dock is on the float in front of the hotel, and moorage with power is available. There are marine repair facilities in Lund, one specializes in stern drives and outboards, the other in diesel engines, and is capable of hauling boats up to 75 feet in length.

Thulin Passage

Immediately north of Lund you enter **Thulin Passage** between the Copeland Islands and the mainland. It is six miles up this straight, narrow passage to Sarah Point, where you enter Desolation Sound. Depths are more than adequate in the passage. Along the way you will be passing Copeland Islands Marine Park to port. The park is undeveloped and has no facilities. There are several possible anchorages, but protection is limited in some, and others have hard bottoms. Better anchorages are just ahead, in Desolation Sound. There may be some log rafts tied to the mainland shore in Thulin Passage, using the large mooring rings set into the rock walls.

A fuel facility on a barge is located at the north end of Thulin

Passage. Another mile farther north is Bliss Landing, a privately owned facility.

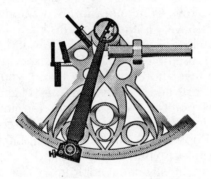

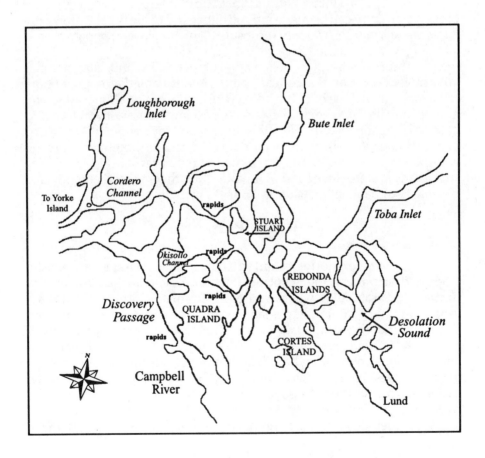

Chapter 3: Desolation Sound and The Discovery Islands

Desolation Sound is entered from the south at Sarah Point, at the north tip of the Malaspina Peninsula. If the weather is clear enough to see the mountain tops, boaters looking northeast, up Desolation Sound, will see one of the most beautiful vistas on the coast. Several peaks over 5,000 feet high are on the mainland and East Redonda Island. This is even more impressive if you look at the chart and discover that, in several places, depths are over 200 fathoms. Fifteen miles away, up Homfray Channel, charts show several depths of almost 400 fathoms, or 2,400 feet. Add this to the heights of the adjacent mountains and you see that they rise almost 8,000 feet, from their bases at the bottom of the inlet.

History records that the weather was not clear in 1792 when Captain George Vancouver sailed these waters while on a surveying and charting mission. Discontent with the rain and the mosquitoes, he named the area Desolation Sound.

In spite of its name, this has become the single most popular cruising destination on the entire British Columbia coast. If you visit during July or August, you will be able to see the vast number of boats for yourself.

Desolation Sound Marine Park is one of the largest in the British Columbia Marine Park system. Metric Chart #3538, scale 1:40,000 and Chart #3555, a harbor chart, cover Desolation Sound. There are no facilities in the park and fires are not permitted on shore. Numerous bays and coves provide good sheltered anchorages. When anchoring, be aware of large tidal ranges. Private property is adjacent to the park. Garbage scows at Tenedos Bay and Prideaux Haven have been removed, and boaters are asked to take their own trash out with them, and deposit it at the drop points and recycling bins at public floats in Campbell River, Squirrel Cove, Cortes Bay, Westview, and Nanaimo. There is a marina at Refuge Cove, and public floats are located at Cortes Bay, Squirrel Cove, and Refuge Cove, all outside of the marine park.

Malaspina Inlet is entered about 1½ miles east of Sarah Point. Eight miles in length, this inlet has several good anchorages. Metric Chart #3559, Malaspina Inlet, Okeover Inlet, and Lancelot Inlet, scale 1:12,000, is helpful when entering. The course is quite straight down to the Isbister Islands, avoiding the charted hazards on either side. Aquaculture operations are along the shorelines. Chart #3538, Desolation Sound and Sutil Channel, scale 1:40,000, will suffice, and is necessary when at the head of the inlet.

Grace Harbour, on the northeast side of Malaspina Inlet, is included in Desolation Sound Marine Park, and offers excellent, protected anchorages in both the inner and outer harbors in five to ten fathoms, soft bottom. Often, this anchorage is less crowded than some others in the park.

Okeover Inlet has a launch ramp and a small public float with no water or power. The harbormaster is the owner of the restaurant on the hill. She will also collect moorage fees. There is space for five or six boats, if the numerous small skiffs haven't filled it. Depth is sufficient to moor on the inside. Okeover Dining Lounge, with a wonderful view of the inlet, is on the hill above the government wharf.

Penrose Bay Marina, in the bay on the southwest side of the Goode Peninsula, has rudimentary float facilities for small sports fishing boats. There is a log breakwater, no power or water, but ice and telephone are available.

Lancelot Inlet and Theodosia Inlet are on the north side of Malaspina Inlet. Isabel Bay is on the west side of Lancelot Inlet, and has protected anchorage west of Madge Island. There are aquaculture facilities along the shoreline. Thors Cove, on the east side of the inlet, has a picturesque anchorage at the south end of the bay, behind the small islet. Again, there are aquaculture operations. Wooten Bay is near the head of Lancelot Inlet and, though open to south and east winds, is relatively protected. Property at Portage Cove is private, and is not included in the marine park.

Theodosia Inlet lies east of Lancelot Inlet, and has a narrow entrance, with a depth of six feet at low tide. Stay in the center of the entry channel. Good anchorage is possible in several places on a mud bottom. The head of the inlet dries, and is sometimes used for log storage. Watch your fathometer.

The widely prevalent aquaculture operations are primarily raising oysters, much of which is shipped to the Orient, mostly in the half-shell state. It is only prudent to minimize wakes to avoid damaging these operations.

Tenedos Bay has high, steep cliffs surrounding it. Although 200 to 350 feet deep in the center, around the shoreline there are coves and niches suitable for anchorage. Anchoring with stern ties to shore is necessary because the bottom is mostly rock, and because of crowded conditions in the summer. Westerly winds can get into this anchorage. There are camping and sanitary facilities on shore.

Prideaux Haven, the most popular spot in Desolation Sound, is part of the marine park. It consists of several sheltered bays. Fires are not permitted on shore. When entering, keep the reef to port. Be aware of a three-foot drying rock close to Lucy Point on Eveleigh Island, and a shelf about 100 yards south of Lucy Point. Clear water allows these hazards to be visible. Melanie Cove, on the east side of Prideaux Haven, is one of the most attractive and popular anchorages in the marine park. Undoubtedly, in the summer it will be crowded, and shore ties will be necessary. A walk of about ½-mile from the head of Melanie Cove leads to Laura Cove, along an old logging road and a stream. Additional anchorage in Prideaux Haven is found in six to eight fathoms in Eveleigh Anchorage at the southwest side of Eveleigh Island. It should be approached from the west, not from the east.

Laura Cove, just east of Prideaux Haven, is best entered at half-tide or better. Entry is between the rock off Copplestone Island and Copplestone Point. This is a small, well protected anchorage, in four to five fathoms, mud bottom. Because of its popularity, shore ties will probably be necessary.

Across the sound, on West Redonda Island, is **Refuge Cove**. It is the site of the Refuge Cove Store and government floats with 1,000 feet of mooring space. One float is owned by the store for the use of its customers. Water and limited power are available. The store and fuel float have gas, diesel, propane, and a good stock of groceries and meat in the summer months. In off-season, supplies may be somewhat limited. There is also a post office and liquor store, as well as a laundry and showers. Marine charts and fishing supplies are also available. No facilities for garbage disposal.

Before 1930, the settlement had a population of over 200 residents. Logging, agriculture, and fur farming were active in the vicinity.

Cortes Island is opposite West Redonda Island. Named for Hernando Cortes, the conqueror of Mexico, it has a good road system that links residents in settlements such as Squirrel Cove, Cortes Bay, Manson's Landing, Gorge Harbour, and Whaletown. From Whaletown, it is possible to reach Vancouver Island by ferry, first to Heriot Bay on the east side of Quadra Island, and then from Quathiaski Cove on Quadra's west side to Campbell River on Vancouver Island. A local van service has been available to make this connection.

Squirrel Cove is about three miles west of Refuge Cove. The church on the Indian reservation is clearly visible as you approach the village. It is the site of a public wharf and floats, usually very crowded, and has a garbage deposit available. However, because the island landfill is nearly full, it is doubtful that the garbage drop will exist much longer. The Squirrel Cove Store, adjacent to the floats, has a good stock of groceries, a liquor store, and propane. No fuel is available.

Cortes Bay, located on the southeast side of Cortes Island, is 3½ miles west of Sarah Point. It has a public float, anchorage, and a private yacht club outstation open to members only. The latter is the converted Cortes Bay Marina, which has not been in operation for several years. The narrow entrance has a beacon with a flashing light marking it; keep it to starboard when entering. The bottom of the bay has anchorage depths of 40-50 feet. The bottom is very soft, and it is said that some anchors may drag when southeast seas or northwest winds get into the bay. We have never had any problems here.

The Discovery Islands

North of Desolation Sound, at the north end of the Strait of Georgia, the Inside Passage is partially blocked by a large group of islands that extend for about 50 miles, until the route opens up again into Johnstone Strait. This group is sometimes called the Discovery Islands. Tides flood from both ends of Vancouver Island and meet near the southern edge of these islands. Because of the restrictions that the islands create, it is necessary to traverse some rapids, where tidal currents can reach as high as 16 knots. Many boaters do not venture through this area north of Desolation Sound, and are missing some of the best cruising waters on the coast.

The name, Discovery Islands, comes from Discovery Passage, which separates Vancouver Island from Quadra Island. Captain Vancouver named this passage for his ship, the *Discovery*, when Lieutenant Johnstone and his men from the *Chatham*, Discovery's escort ship, returned from the north, after circumnavigating this archipelago. When doing so, they observed the tides flooding from the northwest down what is now named Johnstone Strait. This proved that Vancouver Island really was an island, and that, by continuing northwest, they could reach the open sea again.

Lewis Channel

The shortest, and easiest, route north from Squirrel Cove is to round Junction Point and continue up Lewis Channel for seven miles, then another nine miles up Calm Channel to Harbott Point on Stuart Island. Tides in Lewis and Calm Channels flood from the northwest and, in the vicinity of Junction Point, meet the flood tides coming up the Strait of Georgia from the south. Tidal streams here are relatively weak. Metric Charts #3538 and #3541, both on a scale of 1:40,000, apply to these waters. Two miles north of Junction Point, three-mile-long Teakerne Arm indents West Redonda Island. It is the site of a marine park and a dinghy float. Anchoring is not recommended because of exposure to northwest winds and a poor holding bottom. An attractive waterfall in the northeast corner cascades from Cassel Lake. Captain Vancouver anchored here, and his men used the falls for bathing.

When you leave Lewis Channel, steep sided Raza Island will be obvious to starboard. About 2½ miles south of Harbott Point, you will note the native village on the mainland, or starboard side, dominated by a prominent church building. The village is very appropriately named Church House.

Before continuing, let us describe three alternate routes from Desolation Sound north to Stuart Island.

Alternate Route #1, Homfray Channel

If the weather is clear, the most scenic route is the easternmost, following Homfray Channel, around East Redonda Island. Use Metric Chart #3541, Approaches to Toba Inlet, scale 1:40,000. You will be cruising between mountains 5,000 feet to almost 6,000 feet high on both sides of the channel. This route to Stuart Island is about 16 miles farther than traversing Lewis Channel, but is well worth it if time and weather permit. If beginning from an anchorage in Prideaux Haven, it is only about ten miles longer.

Forbes Bay, on the east side of the channel, is too deep and exposed for anchorage. Atwood Bay, four miles north of Forbes Bay, is also deep, but not quite as exposed. Anchorage is possible in the small bight at the head of the bay. Tidal currents in Homfray Channel are usually less than 1½ knots, flooding south in the northern section and north in the southern section.

At Hepburn Point, the north end of East Redonda Island, Homfray Channel joins Pryce Channel coming in from the west, and 20-mile long **Toba Inlet** to the northeast.

The scenery in Toba Inlet is very good, with mountains as high as 8,000 feet surrounding it. The inlet is very deep and anchorages are scarce. We have used one in the northwest corner of Brem Bay in 16 fathoms, as a temporary anchorage. It is fairly open to south and east winds. There is an old rock breakwater at the mouth of Brem River that is said to provide some protection, but we have not tried to anchor in that vicinity. Past Brem Bay, the water becomes increasingly clouded by glacial silt, and, by the time you reach the head of the inlet, visibility in the water is down to a foot or so. The head of the inlet shoals very rapidly, and, with the cloudy water, maneuvering is very tricky. Anchorage would be difficult, and there is no protection from the frequent up and down inlet winds. Toba is best done as a day's cruise, returning to Walsh Cove in Waddington Channel for a more protected overnight anchorage.

An interesting spot is so-called "Blue Ice Cove" on the south side of Toba Inlet about 7½ miles east of Brem Bay. This is a local name, and does not appear on charts. Throughout most of the summer, a snow bank is usually found in the ravine at the head of this little bight. Temporary anchorage is possible at the head of the bay if you want to go ashore to get some snow or ice to put in a cooler.

Alternate Route #2, Waddington Channel

The second alternate route north is through Waddington Channel between East and West Redonda Islands, using Charts #3538 and #3541. There are half-a-dozen possible anchorages in this eight-mile-long channel and in Pendrell Sound on the east side of the passage. This is also the location of Roscoe Bay and Walsh Cove Provincial Marine Parks.

Waddington Channel is entered between Horace Head and Marleybone Point. The first anchorage is in Roscoe Bay, just to the north of Marleybone Point. Because of the drying shoal in the entrance, entry and departure are only possible at, or near, high tide. There are well protected anchorages in four to seven fathoms. This is a provincial marine park. Black Lake, with fishing and swimming opportunities, is within walking distance.

The next anchorage is at the un-named island off the west shore, about a mile northwest of Church Point. Good holding bottom is in the passage between this island and West Redonda Island. Beware of the rock and shoals in the bay on the north side of the island. Aquaculture operations are present, and may affect your choice of an anchorage.

Five-mile long **Pendrell Sound**, across from Church Point, almost divides East Redonda Island into two separate islands. Oyster production is prevalent, and to protect the spat, very small oysters, speeds are restricted to four knots in the north half of the sound. Water temperatures are quite high, making this a good place for a dip. Anchorage is possible at the head of the sound, as well as in the vicinity of the small island about 1½ miles south. The latter anchorage is between the island and the shore, in front of the entrance to the lagoon.

Allies Island, on the west side of the channel two miles north of Church Point, offers anchorage in the bay on its northwest side. Again, aquaculture operations are present. A small bight on the west side, about one mile north of Allies Island, is another possible anchorage. A shore tie may be necessary.

Doctor Bay, two miles farther north can be another possible anchorage, if the salmon aquaculture operations leave enough room.

Walsh Cove Marine Park is one mile south of the north entrance to Waddington Channel. Enter from the south, not through False Pass on the north side of Gorges Island. There are anchorages along the west side of the cove. Most of these anchorages have a hard bottom, making shore ties necessary. We usually anchor in the center of the bay in 15 fathoms, where the bottom is soft, and there is plenty of room. Boaters who do not have an electric winch, or sufficient length of anchor rode, may prefer the shoreline anchorages.

Dean Point, with its light, marks the north end of Waddington

Channel, and its junction with Pryce Channel. Dean Rock lies in the center of the channel about one-fourth mile south of Dean Point. In the past, bottom fishing has been good around this rock. Pryce Channel leads west seven miles to steep-sided Raza Island. Raza may be passed on its north side via Raza Passage or on its south side via Deer Passage. Tides, which do not exceed one knot, flood to the east and ebb to the west in Pryce Channel.

After passing around Raza Island you enter Calm Channel, where the course is north-northwest, either five or seven miles to Harbott Point on Stuart Island, depending on which side you choose to pass Raza Island.

Six-mile-long **Ramsay Arm** lies to the north of Raza Island. This arm is too deep and exposed for suitable anchorages. Frances Bay, just west of the entrance to Ramsay Arm is exposed to east winds coming down from Toba Inlet, but does have anchorage in ten fathoms or less at its head. Because of down-inlet winds, this can be an uncomfortable anchorage at times.

Alternate Route #3, Sutil Channel

A third route from Desolation Sound to Stuart Island is to pass on the west side of Cortes Island, through Sutil Channel to its junction with Calm Channel, using Charts #3538 and #3541, both Metric, on scales of 1:40,000. To accomplish this, it is necessary to first go through Baker Passage, between Hernando Island (again named for Hernando Cortes, conqueror of Mexico) and Twin Islands, and Cortes Island to the north. When rounding Sutil Point, the southern tip of Cortes Island, be certain to pass to the south of the big red bell buoy 020 marking the shoal off Sutil Point. The buoy is about one mile southwest of the point.

Manson's Landing is southeast of the entrance to Gorge Harbour. It has a wharf, public floats, store, and a small marine park. Anchorage is possible in the bay northwest of the public floats. Fuel, water and some provisions are available.

Gorge Harbour, five miles north of the Sutil Point buoy, offers good protected anchorage, and is the site of the Gorge Harbour Marina and Resort. The gorge that forms the harbor's entrance is ½-mile long and, in the narrowest section, is only 200 feet wide. Least depths are 36 feet. Currents can run as high as four knots at springs, but entry is possible at any time. The resort, owned by Glen and Verlie Carleton, has moorage, power, water, fuel, propane, a well-stocked store and restaurant. A laundromat, showers, rooms and campground are also available.

Marina Island, named for Cortes' Indian mistress, lies off the southwest side of Cortes Island. When going north, it can be passed on either side. If on the west side, be sure to stay south of the buoy marking the end of the long shoal south of the island. If on the east side, passage is through Uganda Passage. This is not as difficult as it may appear on Chart #3538. About one mile north of Uganda Passage you will pass the settlement of **Whaletown**, the terminus of the Cortes Island-Quadra Island ferry. There is a small public float and a store. No fuel is available.

On Quadra Island, five miles west of Whaletown, is the much larger settlement of **Heriot Bay**. Drew Harbour and Rebecca Spit Marine Park are east of Heriot Bay. Anchorage is possible in Drew Harbour in the bight on the west side, near the tip of Rebecca Spit, but be sure that you will have sufficient depth at low tide if you are near shore. Better anchorages are at the head of the bay in four to six fathoms, mud bottom. Private buoys and floats are in this vicinity.

Heriot Bay is the location of the Cortes Island-Quadra Island ferry terminal, a large wharf with public floats and garbage deposit, and the Heriot Bay Inn and Marina. Moorage with power and water, gas, diesel, propane, lodging, restaurant, pub, laundry, showers, and a large camp-ground are available. The first inn was built in 1894, and has been replaced twice because of fires. The Island Market/Shopeasy is a short distance up the road from the inn. Anchorage is also possible in the bay to the west of the public wharf.

North of Heriot Bay, Hoskyn Channel leads to Okisollo Channel, separating Quadra Island from Read, Maurelle, and Sonora Islands. Hoskyn and Okisollo Channels are described as an alternate route in Chapter 4.

The description of Sutil Channel continues in this chapter. Sutil extends along the east side of Read Island, separating Read Island from Cortes Island. Several possible anchorages are along Sutil Channel. These include Burdwood Bay and Evans Bay on Read Island, and Coulter Bay, Carrington Bay, and Van Donop Inlet on Cortes Island.

Burdwood Bay has anchorage, with protection from all but south winds, in the small bay behind a group of islands in the southern portion. Evans Bay has a public float on the southwest side of the bay. It is exposed to north winds. Bird Cove has some anchorage and, farther north in Evans Bay, there is anchorage behind the islets which protect a cove. Although open to southerly winds, the easternmost of the two arms at the head of Evans Bay, offers the best anchorage in five to six fathoms in the center. Swimming is possible because the water is warmer than usual for this area.

On the southeast side of Sutil Channel, the first anchorage on Cortes Island is in Coulter Bay, where there is protection from all but north and northeast winds. Carrington Bay, a mile farther northeast has some anchorages, but the bottom is rock and currents from the lagoon at the head of the bay can be strong enough to cause anchor dragging. By far the best, and most popular, anchorage is in **Van Donop Inlet**. There is excellent protection and good holding bottom in this narrow 2½ mile long inlet. A rock, marked by kelp, is in the center of the narrows. It can be passed on either side, but the starboard side when entering is preferred. The best anchorages are in the wide part of the bay towards its head, or in the cove at the very head of the bay. Check your tide tables and fathometer to be sure that you will have enough clearance under your boat at low water.

At Bullock Bluff, the north end of Cortes Island, Sutil Channel joins Calm Channel. It is about 7½ miles northwest to Harbott Point on Stuart Island.

Forty-mile-long **Bute Inlet** takes off to the northeast at Stuart Island. In fact, Stuart Island lies in the mouth of the inlet. The average width of the inlet is about two miles and the mountains range from 5,000 to 6,000 feet high along its sides in the first half, to 8,825 foot Southgate Peak, above Waddington Harbour, at the head of the inlet. Depths of over 2,000 feet are prevalent in the lower section and there are depths of 600 to 800 feet near the head of the inlet. Use Metric Chart #3542, on a scale of 1:40,000.

As in all of the big mainland inlets along the coast, winds are unpredictable and can come up very suddenly. Prevailing wind patterns, especially on sunny days when the land masses warm, are for strong up-channel winds in the afternoon, and a reverse flow at night when the land cools. Because of heavy inflows of fresh water from rivers which are carrying the melt water from glaciers and snow fields, there is an overlay of fresh water in Bute Inlet. This creates a one to two knot outflow most of the time. When a strong up-inlet wind opposes these currents, rough conditions can occur.

Because of the extreme depths and lack of protection, anchorages in Bute Inlet are poor at best. The best of these would be in Orford Bay or at the head in Waddington Bay, off the flats. The depths at the head shoal rapidly and the murky glacial water makes it impossible to see to any depths. In spite of the beautiful mountain scenery to be viewed, the probability of strong winds, and the lack of good anchorages make Bute Inlet a risky place to cruise. Rachel and I went as far as Orford Bay several years ago, but did not anchor because our small boat did not have sufficient anchor rode.

Taming The Rapids

There are four large rapids in the Stuart Island area. These are created by the restrictions to the outflow and inflow in the channels, caused by Stuart and several smaller islands. Our course from Harbott Point will take us through Yaculta, Gillard and Dent Rapids. Currents run to seven knots in Yaculta and Gillard, and nine knots in Dent Rapids.

Volume 6 of the Canadian Tide and Current Tables gives the times of tidal changes, and the maximum speeds to be expected. The times given are for Gillard, with the differences for Yaculta and Dent. Don't forget that all times shown are Standard Time, not Daylight Savings Time. These rapids are not to be taken lightly, but by making a transit at or near times of slack tide there should be no problems. The best time to go through the rapids, if you are going to continue north and west, is near high tide, so that you will have a following ebb tide behind you in Cordero, Chancellor and Wellbore Channels. This means leaving Harbott Point 45 minutes, or so, before high slack. This should get you through Gillard Rapids about slack and clear of Dent Rapids, the worst one, before it has built up too much.

If traversing at the end of a flood tide, after leaving Harbott Point, site of a private sportsfishing camp, keep close to the Stuart Island shore to take advantage of the backwater, until reaching Kellsey Point. Then cross to the Sonora Island shore to take advantage of another backwater. Keep an eye on the charts for shoals. Use the inset on Metric Chart #3543, scale 1:40,000 for the rapids, and continue on this chart through Cordero and Chancellor Channels.

After clearing Yaculta Rapids, you will see some private sportsfishing facilities on Sonora Island and, on the Stuart Island shore, you will come to Big Bay, site of breakwater-protected public floats, and, to the left of these, Big Bay Marina Resort. Owned by Bruce and Kay Knierim, Big Bay Marina Resort offers moorage with water and power, fuels, a well stocked store, showers, laundry, restaurant and accommodations. Slow down when entering Big Bay because currents and the topography of the bay magnify washes.

The presence of several fish camps so close to each other tells you that there must be good salmon fishing here. If you are interested in getting some local help, it may be a good idea to go into Big Bay Marina and Resort and hire one of their guides. In these turbulent waters some local knowledge and a smaller, more maneuverable skiff, can be very helpful.

Gillard Passage and Gillard Rapids lie between Jimmy Judd and Gillard Islands. This passage is short, straight and deep.

Dent Rapids is two miles farther along. Favor the Sonora Island shore to avoid the "Devil's Hole", a whirlpool that builds up south of the point near the light on Little Dent Island.

The fourth rapids, Arran Rapids, is on the north side of Stuart Island, and leads to Bute Inlet. Currents run from seven to nine knots. These rapids are off your course if heading north and west.

Cordero Channel

The preferred course continues along Cordero Channel, which

stretches west for 17 miles from the light on Little Dent Island to Lyall Island Light in the mouth of Loughborough Inlet, where it joins Chancellor Channel. Floats for moorage are in three locations, and there are also several anchorages in this stretch. The prominent peak on the north side of the channel is 5,485 foot Estero Peak. Views are particularly imposing when coming down the channel from the west. All waters in Cordero Channel flood to the east and ebb to the west.

Three and a half miles northwest of Dent Island Light is Hall Point, where Nodales Channel leads off to the southwest. Across from Hall Point is the entrance to three-mile-long Frederick Arm. Eight-mile-long Nodales Channel runs southwest to Chatham Point, where the weather reporting lighthouse is located. At Chatham Point, Discovery Passage to the south meets Johnstone Strait to the west. These areas will be covered later in this chapter.

Nodales Channel

Off Nodales Channel, several good anchorages are in Thurston Bay Marine Park on Sonora Island. The park is undeveloped. For nearly 30 years, Thurston Bay was headquarters for the British Columbia Forest Service. The station was shut down several years ago. Anchorage is possible in the north part of Thurston Bay, behind Block Island, and in Anchorage Lagoon at the south end of the bay. Cameleon Harbour has excellent, well protected anchorages toward its head, on the starboard side, as well as in Handfield Bay in depths of three to four fathoms, all soft bottoms. Be cautious when entering Handfield Bay because there are numerous hazards. It is, however, the nicest anchorage, if someone hasn't beaten you to it.

Hemming Bay is across Nodales Channel from Thurston Bay and offers some anchorages at its head behind the islets on the port side. The bottom is rocky and not good holding ground. The anchorages in Thurston Bay and Cameleon Harbour are superior.

Opposite Nodales Channel, **Frederick Arm** has a good anchorage at its head, in the northwest corner in ten fathoms. It is open to south winds. Four-mile-long Estero Basin can be explored at or near high tide in a dinghy. The entrance is impossible at low tide, and currents are strong. Fishing for cutthroat trout is said to be good in this basin. Don't wait too long for your exit, or you may run into some trouble.

Two and a half miles west of the entrance to Nodales Channel, **Shoal Bay** lies on the south side of Cordero Channel. Phillips Arm is on the north side. Before World War II, the town of Thurlow in Shoal Bay was a thriving place with two gold mines and three saloons. Business also came from those operating two additional gold mines in Phillips Arm. Today, all that remains at Shoal Bay are the government wharf and floats, the vacant store building at the head of the wharf, the big building housing the Shoal Bay Lodge, and a few private homes. Moorage has always been available at the government floats. Through the years, the lodge has been closed and re-opened several times. In 1992, it became a fishing resort, welcoming boaters to its restaurant and lounge. Water is accessible on the floats when the harbormaster turns it on. A sign informs you when that will be. Anchorage in Shoal Bay is not very desirable because most of the bay is very shallow, and it is wide open to winds coming from Phillips Arm.

Anchorages in **Phillips Arm** are in Fanny Bay or at the head of the arm in ten to 15 fathoms. The bottom shoals rapidly at the head, and must be approached carefully. Better protection is found in Fanny Bay. If planning to fish, be sure to check the current British Columbia fishing regulations. Waters of Phillips Arm have been closed for several years.

Bickley Bay is on East Thurlow Island, about 1½ miles west of Shoal Bay. There is anchorage in three to six fathoms near the head, mud bottom. An aquaculture operation may be located on the port shore. Slow down and favor the port side when entering the bay. Open to northwest winds, currents may also invade the area, making anchor dragging possible.

Two miles west of Bickley Bay, the Lorte Island Light is on the starboard side of the channel. In the cove just east of Lorte Island, is Camp Cordero Lodge, owned by Reinhardt and Doris Kuppers. They have moorage, a restaurant serving German food, and lodging.

A mile and a half west of Lorte Island, Cordero Channel turns northwest to pass through Greene Point Rapids, and Mayne Passage opens to the south and west, leading to Johnstone Strait, a distance of five miles.

Mayne Passage floods north and ebbs south, with currents running to five knots in the narrow sections. Blind Channel Resort is on West Thurlow Island, 1½ miles down Mayne Passage. Since 1970, the Edgar Richter family has operated the resort, and has developed it into a first class facility. They offer moorage with power and water, fuel, propane, a well stocked store, liquor outlet, post office, laundry, and showers. A restaurant specializing in German style cooking is open during the boating season.

Returning to Cordero Channel, Greene Point Rapids run to seven knots on big spring tides, ebbing northwest and flooding southeast. If you left Dent Rapids at high slack and are planning to transit all of Cordero Channel with a following ebb tide, Greene Point Rapids may be running fairly strong when you arrive. We have always gone through at all states of the tide without any difficulty, but deep-keeled sailboats may find the swirling currents uncomfortable. Keep to the west side, avoiding the light on Griffith Island where the turbulence is most severe.

Three and a half miles west of Greene Point Rapids is Lyall Island, with its light, marking the end of Cordero Channel.

Chancellor Channel

Chancellor Channel continues west for seven miles until it joins Johnstone Strait. Information regarding Johnstone Strait is found in the next chapter.

At Lyall Island, 18-mile-long **Loughborough Inlet** branches to the north. When currents aren't too strong, there usually is good fishing for bottom fish, especially Ling Cod, on the reef between Lyall Island and Grismond Point. Be sure to check the size limit on Ling Cod in the fishing regulations. It has been increased recently.

If it is a clear day, the spectacular scenery makes a trip into Loughborough Inlet well worth while. Beautiful mountains, on both sides of the inlet, reach heights of over 5,000 feet. Depths are too great for anchorage in most of the inlet, and there are no facilities. However, anchorage is found in Beaver Inlet and Sidney Bay, and a deep anchorage may be possible near Heard Point at the extreme head of the inlet, exposed to winds up and down the inlet. If you do go past Sidney Bay, beware of the rock shown on the chart off Cosby Point. It is located farther out than indicated.

Beaver Inlet lies to port, about 3½ miles up the inlet on the west side, and has anchorage at its head in six to seven fathoms, mud bottom. It provides good protection, except when west winds funnel through. Avoid anchoring too far in, at the head of the inlet. Years of logging have left debris on the bottom that may foul your anchor. A small bight on the south shore is attractive, and appears to offer a cozy shelter. However, this niche is shallower than may be desirable.

Sidney Bay, on the other side of Mary Point, offers better protection in a west wind, and has an anchorage basin at the head.

Four and a half miles west, in Chancellor Channel, is D'Arcy Point at the junction with **Wellbore Channel**. Heading off to the northwest, Wellbore Channel offers the most protected route to Johnstone Strait. It avoids the vicinity of Helmcken Island, the worst section of Johnstone Strait.

Forward Harbour, an excellent anchorage, is only five miles away, just beyond Whirlpool Rapids. Currents in Whirlpool can run to seven knots, but it is very short, straight, and deep. We have always gone through in our 7½ knot *Sea Otter* regardless of the state of the tide or direction of the current. The current floods to the southeast and ebbs to the northwest.

A small indentation to port in the entry channel to Forward Harbour is large enough to accommodate one or two boats. However, it is open to wakes of boats as they pass to go to the better, well protected

51

anchorages in Douglas Bay. The most popular space is off the crescent shaped beach in five to seven fathoms. We prefer to anchor farther out in ten fathoms. The softer bottom is better holding, and there is more room to swing. We once spent several days in Forward Harbour waiting for a gale in Johnstone Strait to abate. Farther into the bay is the Forward Harbour Fishing Lodge, a relatively new development with moorage, showers, and laundry. Use Metric Chart #3544, scale 1:25,000. You should be able to get weather on WX-4, Comox, via Sonora Island repeater, or on WX-1, Comox via Alert Bay repeater.

One mile north of the entrance to Forward Harbour, Wellbore Channel joins Sunderland Channel and the course turns west down Sunderland Channel to Johnstone Strait.

Sunderland Channel Vicinity

Bessborough Bay has an anchorage at its head in five to six fathoms, soft bottom, but wide open to seas coming in from the west. Topaze Harbour lies to the northeast and offers anchorages at its head, and in Jackson Bay. Since these anchorages have only limited protection, Forward Harbour is a much better choice.

Seven miles west, Sunderland Channel joins Johnstone Strait, at Yorke Island. During World War II, Yorke Island was fortified and armed with heavy artillery. Enemy ships trying to attack the Vancouver, or Victoria areas via the "inside" of Vancouver Island would have to pass here. No enemy ships ever appeared, but Yorke Island was an important part of the coastal defense of British Columbia.

Prideaux Haven

Petroglyphs, Robber's Nob, Port Neville

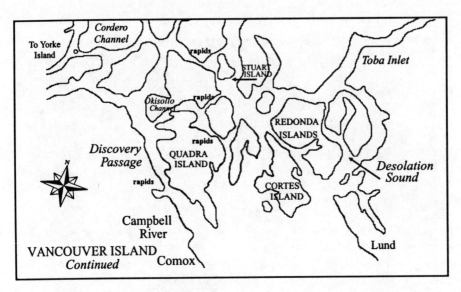

Cordero Channel

To Yorke Island

rapids

STUART ISLAND

Toba Inlet

Okisollo Channel

rapids

REDONDA ISLANDS

rapids

Discovery Passage

N

QUADRA ISLAND

Desolation Sound

rapids

CORTES ISLAND

Campbell River

Lund

VANCOUVER ISLAND
Continued

Comox

To Comox

Gibsons

BOWEN IS

Horseshoe Bay

Strait of Georgia

Vancouver

Fraser River

Silva Bay

GABRIOLA IS.

Nanaimo

VALDES IS.

White Rock

Blaine

THETIS IS.

GALIANO ISLAND

GULF ISLANDS

Ladysmith

Point Roberts

SALTSPRING IS.

Ganges

PENDER ISLANDS

Maple Bay

Cowichan Bay

Bedwell Harbour

Saanich Inlet

Sidney

Haro Strait

VANCOUVER ISLAND

Victoria

SAN JUAN ISLANDS

N

CANADA

UNITED STATES

Strait of Juan de Fuca

Chapter 4: East Coast Vancouver Island

Although the eastern shore of Vancouver Island cannot properly be said to be part of the mainland coast of British Columbia, these waters definitely include important routes to the north coast. Therefore, this chapter will cover the waters between Victoria and Kelsey Bay, where we enter areas described previously.

Victoria, the capital of British Columbia, was established in 1843 by the Hudson's Bay Company. It became their main trading post when other posts, previously located on the Columbia River, Fort Vancouver, and the two posts to the north, were abandoned. Families, including those from Taku in Alaska and Fort McLoughlin at Bella Bella, moved to the new Fort Victoria. For many years it was the only European settlement of any size in all of British Columbia. Today, it is truly a beautiful and interesting city to visit. In 1994, the population of greater Victoria was 300,000, and growing rapidly.

Several marine facilities are located along the Inner Harbour of Victoria. These waters are also used by float planes for landings and takeoffs; look out for them. A beacon has been installed on Berens Island, off Work Point. Float plane pilots activate this beacon when landing or taking off. Metric Chart #3415, scale 1:6,000, is the best chart of Victoria.

The first moorage is the commercial fishing fleet basin to starboard when entering, just west of the large Laurel Point Inn. During the summer season, when the fishing boats are out, this moorage is available to pleasure craft. The best moorage of all, if there is room, is on the city-owned floats right in front of the Empress Hotel. Additional floats for pleasure craft are just north, next to the old Coho ferry dock. Farther into the harbor, toward the Johnson Street Bridge, moorage with power and water is available at the public Rithet Basin. Customs clearance is at the Customs Jetty, adjacent to Rithet Basin. There is a small public float near the Johnson Street Bridge. All of these floats are near the city center.

Victoria is a great tourist center, and, in summer months, will be very crowded. Attractions, in addition to the extensive variety of shops, include the Empress Hotel, where, with reservations, you will enjoy afternoon tea, and the Provincial Museum, which we consider to be one of the best that we have ever seen. All are within easy walking distance of any of the previously mentioned moorages.

Oak Bay, located on the southeast side of Victoria, is the home of the Oak Bay Marina. It has moorage with power and water, gas and diesel fuels, showers, and laundry facilities. The entrance is between Turkey Head and the light on the breakwater on the south side of Mary Tod Island. Metric Chart #3440, scale 1:40,000, covers this area, and if you are going into Oak Bay, Metric Chart #3424, Oak Bay, would be very helpful.

Customs clearance may be done at Oak Bay Marina, usually by telephone. There is frequent city bus service to downtown Victoria.

Cordova Channel

Sidney Spit Provincial Marine Park is located on the northwest end of Sidney Island, two miles east of downtown Sidney. There are over 30 mooring buoys, and anchorage is also possible, but be cautious about going too far south because it is very shallow. The southern bay is a drying flat. Open to winds from most directions and wakes from passing boats, this anchorage can be uncomfortable. However, it is still very popular. A float for shore access, as well as overnight moorage, is also available. On shore are picnic facilities and campsites. A passenger ferry that runs several times a day connects the park with Sidney from May 15 to September 30.

Sidney, a town of 10,000, is 14 miles north of Oak Bay, at the north end of the Saanich Peninsula. It is reached by traversing either Sidney or Cordova Channels, one on each side of James Island. Metric Chart #3441, scale 1:40,000 should be used.

Three large marinas in the Sidney vicinity accommodate transient boats. These are Port Sidney Marina, Van Isle Marina, and Canoe Cove Marina. Metric Chart #3476, scale 1:10,000 is helpful. Customs may be cleared by telephone from each of them. See Appendix A for customs information. Port Sidney Marina is located next to downtown Sidney. The approach is between the red and green spar buoys, and entry between the two arms of the rock breakwaters. Do not attempt to enter from the north. They do not have fuel or repair facilities, but there is moorage with power and water. Several restaurants and shops are located just above the floats, and it is only a block to the foot of Beacon Avenue, the main street of Sidney. Our favorite eating place is the Mozart Cafe on Beacon Avenue. There are large grocery stores located along Beacon Avenue, as well as several banks, post office, and liquor store.

Van Isle Marina, situated on the south side of the entrance to Tsehum Harbour, is about a mile north of the center of Sidney. It has a new breakwater and has been enlarged to accommodate vessels to 160 feet in length. Fuel, repairs, power, water, showers, and laundry are available.

Canoe Cove Marina, another full service marina, is located ½-mile to the northwest, in Canoe Cove, off Iroquois Passage. Water, repairs, laundry, showers, fuel, and moorage are accessible.

Sidney to Dodd Narrows and Nanaimo

Leaving the Sidney vicinity, with Dodd Narrows and Nanaimo as your destination, there is a choice of routes. You will pass either side of Saltspring Island, the largest of the Gulf Islands. Passage on the west side of Saltspring is via Satellite Channel, Sansum Narrows, and Stuart Channel. On the east, there are two routes, which wedge the Pender Islands in between them. One is through Moresby Passage to Swanson Channel and Trincomali Channel, and the other is farther east, by Boundary Pass to Bedwell Harbour, Plumper Sound, Navy Channel, and then to Trincomali Channel.

Route #1: Bedwell Harbour, Plumper Sound, Navy Channel to Trincomali Channel

First, we will describe the route which is farthest east and will include a stop at **Bedwell Harbour**, located on South Pender Island. This is the site of Bedwell Harbour Resort, a Canadian Customs Office, and a marine park. Use Metric Charts #3441, scale 1:40,000, and #3477, various scales. The resort has moorage, with water and power, gas and diesel fuel, a laundromat and showers, as well as a store, restaurant, and guest rooms.

See the Appendix A for complete information regarding customs. Clearance is accomplished, not by telephone, but by checking in to the Customs Office. A customs officer may visit the boat. The office is open from May 1 to September 30.

Beaumont Provincial Marine Park is ½-mile north of the resort. There are several mooring buoys and camp and picnic sites.

Pender Canal, located at the head of Bedwell Harbour, was constructed in 1903. It separates North and South Pender Islands. A bridge over the canal has a minimum clearance of 26 feet. Minimum depth is seven feet and minimum width is 40 feet. Maximum current is four knots at spring tides, flooding to the north and ebbing to the south. When heading north, passage is between the red buoy to starboard and the green spar buoy to port.

The north end of the canal connects with Port Browning. Anchorage can be found in five to seven fathoms on a mud bottom, with protection from all but east winds, but exposed to the wakes of all passing craft. A small public wharf is on the north side, and the Port Browning Marina Resort is at the head of the bay. The marina has moorage, with water and power, laundromat, showers, a restaurant and well stocked store. A shopping center, including a drug store and liquor store, is a five minute walk from the marina. Exiting Port Browning, Plumper Sound and Navy Channels lead west and meet Swanson Channel at Stanley Point on the north tip of North Pender Island.

Route #2: Moresby Passage, Swanson Channel to Trincomali Channel

The other route along the east side of Saltspring Island traverses Swanson Channel, passing Otter Bay and Port Washington, on Pender Island. Otter Bay is the site of a ferry landing and the Otter Bay Marina. Moorage with power and water, laundry, showers, and store are available.

Opposite Otter Bay, across Swanson Channel into Captain Passage, is **Ganges**, the largest community in the Gulf Islands. It is situated at the head of Ganges Harbour. Use Metric Chart #3441, scale 1:40,000. Metric Chart #3478, Plans Saltspring Island, is helpful.

Transient moorage is available at the Government Boat Basin, located behind the breakwater south of the Grace Peninsula, at the public float on the north side of the Peninsula and at marinas located at the head of the harbor. During summer months, short term shoppers' moorage is also located on the north side of the peninsula, and anchorage is possible throughout the harbor. Ganges Marina has transient moorage with power and water, gas and diesel fuels, showers, laundry and ice. Salt Spring Marina, Ltd. has moorage with water and power, showers, laundry, and a marine pub with full dining menu. Nearby, repairs and haul-outs are available at Harbour's End Marina.

Ganges has over 100 businesses of all types, including banks and a post office. All are within easy walking distance of the wharves. Saltspring Island is well known for the quality pieces created by its artists and craftsmen, whose works are displayed in the numerous shops in Ganges. Ganges is a fast growing community but still retains much of its small town charm.

Saltspring Island has three B. C. Ferry landings. One route connects Fulford Harbour to Swartz Bay on Vancouver Island, where connections can be made by ferry to Tsawwassen on the mainland. Another ferry runs from Long Harbour, at Ganges, to other Gulf Islands and to Tsawwassen. The third ferry links Vesuvius, on the west side of Saltspring, to Crofton on Vancouver Island.

Trincomali Channel

Swanson and Navy Channels join Trincomali Channel at the north end of North Pender Island. Trincomali Channel then leads northwest for 20 miles to the light on Danger Reef, where it joins Stuart Channel. Stuart Channel extends to Dodd Narrows, six miles farther northwest.

Active Pass, on the east side of Trincomali Channel, separates Galiano Island from Mayne Island. Tidal currents can run to eight knots, flooding to the east and ebbing west. There is heavy traffic in Active Pass because it is used by the British Columbia ferries running from Tsawwassen (Vancouver) to Swartz Bay (Sidney) and the inter-island ferries. It is also used by large ships, tugs with barges, and commercial fishing boats, as well as pleasure craft. Times of tidal changes and current velocities are listed in the Canadian Tide and Current Tables, Volume 5. Active Pass was named after the United States revenue and surveying vessel the *U.S.S. Active*, which was the first naval vessel to transit the pass. At its east end, Active Pass opens into the Strait of Georgia.

Montague Harbour, on Galiano Island, is three miles north of Active Pass. Protected by Parker Island, Montague Harbour offers sheltered anchorage throughout in four to ten fathoms on a soft bottom; just don't anchor in the path used by the ferry whenever it approaches or leaves its dock. Moorage is found at a small public float adjacent to the ferry landing and at Montague Harbour Marina. The marina has power and water on the floats as well as gas and diesel fuels, and provisions.

Montague Harbour Marine Park, located at the north end of the bay, was established in 1959, the first marine park in British Columbia. There are numerous mooring buoys, moorage floats, and a dinghy float. Camp and picnic sites are popular. Moorage and camping fees are charged. Metric Chart #3442, scale 1:40,000 should be used.

Continuing north in Trincomali Channel, near mid-channel at the base of the Secretary Islands, is Wallace Island, site of a provincial park. Park acreage consists of Conover Cove and all but two parcels on Princess Bay. Both bays are on the west side of Wallace Island, and are separated by an anvil shaped peninsula. They offer protected, very shallow anchorages. Caution is needed because not only are the entrances shallow and narrow, but a series of ledges lie off shore of Wallace Island. These are clearly shown on Metric Chart #3442.

Continuing north, you pass Kuper and Thetis Islands. Clam Bay, located between the islands, is a large, relatively protected anchorage, with depths of three to five fathoms on a soft bottom.

Boat Passage, separating Thetis and Kuper Islands, connects Clam Bay with Telegraph Harbour. It is a dredged channel which dries at low tides. Consequently, it should be attempted only at or near high tide. A measurement scale, mounted on pilings at either end of the passage, shows the depth of water in the channel. Many boats use it, and we have done so, but do not recommend it for inexperienced mariners. It is much safer to approach Telegraph Harbour by going along the west side of Kuper Island.

Porlier Pass, on the east side of Trincomali Channel, leads to the Strait of Georgia. It separates Galiano and Valdes Islands. Currents flood to the north and ebb to the south, reaching nine knots on big spring tides, making passage at or near slack tide recommended. Use Metric Chart #3443, scale 1:40,000.

Trincomali Channel meets Stuart Channel, to the west, and Pylades Channel, to the east, in the vicinity of Pylades Island, five miles northwest of the west end of Porlier Pass.

Pylades Channel, Gabriola Pass

Pylades Channel runs another four miles northwest to Gabriola Passage, which, in turn, runs east to the Strait of Georgia.

Pirates Cove Marine Park is on the east side of DeCourcy Island, on the west side of Pylades Channel. Caution advised when entering to avoid the shoal to port, which extends well past the day beacon marking it. A shoal to starboard is marked by a red buoy. Pass between the day beacon and the buoy. There are campsites and drinking water on park land, and dinghy docks for shore access. This anchorage is not the best, in spite, or because of its popularity. The bottom does not hold too well, and when this is compounded by insufficient scope, due to crowding, anchor dragging can be common. Rings for stern ties are embedded in the rocks. The parks department requests that you do not tie to trees because of the possibility of damage to them.

Gabriola Passage, at the north end of Pylades Channel, separates Valdes from Gabriola Island. Currents flood to the east and ebb to the west, reaching a maximum velocity of eight knots at big spring tides. Times of tidal changes and velocities are given in Volume 5 of the Canadian Tide and Current Tables.

Two miles north of the east end of Gabriola Passage lies **Silva Bay**, site of marinas and a private yacht club facility. The largest marina, Silva Bay Resort, has been purchased and refurbished. It offers moorage, fuel, haul outs, restaurant, laundry, and store. Another is Pages Resort Marina, with moorage, power, gas and diesel fuels. Lastly, the Silva Bay Boatel has moorage with water and some power, provisions, and laundry. Anchorage is also possible in the bay. From Silva Bay, it is 21 miles across the Strait of Georgia to Welcome Pass on the mainland side of the strait. This route avoids the restricted area Whiskey Golf (WG) but has no havens in case of bad weather.

False Narrows, at the north end of Pylades Channel, lie between Mudge and Gabriola Islands. Passage is not recommended, because of shallow depths and many rocks.

Rather than False Narrows, the recommended, and commonly used passage to Nanaimo, is through Dodd Narrows, at the head of Stuart Channel.

Route #3, Western Route: Colburne Passage, Satellite Channel, Sansum Narrows to Stuart Channel

The western route from Sidney to Dodd Narrows and Nanaimo is around the west side of Saltspring Island. As you head through Colburne Passage, using Metric Chart #3441, scale 1:40,000, you will pass the B.C. Ferry Terminal at Swartz Bay. Ferries arrive from and depart for Tsawwassen, for Vancouver, as well as to several of the Gulf Islands. One of these ferries runs to Fulford Harbour five miles to the north on Saltspring Island.

Fulford Harbour has a small public wharf with floats near the ferry dock, and Fulford Marina near the head of the bay. The marina has moorage with power and water, gas and diesel fuels, and showers. It is a short walk into town. Anchorage is possible near the head of the harbor in five to seven fathoms, mud bottom, but open to southeast winds.

Satellite Channel

Satellite Channel lies along the south and southwest sides of Saltspring Island, and leads to Sansum Narrows. Twelve-mile-long **Saanich Inlet** is to the south, along the west side of the Saanich Peninsula. The appropriate chart is Metric Chart #3441. The community of **Mill Bay** is on the west side of the inlet, near its entrance. A ferry connects Mill Bay with Brentwood Bay, on Saanich Peninsula. Mill Bay Marina has moorage, gas and diesel fuels, laundry, and showers. A shopping center, with grocery and liquor store, is a block away. **Brentwood Bay** is the largest community in the inlet. It is located seven miles up the inlet, and has public floats and two marinas which accommodate transient boats. Brentwood Inn Resort and Marina has moorage, power, water, a restaurant, and lodging. Anglers Anchorage Marina, largest in the inlet, is a Canadian Customs port-of-entry; check-in is by telephone. They offer moorage with power and water, gas, diesel, showers and laundry.

Butchart Gardens, with its dinghy dock for shore access, can be reached by dinghy from Brentwood Inn or Anglers Anchorage Marinas, by tying to a buoy in the Butchart Garden cove near the entrance to Tod Inlet, and from anchorage farther into Tod Inlet. Tod Inlet provides protected anchorage in two to three fathoms on a mud bottom. At the head of Saanich Inlet, in Finlayson Arm, Goldstream Boathouse has moorage with power and water, and gas.

Heading north from Satellite Channel, Cowichan Bay opens to the west, at the south end of Sansum Narrows. The community of **Cowichan Bay** has public floats, as well as small marinas. Anchor Marina, Bluenose Marina, and Pier 66 all have moorage with power and water. In addition,

Pier 66 has gas and diesel fuels. Lodging and restaurants are in the community. On the north side of Cowichan Bay, Genoa Bay Marina and anchorage are found in Genoa Bay. Genoa Bay Marina, has moorage with power and water, showers and a laundromat. There is a restaurant and a store with baked goods. Protected anchorage, often amidst log storage, is in Genoa Bay in three to five fathoms, mud bottom.

Sansum Narrows

The shorelines become steeper as you approach Sansum Narrows, particularly on the Saltspring Island side. Tides flood to the north and ebb south, reaching three knots in the narrowest section and one to two knots in wider parts of Sansum Narrows. Because it is a popular sports fishing area and there are several aquaculture operations, there is a speed limit in these waters.

On the west side of the narrows is **Maple Bay**, with the Maple Bay Marina, Maple Bay Yacht Club, public floats, fuel floats, repair yards, restaurants, and stores.

Maple Bay Marina has moorage with power and water, showers, and laundry. A well stocked store and a licensed restaurant are also located at the marina. Quamichan Inn, a favorite dining spot, is located along the road to Duncan, with complimentary limo pick-up and delivery at Maple Bay and Genoa Bay marinas and at the Maple Bay Yacht Club.

Stuart Channel

Stuart Channel runs 20 miles northwest, along the Vancouver Island shoreline, from Sansum Narrows to Dodd Narrows. Use Metric Chart #3442, scale 1:40,000. A ferry runs from Crofton on Vancouver Island to Vesuvius which is on Saltspring Island, two miles north of Grave Point, the north end of Sansum Narrows. **Vesuvius** is named for a British warship. There is a very small public float just north of the Vesuvius ferry dock. Its size was more than doubled in 1994, so it can now handle four or five medium sized boats. The Vesuvius Inn, a good place for lunch or dinner, is just above the floats.

Crofton has a set of public floats behind the breakwater next to the ferry landing. Half of the moorage is reserved for commercial fishing boats.

The town of **Chemainus**, on Vancouver Island, is four miles north of Crofton. It is the oldest deep sea port on Canada's west coast. Four public floats are in the small harbor next to the Chemainus-Thetis Island ferry landing. In 1980, fearing that the lumber mill in this one-industry-town was going to shut down, the residents, with the help of the Provincial

Government, established a Downtown Revitalization Project. More than 30 large murals, painted from photographs depicting the logging industry and events connected with it are painted on buildings throughout town. Chemainus has thus become a large outdoor art gallery. The project has been very successful, attracting thousands of tourists. Consequently, tourist oriented shops, arts theater and a variety of eating places have been built. If the small public floats are crowded, it is possible to moor in one of the Telegraph Harbour marinas, take a short walk to the Thetis Island Ferry Terminal and take the ferry across to Chemainus.

Telegraph Harbour, between Thetis and Kuper Islands has two large marinas. Thetis Island Marina, owned by Paul and Dawn Deacon, is the first one that you come to when entering from the south. It has moorage with power and water, gas and diesel fuels, laundry, showers, and a store. Telegraph Harbour Marina, whose owners are John, Jan and Julie Ohman, is located at the head of the harbor. It has moorage with power and water, showers, laundry, gas and diesel fuels. On shore is a cafe, store and playground.

Boat Passage runs from Telegraph Harbour east between Thetis and Kuper Islands to Clam Bay. The channel dries and should be used only at or near high water, if at all.

Ladysmith is an attractive community of about 5,000 people located on Vancouver Island, five miles west of Telegraph Harbour. There is moorage at public floats, as well as at two marinas. The Ivy Green Marina has transient moorage only when permanently moored boats are away. A repair yard is adjacent. Manana Lodge and Marina, on Page Point on the east side of Ladysmith Harbour, has moorage with power and water, gas and diesel fuels as well as showers, laundry, a restaurant, and accommodations. Metric Chart #3443, scale 1:40,000 covers this area.

The Inn of the Sea is located on the west side of Stuart Channel, ½-mile north of Yellow Point. It has moorage with power and water, restaurant, and accommodations. Approach from the southeast to avoid shoals shown on the chart. There is not much protection from winds. Nine miles north up Stuart Channel is Dodd Narrows, and it is another five miles to Nanaimo.

Dodd Narrows, Northumberland Channel

Tugs with barges or log rafts use this narrow passage, as well as pleasure and commercial fishing boats. Currents can attain eight to ten knots, so passage at or near slack tide is recommended. Times of tidal changes and velocities are given in Volume 5 of the Canadian Tide and Current Tables.

It is five miles via Northumberland Channel from Dodd Narrows to Nanaimo Harbour. Keep to the east side of the channel until you can clear the light on Jack Point and head west into Nanaimo Harbour.

With a population of approximately 60,000, **Nanaimo** is the second largest city on Vancouver Island, and is growing rapidly. Because of extensive development by the Nanaimo Harbour Commission, the waterfront park areas, moorages, and buildings have changed dramatically in the last ten years.

There are several facilities for boaters, including the new Cameron Island Marina and the moorage floats at the Commercial Inlet Basin. If approaching from the south, you round Cameron Island and the new 600 foot Visiting Vessel Pier. Moorage for cruise ships and large craft is found at the pier. Smaller pleasure boats are accommodated at floats, with power and water, inside the pier, near the fuel float and in the inner basin. With the exceptions of the "B" float and the tug float in the inner basin, all floats are open to pleasure craft. In total, 9,000 feet of moorage is available on a non-reserved basis. Facilities and services include showers, laundry, restrooms, gas, diesel, and Eco-Barge waste pump-out. The Wharfinger can be reached by calling on VHF Channel 67.

A promenade, 2½ miles in length, rims the waterfront, connecting the boat basin with parks and other attractions to the north, along Newcastle Island Passage. In the immediate vicinity of Commercial Inlet Basin moorage is Pioneer Waterfront Plaza, a public plaza featuring concessions and retail shops. Harbour Park Mall, located on the hillside across the street, has a large supermarket, a Government Liquor Store, and many small shops. Nanaimo has all of the amenities that you would expect to find in a city of its size. Bus and taxi service connects with parts of the city and other Vancouver Island communities. Scheduled passenger service is provided by float plane to Vancouver and charter flights to Victoria can be arranged.

Nanaimo has an interesting history, and many historic buildings are featured on a walking tour of the downtown. When coal deposits were discovered in 1849 and the Hudson's Bay Company began mining in 1852, Nanaimo soon became an important coaling station, and mining continued for about 100 years.

Newcastle Island Passage

Newcastle Island lies across Newcastle Island Passage from Nanaimo. The entire island is a provincial marine park. A public float, and good anchorage are in Mark Bay, on the south side of the island. In the summer, a passenger-only ferry connects the island with the city. In addition to the marine facilities, the park offers camping, picnic sites, and hiking trails. A popular pub and restaurant, Dinghy Dock Pub, is nearby.

Newcastle Island Passage has a great variety of marine-oriented businesses and facilities, including the Nanaimo Yacht Club. Several of these offer transient moorage. See the Appendix of this book.

Departure Bay, at the north end of the passage, opens into the Strait of Georgia. B.C. Ferries has a large terminal facility in Departure Bay, from which ferries depart for Horseshoe Bay, north of Vancouver and Tsawwassen, south of Vancouver.

North From Nanaimo

It is 4½ miles from either the Port of Nanaimo floats, or Newcastle Island Marina Park, to Neck Point, using Metric Chart #3458, scale 1:20,000.

Our route takes us west for 7½ miles, past Nanoose Harbour, to Schooner Cove Resort Hotel. Using Metric Chart #L/C3512, scale 1:80,000. In addition to moorage with power, and water, the facility offers a coffee shop, restaurant, pub, accommodations, and golf course. Gasoline is available. No diesel.

Ballenas Island Lighthouse is 3½ miles north of Schooner Cove. If crossing the Strait of Georgia at this point, it is nine miles to Upwood Point, on the south end of Texada Island. This is not only the most sheltered route across the Strait of Georgia from Nanaimo, it is also the one that should be used when the Canadian Forces Torpedo Test Range WG (Whiskey Golf) is active. From Upwood Point, it is then only eight miles across Malaspina Strait to Pender Harbour on the mainland. Pender Harbour is covered in Chapter 1. Before crossing, it is only prudent to check the weather forecast and sea conditions. Particular attention should be paid to the reports from Ballenas Island and Entrance Island on the south side of the strait, and Merry Island on the north side.

Continuing west, along the shoreline of Vancouver Island, it is another nine miles to **French Creek**, where a dredged channel, minimum depth three feet, leads to a public wharf and floats with power, water, and fuel. There is also a launching ramp.

Three more miles west, you pass the resort community of **Qualicum Beach**. There are no facilities for boaters, though un-protected anchorages are available offshore.

The highest island that looms ahead is Hornby Island. Just to the west, and extending nearly parallel to the Vancouver Island coast, is low-lying Denman Island. As you get closer, you will be able to make out the large set of buildings around the Chrome Island Lighthouse off the south end of Denman Island. Use Metric Chart #L/C3513, scale 1:80,000. To the north, off the north end of Lasqueti Island, the prominent Sisters Island Lighthouse can be seen.

The most protected and interesting route to Comox is via **Baynes Sound**, between Denman and Vancouver Islands. Be sure to pass starboard of the green buoy P39 marking the shoals off Mapleguard Point when entering this passage. It is 16 miles northwest to Comox Harbour, using Metric Chart #3527, scale 1:40,000.

Comox offers a choice of marina operations. Black Fin Pub and Marina has transient moorage. Desolation Sound Yacht Charters, Bob Stevenson owner, is based there and their boats sometimes occupy many of the slips. Fuel, power, water, showers, and laundry are available. Comox Municipal Marina has many slips for small craft, limited space for larger boats. Power and water are available. Des Reid Marina (Comox Bay Marina) has transient moorage, power, water, showers, laundry, and haul-out. Government floats, with power and water, are open when the fishing fleet is out. New floats have been added, with power and water. The Courtenay Valley area, which includes Comox, is growing very rapidly, and a more orderly marine development is probable in the future. The city is looking for an operator/developer for their floats.

Departing Comox to head north in the Strait of Georgia, it is first necessary to cross the Comox Bar. From the light on Goose Spit, at the entrance to the harbor, head for Sandy Island. Proceed about two miles on that course, until you can see the three red buoys that should be lined up to indicate the proper course, as shown on Chart #3527. The range markers shown on this chart are lights only, so are of no benefit during daylight hours. Keeping the red buoys to port, the smoke from the Powell River Pulp mill, across the Strait of Georgia, should be dead ahead, more or less. The chart shows a least depth of over two meters, so even on a low tide most boats should have plenty of water. Continuing on the same course about two more miles, you must first round East Cardinal Buoy "PJ", black with a yellow band to clear the shoals around Cape Lazo.

For a description of Cardinal Marks, or buoys, see page 80 of Canadian Chart 1, Symbols, Abbreviations, and terms. This 112 page book explains all of the different symbols that appear on your marine charts, and is a very necessary adjunct to your charts.

Heading north or northwest up the Strait of Georgia, use Metric Chart #L/C3513, scale 1:80,000. If going to Campbell River, the course is along the shore of Vancouver Island until you enter Discovery Passage. It is about 22 miles from Cape Lazo to the lighthouse on Cape Mudge. It is a weather reporting station, so you can be aware of the wind and sea conditions at Cape Mudge. The same is true at Cape Lazo. Comox Coast Guard on WX-1 covers this area.

If your destination is Desolation Sound, Cortes Island, or Sutil Channel, your course will take you past, or close to, rocky Mitlenatch Island. Because it is the nesting ground for many sea birds, it is designated as a Nature Reserve. During the nesting season, visits ashore are restricted. If heading for Manson's Landing, or Gorge Harbour on the west side of Cortes Island, be sure to clear the big red bell buoy 020, off Sutil Point, or you will run aground on the shoal that it marks. The Sutil Point vicinity is covered in Chapter 3. If you wish to take an alternate route through Sutil, Hoskyn, and Okisollo Channels to reach the Chatham Point vicinity and Johnstone Strait, see the description that follows information regarding Discovery Passage.

Discovery Passage

Discovery Passage is entered at Cape Mudge. Metric Chart #3539, scale 1:40,000 should be used. Another Metric Chart, #3540, Approaches to Campbell River, scale 1:10,000 is helpful. Discovery Passage separates Vancouver and Quadra Islands. Tidal currents flood to the south and ebb to the north, attaining speeds of five to seven knots on big tides. These currents meet those coming around the south end of Vancouver Island between Cape Mudge and Cape Lazo. Strong tide rips can occur where the two flood tides meet. Especially strong tide rips occur in the vicinity of Cape Mudge when a flood tide meets south or southeast winds coming up the Strait of Georgia. Even fairly large vessels can get into difficulty, so caution is advised when these conditions exist. Discovery Passage, named for Vancouver's ship is the main shipping route between the Strait of Georgia and Queen Charlotte Strait to the northwest. It is used by cruise ships, ferries, tugs with barges or log rafts, as well as numerous commercial fishing boats and pleasure craft.

Campbell River, population 21,175, is on the Vancouver Island side of Discovery Passage. It is the largest community on the island north of Nanaimo. At one time it was the best known salmon fishing area on the coast, however, in recent years, this emphasis has moved farther north, first to Port Hardy and Rivers Inlet, and then to Hakai Passage and the Queen Charlotte Islands.

Campbell River has marinas as well as a large public boat basin. The latter is located behind the rock breakwater just south of the Quadra Island ferry terminal. Moorage, gas and diesel fuel, and showers are available, but it is often crowded with commercial fish boats. Among the private marinas is Discovery Marina, adjacent to the ferry terminal. It has moorage with power and water, as well as gas and diesel fuels, propane, CNG, showers and laundry. The newest development is Discovery Harbour Marina, located about ½-mile farther north. Located behind a breakwater, it has moorage with power and water, gas, and diesel fuels and showers. Because it is larger, it may be the easiest place to find moorage space. Freshwater Marina is located inland, up the Campbell River, and can only accommodate small boats. It has moorage with power, water, gasoline, and ice.

Campbell River has a wide selection of restaurants, hotels, motels, as well as shopping facilities and a large hospital. It is connected to Vancouver and Victoria by bus and air services, and to Quadra Island by ferry.

Quadra Island, on the east side of Discovery Passage was named for the Spanish explorer, Quadra, who explored the coast at the same time as Vancouver. They became good friends, and Vancouver originally named Vancouver Island "Quadra and Vancouver Island", but this was changed by the British Admiralty who said the name was too long and unwieldy. Quadra had to settle for having his name on the smaller island. **Quathiaski Cove** on Quadra Island has moorage with power at the public floats. Gas and diesel fuel are available at a nearby facility. Provisions, a liquor store, a post office, a restaurant and small shopping center are nearby. Quathiaski Cove is the eastern terminus of the Campbell River-Quadra Island ferry.

Well-known April Point Marina is about 1½ miles north of Quathiaski Cove. It has 6,000 feet of moorage space with power and water, restaurant, accommodations, guide service and fishing charters.

Gowlland Harbour, near April Point, offers good anchorages in six to seven fathoms, soft bottom, and very good protection. Entry is around the north end of Gowlland Island; do not attempt the rock-strewn southern entrance.

When proceeding north and west from the Strait of Georgia to Queen Charlotte Strait, it is necessary to go through at least one set of rapids. Discovery Passage has only one, Seymour Narrows, while the other routes through the Discovery Islands have three or more. **Seymour Narrows** makes up for this by being much faster, up to 16 knots on big spring tides. Located seven miles north of Campbell River; passage is definitely at or near slack tide, using the inset on Metric Chart #3539. Times of slack tide and maximum velocities are given in Volume 6 of the Canadian Tide and Current Tables. In 1958, Ripple Rock, which is in the center of the narrows, and had been responsible for many ship wrecks and lost lives, was partially removed by the largest non-nuclear explosion in the world. To accomplish this, a tunnel was driven from shore, a cavity hollowed out, and packed with explosives. The explosion vaporized the top of the rock, killing many fish, but removing a dangerous obstruction.

After passing Seymour Narrows, Discovery Passage continues north for another 12 miles to Chatham Point Lighthouse, where it meets Johnstone Strait. Brown's Bay Marina is located on the Vancouver Island shore about ½-mile north of the north entrance to Seymour Narrows. It has moorage, power, water, gas and diesel fuels. Note the unusual breakwater, a series of floating railroad tankers tied together. The Island Highway connects it with Campbell River.

Kanish Bay, on Quadra Island, about 7½ miles north of Seymour Narrows has several good, protected anchorages. The Chained Islands on the south side of the bay have anchorages in ten to 15 fathoms, mud bottom. Granite Bay, in the southeast corner of Kanish Bay, has a protected anchorage in four to seven fathoms on a mud bottom. The village of Granite Bay, now gone, was located here; it had a small hotel and public school. Small Inlet, in the northeast corner of Kanish Bay has well protected anchorages in three to six fathoms, soft bottom. There is a minimum depth of eight feet in the entrance.

The west entrance to Okisollo Channel, which will be described later in this chapter, is 1½ miles north of Kanish Bay.

Chatham Point Lighthouse, three miles north of Okisollo Channel is at the junction of Discovery Passage, Johnstone Strait and Nodales Channel. Otter Cove, just south of Chatham Point, offers shelter if a west wind is blowing in Johnstone Strait. Enter north of Limestone Island, and anchor near the head; the bottom is rock.

Nodales Channel runs eight miles northeast from Chatham Point to join Cordero Channel, a more protected route than Johnstone Strait. There are several good anchorages in Thurston Bay Marine Park, on the east side of Nodales Channel that are described in Chapter 3.

Alternate Route to Chatham Point Vicinity and Johnstone Strait: Sutil Channel, Hoskyn Channel, Okisollo Channel

An alternative route from the Cape Mudge vicinity through the Discovery Islands is by Sutil Channel to Hoskyn Channel and through Surge Narrows to Okisollo Channel. This by-passes Campbell River and joins Discovery Passage at the north end of Quadra Island.

Surge Narrows, the southern entrance to Okisollo Channel, is reached via Hoskyn Channel, seven miles north of Heriot Bay. See Chapter 3 for description of Heriot Bay. Hoskyn Channel, between Quadra and Read Islands, leads to the small settlement named Surge Narrows, and on to the narrows themselves. At the settlement are some public floats, but no other facilities.

Whiterock Passage connects Hoskyn Channel with Calm Channel. This passage avoids the strong currents in Surge Narrows. The dredged channel has a least depth of six feet, and currents of only two knots, flooding north and ebbing south. There are two sets of range markers in the passage. Use the inset on Metric Chart #3537, scale 1:10,000.

Tides in Surge Narrows flood south and ebb to the north, reaching 12 knots on the flood and 10 knots on the ebb during big spring tides. At maximum velocities there can be a wall of water four feet high in the passage. The strongest currents occur in Beazley Passage. The inset on Chart #3537 should be used. Okisollo Channel, which is 12 miles long, runs along the east and north shores of Quadra Island.

Five miles north of Surge Narrows, the **Hole-in-the-Wall** branches off to the east. It connects Okisollo and Calm Channels. Rapids at its west end can run to 12 knots and should only be traversed at or near slack tide. Anchorage is possible in Florence Cove in ten to 15 fathoms.

The Upper Rapids in **Okisollo Channel**, just north of the Hole-in-the-Wall, should be traversed at or near slack tide. Currents can reach nine knots, flooding south and ebbing north. The Lower Rapids, one mile west of Upper Rapids can be avoided by passing north of the Okis Islands. Okisollo Channel continues west another five miles to Granite Point where it joins Discovery Passage.

Good anchorages along Okisollo Channel are in the Octopus Islands Marine Park, Waiatt Bay, and Owen Bay. Octopus Island Marine Park is entered from Bodega Anchorage, traversing the narrow passage between Quadra and the Octopus Islands. Mid-channel depths are 15 to 20 feet, but there are several rocks at the south end of the passage. The best anchorages are in the second bay in one to two fathoms, mud bottom. Large Waiatt Bay can also be entered through this passage and has anchorages in three to six fathoms throughout, on mud bottom.

Owen Bay, northeast of the Upper Rapids has a public float and numerous good anchorage possibilities in four to eight fathoms, mud bottom, and good protection.

From the junction of Okisollo Channel and Discovery Passage, it is three miles north to Chatham Point Lighthouse. This area is described earlier, in the last paragraph regarding Discovery Passage.

Johnstone Strait

Johnstone Strait runs 54 miles northwest, along the Vancouver Island shoreline, from Chatham Point to the Blinkhorn Peninsula. It has a well deserved reputation for rough sea conditions, usually due to strong northwest winds opposing an ebb tide. Johnstone Strait has a strong residual westerly ebb current, and, on some days, little or no flood currents. The section in Volume 6 of the Tide and Current Tables under Johnstone Strait-Central, represents conditions at a point 1½ miles west of Port Neville, and does not represent conditions in other parts of the strait. Tides flood to the east and ebb to the west.

About 5½ miles west of Chatham Point, Mayne Passage, another "escape" route to Cordero Channel, enters Johnstone Strait. It is described in Chapter 3. Blind Channel Resort, with moorage, fuel, provisions, and restaurant is on the West Thurlow Island shore. Use Metric Chart #3543, scale 1:40,000.

Helmcken Island lies in the center of Johnstone Strait, 17 miles west of Chatham Point, and creates some of the worse sea conditions in the entire strait. Strong currents and tide rips may be encountered at Ripple Point, in Race and Current Passages, and at Earl Ledge. In Current Passage, currents can attain five knots on the ebb and three knots on the flood. In Race Passage, currents can reach seven knots on both the flood and ebb. Chancellor Channel, between West Thurlow and Hardwicke Islands is an alternate route, leading to Wellbore Channel, if conditions are too rough around Helmcken Island. An automated weather station on Helmcken Island gives wind velocities, but does not report sea conditions.

Kelsey Bay is on Vancouver Island, about 2½ miles west of the western end of Helmcken Island. There are some public floats behind the breakwater, but they are usually jammed with commercial boats. No fuel is available, nor is there a store.

Yorke Island, 2½ miles north of Kelsey Bay, and additional coverage of Johnstone Strait are contained in Chapter 3.

Seymour Narrows

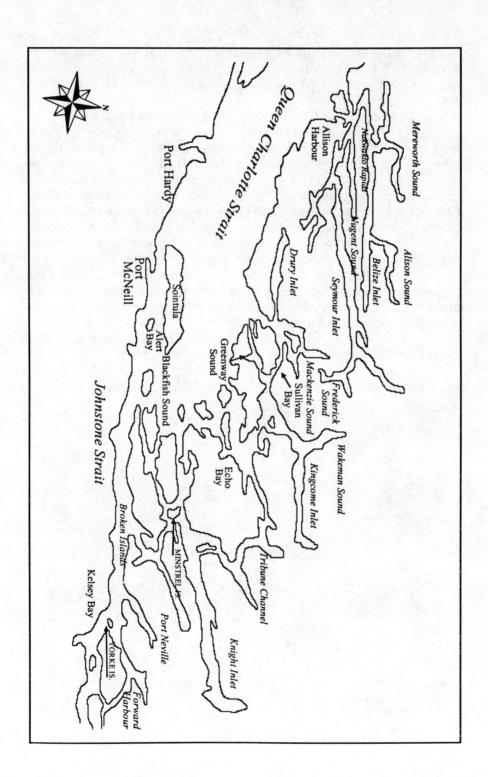

Chapter 5: Johnstone and Queen Charlotte Straits

Yorke Island to Port Hardy

The section of Johnstone Strait that stretches from Yorke Island to the Blinkhorn Peninsula, where the strait ends, is 31 miles long. The eastern section of the strait, which runs 23 miles to Chatham Point Lighthouse, was covered in Chapter 4.

Johnstone Strait has a well deserved reputation with pleasure boaters for rough water conditions. These conditions often result from an ebbing current to the west opposing some wind coming from the west. Tides flood to the east and ebb to the west at rates of 1.5 to 2.5 knots. There is a strong residual westerly current resulting from fresh water flows from the various inlets, and on some days there is little or no flood current in Johnstone Strait. The tidal predictions in Volume 6 of the Tide Tables for Johnstone Strait (central) are for a point about one and a half miles west of Port Neville. In spite of its reputation, the sections from Yorke Island to the Broken Islands, 13 miles, or to the light on the Blinkhorn Peninsula, the west end of Johnstone Strait, 31 miles, are usually not difficult to traverse. We have done it over 35 times, and have only had uncomfortable conditions half a dozen times. On one occasion, however, we did spend three nights in Forward Harbour waiting for a gale to subside.

The best way to avoid trouble in Johnstone Strait is to traverse it as early in the day as possible, avoiding the wind that usually comes up in the afternoon, especially on clear days. If the wind does come up when you are heading west, you can always duck into Port Neville about four miles west of Yorke Island; or go on to Broken Islands, another nine miles west, and take the sheltered scenic inside route through the islands. For now, we will continue west along the Vancouver Island shore until we reach Port Hardy, about 63 miles west of Yorke Island. We will cover the "inside" route in Chapter 7.

Johnstone Strait always has a lot of traffic along it, cruise ships, ferries, tugs with barges and log rafts, and commercial fishing boats, as well as pleasure craft. The tall mountains, especially those on Vancouver Island, create some very nice scenery. Recent heavy logging activities are very apparent on the mountains on both sides of Johnstone Strait.

Blenkinsop Bay lies about two miles northwest of Yorke Island, but does not afford good anchorage. The head of the bay is shallow, and all of it is exposed to west winds coming down Johnstone Strait.

Port Neville, two miles further west, is a better choice if seeking shelter. The only remnants of the former community are the post office in the building at the head of the wharf, which is open intermittently, usually when the mail plane arrives, and the Hansen residence. There is a small public float at the wharf. As at all public floats, rafting is mandatory. It is also possible to anchor on the west side of the inlet, but tidal currents, sometimes carrying drift wood, can be strong, running to as much as three knots. Ole Hansen, a long time resident of Port Neville, lives in the house just west of the floats, and monitors VHF Channel 6, answering to "Sea Scout III". He will give mariners local weather and water conditions for this section of Johnstone Strait.

The most protected anchorages in seven-mile-long Port Neville are about two miles past the public floats, in the vicinity of Robber's Nob. The best one is in the niche southeast of the little island across the inlet from Robber's Nob, in five fathoms, mud bottom and good protection. The second is on the east side of Robber's Nob, which has some cabins on it. Indian petroglyphs are said to be found on the northwest side of Robber's Nob.

Another well protected anchorage is on the south side of the inlet, three miles further northeast, and just past the narrows. A large, active logging camp was on the north side of the inlet, at its head in 1993. Charts #3545 or #3564, both Metric, should be used in Port Neville. A perusal of either chart will show that, in settled weather, it is possible to anchor almost anywhere in Port Neville in four to ten fathoms, mud bottoms.

Nine miles west of Port Neville is the Broken Islands Light, where shelter may be found in nearby **Port Harvey**, or you can turn into Havannah Channel, and go through the islands. There is a well protected anchorage at the head of Port Harvey, north of Range Island in five fathoms, mud bottom. Use Chart #3564. There are beautiful views from this spot of the Bonanza Range of mountains on Vancouver Island, across Johnstone Strait. During the last ten years there has been some development in Port Harvey, mostly float houses, but there are some new homes on land as well. It is a popular anchorage, but there is plenty of room for a number of boats without crowding. Don't go too far to the east because it shoals rapidly. See Chapter 7 for the inside route from Havannah Channel.

Continuing west in Johnstone Strait, it is 14 miles farther to the light on Cracroft Point on West Cracroft Island. Possible anchorages on the shore of West Cracroft Island are found in Forward Bay, Boat Bay and Growler Cove. The best anchorage in Forward Bay is at the west end of the bay, north of the Bush Islands, with good protection from west winds. Boat Bay is just east of the light on Swaine Point, and offers shelter north of the islet lying about one-eighth of a mile off shore. When entering Boat Bay, beware of the foul ground around the entrance. Growler Cove is about two and a half miles west of the Swaine Point Light, and is entered between the Sophia Islands and Baron Reef. Anchorage is possible in five to seven fathoms at the east end, open to west winds.

Robson Bight, on the Vancouver Island shore across from Swaine Point Light, was named for Lieutenant Commander Charles Robson of the Royal Navy. It has been designated as a protected reserve for Killer Whales, which are very common in this section of Johnstone Strait. The whales use the shallow beaches to rub barnacles off their backs. About two thirds of the pods, or groups of Killer Whales, that travel between British Columbia and the State of Washington are found in this area for part of each year. Boaters are required to stay at least one half mile off shore in the Robson Bight area, and to give the whales themselves a wide berth. You will probably see one or more excursion boats from Telegraph Cove or Port McNeill taking people to see the whales.

Broughton Strait

At Cracroft Point, Johnstone Strait continues west for another four miles to the light on the Blinkhorn Peninsula, on Vancouver Island. Broughton Strait is a continuation of Johnstone Strait and, at its west end, leads into Queen Charlotte Strait. Use Metric Chart #3546, scale 1:40,000. It was named by Captain Vancouver for the master of his escort ship, the *Chatham*, Lt. Commander William Broughton. Blackney Passage goes off to the north at Cracroft Point, and leads into Blackfish Sound, which in turn runs into Queen Charlotte Strait. Anchorage and moorage facilities in the Blackfish Sound area are covered in Chapter 7. Currents in Blackney Passage run to four knots, ebbing north and flooding south. The flood currents coming around both the north and south sides of Hanson Island meet off Cracroft Point, and create some very strong tide rips. The north side of Cracroft Point is a very popular spot for salmon fishing; you will usually see a lot of small boats there.

The tiny settlement of **Telegraph Cove** is on the Vancouver Island shore, about two miles west of the Blinkhorn Peninsula Light. It is a very popular spot for trailer boaters, who camp and launch there to fish the local waters. In 1993, a developer had taken over much of Telegraph Cove, removing the small saw mill that had been a land mark since the establishment of the community. There are no facilities for moorage for any craft over 25 feet. A small store and post office, as well as a campground, a launching ramp and floats for small boats are in the cove. Gas is available.

Beaver Cove lies immediately west of Telegraph Cove, and is the site of a large logging operation. It is not a good anchorage because of the depths, and the presence of many sunken logs on the bottom, resulting from the saw mill that operated in the past. One interesting fact about Beaver Cove is that one of the last logging railroads terminates there, bringing logs from the interior of Vancouver Island to the salt water, where they are loaded onto log carriers.

Weynton Passage, between Hanson Island and the Pearse Islands, leads from Johnstone Strait to Blackfish Sound, which is the east end of Queen Charlotte Strait. Tidal streams can attain as much as six knots at times. There are heavy tide rips near both shores and near Stubbs Island. Times and rates of maximum currents as well as slack water are in the Tide and Current Tables, Volume 6.

The village of **Alert Bay,** four miles west of Beaver Cove, is on the south and west sides of Cormorant Island, across Broughton Strait from the large delta of the Nimpkish River. Currents can run to four knots in Broughton Strait, and large tide rips may be encountered. Alert Bay is the oldest European settlement in this area, with a population of about 700, many of whom are native Indians. It was named after a ship of the Royal Navy, *HMS Alert*. It is a commercial fishing port, and supply point for much of this area. Weather reports previously broadcast on VHF Channel WX-1 from the Alert Bay Coast Guard Station, now come from Comox Coast Guard. Repeaters at Alert Bay, WX-1, Port Hardy, WX-2 Holberg WX-4 (21-B) and Calvert Island WX-2, cover about 170 miles of the British Columbia Coast, from Forward Harbour to Ivory Island Lighthouse, 15 miles west of Bella Bella. Call Comox Coast Guard while in this area. A detachment of the Royal Canadian Mounted Police (RCMP or Mounties) is based at Alert Bay.

A small, unprotected public float is in front of the town, and has space for six to eight boats for temporary moorage. A harbor for small boats, with power and water on the floats, is located just north of the ferry dock, behind the breakwater. It is usually crowded with commercial fishing boats. A car-carrying ferry, running on a frequent schedule connects Alert Bay with Port McNeill, five miles to the west, and also to Sointula, on Malcolm Island. Alert Bay has a complete marine fuel facility. Be aware that strong currents can be present when docking. A large grocery and general store is just above the small public float, and the liquor store and post office are in the nearby Government Building. Alert Bay Shipyard has a complete machine shop and repair facilities, three marine ways, and a store carrying marine supplies.

Anchorage in seven fathoms, sand bottom is possible about three tenths of a mile southwest of the breakwater light, but it is exposed to all of the wakes from passing boats and the ferry.

The Kwakiutl Tribe inhabiting Alert Bay have become famous for their artistry and handcrafts. The numerous totem poles around town are proof of these talents. The very tall one near the former school building is one of the tallest in the world. The U'Mista Cultural Centre contains some of the regalia formerly in use in religious and other ceremonies. In the 1920's, most of these works were confiscated by Indian Agents in their attempt to stamp out paganism and the tradition of potlatch feasts. The provincial and federal governments recently returned these items to the Kwakiutls.

Port McNeill, on Vancouver Island, is five miles west of Alert Bay, down Broughton Strait. With a population of 2,641, it is a fishing and logging community, and has, to a large extent, replaced Alert Bay as a supply point for this area. In the past ten years, the Town of Port McNeill has developed the best pleasure boat facility on the north end of Vancouver Island. All of the floats, both for commercial and pleasure craft, are behind the large rock breakwater. The old government floats, used only for commercial boats now, can be seen on the port side, behind the breakwater, as you enter. Each year the town has been adding new floats for pleasure boats. Power and water are available. A garbage drop is at the head of the ramp. Complete fuel facilities are located on the float just west of the pleasure boat floats. Reservations are not taken for moorage; it is on a first come basis. If the floats are full, it is possible to anchor out in the harbor and dinghy in, but be aware that the harbor is a busy float plane airdrome, and don't anchor in their landing and take-off area.

Most of the commercial center of the town is within a block of the floats. It includes the post office, a bank (open 9:30 a.m.-3:30 p.m. weekdays), a well-stocked grocery and general store, a large drug store, several restaurants, a marine supply and sporting goods store and a laundromat. A Provincial Liquor Store and a second grocery store, are two blocks away. Showers are available in the hotel. A hospital is accessible. The combination of the new, improved facilities and the convenience of having the downtown business district handy to the floats has made Port McNeill a favorite destination and provisioning spot for many boaters.

Port McNeill also has excellent transportation facilities. Bus service connects it with Port Hardy, Nanaimo (with connections to Vancouver) and Victoria. In addition, there is van service leaving from the bus stop, one block from the floats, to the Port Hardy airport, about 15 miles away, where two airlines have prop-jet service, non-stop, to Vancouver. Several float plane operations offer frequent service to points in the islands and the nearby mainland. Ferry service also connects Port McNeill with Alert Bay and Sointula. These services make Port McNeill a good point for picking up or dropping off guests.

Sointula, on the south side of Malcolm Island, is four miles northeast of Port McNeill, across Broughton Strait. There is a large public small craft harbor behind the breakwater one mile north of the center of the town. A small public float is located next to the ferry landing, right downtown. It is usually crowded, and only suitable for temporary moorage. The floats in the small craft harbor are marked for commercial boats and for pleasure boats, and have power. Fresh water, a garbage drop and repair facilities are accessible.

Fishing is the chief occupation of Sointula's 1,000 inhabitants. Sointula means "Harmony" in the Finnish language, and was settled by Finnish immigrants at the turn-of-the-century. If you make the one mile walk into town from the boat basin, you will notice how neat the town and its houses are, largely due to the influence of the Finnish settlers. The Co-op Grocery and General Store dates from 1909 and is the oldest and one of the largest co-op stores on the coast. It is very well stocked. There are no marine fuel facilities, but the town has, in addition to the store, a post office, hospital, liquor store, restaurant, bank (open only on certain days), marine hardware and various other shops. It is connected to Port McNeill and Alert Bay by car/passenger ferry. A visit to Sointula is always a pleasant experience.

Queen Charlotte Strait

Broughton Strait ends at Pulteney Point, with its lighthouse, located on the southwest corner of Malcolm Island. Here you enter Queen Charlotte Strait, which connects Johnstone and Broughton Straits with Queen Charlotte Sound to the northwest, and separates Vancouver Island from the mainland. Use Chart #3548, scale 1:40,000. The strait is about 50 miles long and up to 15 miles wide, a big enough body of water to create rough conditions, and it often does just that. Tidal streams are east-southeast on the flood and west-northwest on the ebb. Winds in Queen Charlotte Strait are predominantly from the northwest in the summer. On clear sunny days, the warming of the land masses will cause winds to rise in the late morning and throughout the afternoon, often reaching 25 to 30 knots. When these winds oppose an ebbing tide, conditions can become very uncomfortable. Obviously, the best way to deal with these conditions is to begin any crossing of Queen Charlotte Strait as early in the morning as possible, when it should be smoother.

August and September are the foggiest months of the year in these waters, and present more problems. We often think, or hope, that a fog will burn off as the day progresses, but that is not always the case. On one occasion, during the second week of September, the lighthouse at Egg Island, north of Cape Caution, reported visibilities of one half mile or less, usually one fourth mile or less, 24 hours a day for five straight days. We were out in it the first two days, coming down from Fitzhugh Sound, but spent the last three days in Seymour Inlet, which was fog free, even though its location is very close to Queen Charlotte Strait. Fog is sometimes present in other months all of the way up the coast. For this reason we consider radar an absolute necessity for cruising Queen Charlotte Strait, and all waters north of it, including Southeast Alaska. We have never used LORAN, or GPS, though many boaters find it helpful, but to us these aids would not be as important as radar for Inside Passage travel. There is a lot of traffic in Queen Charlotte Strait and Queen Charlotte Sound, cruise ships, ferries, tugs and barges, commercial fishing boats, and pleasure boats, which must be avoided in the fog. It is a very good idea to become well familiar with your radar before facing a situation in which foggy conditions may be encountered.

An alternative to moorage in Port Hardy, if you don't need supplies, is to anchor in **Beaver Harbour**. The harbor was named for the Hudson's Bay Company ship, *The Beaver*, the first steamship on this coast. Beaver Harbour is about three miles south of the Masterman Islands. There are three entrances to Beaver Harbour, through Daedalus Passage to the north, on the west side of Peel Island, the passage south of Peel Island, or the southern entrance between Deer Island and Thomas Point. One anchorage is on a soft bottom in five to seven fathoms on the west side of the Cattle Islands, with good protection from all but northwest winds. The Shell Islands to the south have several very large shell middens on them. If the wind is from the northwest, a more comfortable anchorage may be in Patrician Cove in the northwest corner of the harbor, in seven fathoms, soft bottom. The largely native settlement of Fort Rupert is at the south end of the harbor. It is the site of a former Hudson Bay Company post, one of the oldest settlements on Vancouver Island, dating back to 1849. Coal was mined here for a while, which was the reason that the post was established. The mines were abandoned when large coal deposits at Nanaimo were discovered and developed.

The entrance to Hardy Bay is 13 miles northwest of Pulteney Point, and the town of **Port Hardy** is four miles into the bay, at its head. Shoals extend from the shore on the west side; be sure to keep all red markers well to starboard when entering Hardy Bay.

Port Hardy, with 5,000 inhabitants, is the largest community and chief supply point for north Vancouver Island. It is a logging, mining, and commercial fishing town. With the 1979 completion of the Island Highway north from Kelsey Bay, tourism, including sports fishing, has also become very important. For boaters heading to the north coast of British Columbia or Alaska, Port Hardy, along with Port McNeill and Alert Bay, is a provisioning and refueling point—the last chance for some distance.

There are four mooring areas, (1) a small public float in front of town, (2) floats near the fueling station outside of the breakwater, and inside the breakwater, (3) a large set of public floats to starboard, often crowded with commercial boats but open to pleasure boats also and (4) to port the floats of Quarterdeck Marine. Quarterdeck Marine, owned and operated by Vern Logan, has water, limited power, fuel, propane, CNG, marine hardware, charts, fishing supplies, showers, laundromat, boat rentals, RV park and 60 ton Travelift for hauling boats. They will take reservations for moorage. Reservations advised in July and August. In recent years, maintenance on these floats has been neglected, resulting in complaints from some boaters.

The town center is located a distance of about one half mile from the last facilities described above, and has a shopping center with a large grocery store, drug store and many other shops. In addition, there is a hospital, post office, liquor store, two banks, an excellent bakery, restaurants and many more facilities. Because of staggered schedules, banking services are offered six days per week. One bank is open Monday and the other is open Saturday. Taxi service is available. When returning to your boat with supplies, the grocery store may pay for the taxi if your purchase is large, and you tell them you are on a boat.

There are three fuel facilities. Two are located at the floats at the head of the bay and another is in Bear Cove, across from the ferry dock.

Port Hardy offers excellent transportation services. Two airlines fly turbo-prop land planes non-stop to Vancouver. Bus service connects with Nanaimo, Vancouver and Victoria, and the British Columbia Ferry, *Queen of the North*, runs to Prince Rupert every other day during the summer months. These make Port Hardy a good location for boating visitors, who are either arriving or departing.

Queen Charlotte Strait

Burial Boxes, Byrnes Island, Blunden Harbour

Ebb Tide, Seymour Inlet

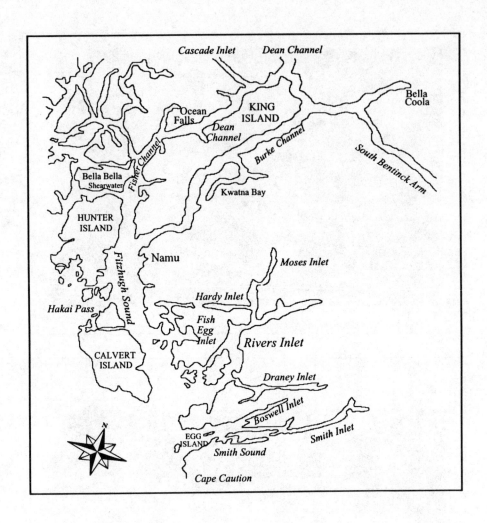

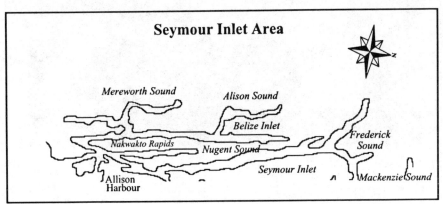

Seymour Inlet Area

Chapter 6: Queen Charlotte Strait and Queen Charlotte Sound

Port Hardy to Cape Caution and Fitzhugh Sound

Heading north, regardless of which of the communities may be your jumping off point, Alert Bay, Port McNeill, Sointula, Port Hardy, or one of the marinas in the Kingcome Inlet area, the waters of Queen Charlotte Strait and Queen Charlotte Sound are the greatest challenge of the entire Inside Passage, all of the way to Skagway. In the last chapter we pointed out the weather conditions that may be encountered. In addition to the wind and fog previously mentioned, tidal currents flow to and from the south in Queen Charlotte Strait and Queen Charlotte Sound, to and from Fitzhugh Sound to the north, as well as in and out of several large mainland inlets. As you near Cape Caution you will begin to meet swells coming in from the Pacific Ocean to the west. When these currents meet, and/or are opposed by some wind or swells, it can be very uncomfortable. The advice given in the previous chapter, to begin a crossing as early in the day as possible, is the best way to avoid trouble. Listen to the weather forecasts and local conditions on Comox Coast Guard, WX-1 Alert Bay, or WX-2 Port Hardy, the night before starting; and in the morning, as you go north, you can pick these broadcasts up first on WX-1, Alert Bay; and WX-2, Port Hardy; WX-4, Holberg (21-B); and later WX-2, Calvert Island. Pay particular attention to reports from Egg Island, Pine Island, Scarlett Point and Pulteney Point. As you get farther north, reports from the Addenbroke Island Lighthouse will give conditions in Fitzhugh Sound.

There are several routes north to Cape Caution. It lies 35 miles north of Port Hardy, and 41 miles north of Pulteney Point Lighthouse which is five miles west of Port McNeill. Basically there are two choices. One is to go straight across Queen Charlotte Strait to Cape Caution. This may be a few miles shorter, but has the most exposure. The second is to follow along the mainland shore, where there are several good places to take refuge in case weather conditions make it advisable to do so.

In spite of all that I have said about the area around Cape Caution, it is not difficult at all if you are well prepared and heed the weather forecasts and lighthouse reports of current conditions. Use Metric Charts #3549, 3550, and #3934, all on scales of 1:40,000. I consider it to have been an easy crossing if we have had good visibility and have taken no spray on the windshield. Sixty to 70% of our crossings fall into that category. Poor visibility, due to fog, has been our biggest problem. We have passed Cape Caution 26 times over an 11 year period (13 each way) and only twice have we been forced to wait for two or three days for better weather.

The first fuel and supply points north of Port Hardy are Duncanby Landing and Dawsons Landing in Rivers Inlet, 50 and 62 miles away, respectively. Namu, 75 miles, and Bella Bella, 100 miles. In 1995 the situation at Namu was uncertain, so check the latest edition of *Northwest Boat Travel* if you are planning to stop there.

The direct route goes by way of Pine Island, then past Cape Caution to Egg Island, 40 miles from Port Hardy and north another 11 miles to Clark Point on Calvert Island, where you should get some relief from the swells coming in from the west. God's Pocket Resort, on Hurst Island off Christie Passage, ten miles northwest of Port Hardy, is a good refuge and jumping off point for departure. It offers moorage, a restaurant, showers and laundry. The restaurant serves three meals a day. Reservations are necessary for dinner. They answer on VHF Channel 73.

Another possible choice is Bull Harbour on Hope Island about 23 miles northwest of Port Hardy via Goletas Channel. There is a public float, not connected to shore. Use inset on Chart #3549. This route is about 15 miles longer to Egg Island than the previously described route via Christie Passage. Do not plan to go around the west end of Hope Island without ascertaining conditions on Nahwitti Bar, which must be crossed. Currents run to five and a half knots and when a west wind meets a strong ebb current there can be very heavy, and dangerous seas, caused by shallowing depths of as little as six fathoms. Western swells, which are usually present, only make conditions worse. If you must go this way, do so near slack tide with little wind.

On all of our trips, save one, we have gone along the northeast side of Queen Charlotte Strait, fairly close to the mainland. Shelter can be found in Blunden Harbour, Allison Harbour, Skull Cove or Miles Inlet.

Blunden Harbour is on the mainland about ten miles north-northeast of Pulteney Point. It is one of our favorite anchorages, and we have visited many times. Metric Chart #3548, scale of 1:40,000, with an inset of Blunden Harbour on a scale of 1:15,000, is essential. There are many hazards in the entrance. Anchorage is in the inner cove in one and a half to four fathoms with a soft bottom. There is excellent shelter from any seas in Blunden Harbour, though the wind can, and will, get in from the west and south over the low-lying land. We have ridden out gales a couple of times without any problems. Our favorite anchorage is south of the old native village site, which can be identified by its large shell midden. Be sure to keep clear of Moore Rock, to the east, when entering or anchoring. The former Indian village located here was a large one, and a visit ashore is worth while. Be aware that it is a reservation, and digging or removing any objects is forbidden. When you land you will be standing on a shell midden, several thousand years old and many feet deep. The scraps of shells are those left from the shellfish that the inhabitants devoured. If you look up into the blackberry bushes above the beach, you can see the ends of the huge log rafters that formerly held up the roofs on the big long houses. The small red cabin on the shore was placed there in 1990 by the natives for use on their visits. We have seen families picnicking here.

There is no trespassing on Byrnes Island because it was formerly used as a burial spot. The bodies were put in wooden boxes and placed high up in the trees. Some of the boxes used to be visible from the water. Blunden Harbour is a popular place for boaters. Crabbing is usually good, if the commercial crabber from Port Hardy hasn't cleaned them out recently. Bradley Lagoon can be explored by dinghy at high tide. The entrance dries more than ten feet at low tide.

The Jeanette Islands Light is six miles northwest of Blunden Harbour; the Browning Islands are along the way. If you look at your chart you will see Mary Rock, two miles south of Jeanette Islands. There are really several rocks which are exposed on a zero tide. In 1793 Captain George Vancouver located Mary Rock the hard way; he put his ship, the *Discovery*, on it near high tide, and came very near to losing her. To keep her from rolling over when the tide fell, the crew propped her up with masts and spars, then took off some of her cargo into small boats to lighten her. They succeeded in getting her off without any great damage when the tide rose, and were able to continue their voyage. Her escort, the *Chatham* also grounded on these rocks. Vancouver named the rock, as well as Cape Caution, the latter probably because of his experience here.

At times, we have very good luck catching salmon, both springs (chinook) or coho (silvers) right in front of the light at Jeanette Islands. Bottom fishing around the kelp beds is always good. From Jeanette Island, it is another seven miles northwest to the light on Harris Island, which marks the entrance to Allison Harbour. After passing Jeanette Island you will probably notice the first swells coming in from Queen Charlotte Sound.

The entrance to **Allison Harbour** is about three miles northwest of Harris Island. The site was once a thriving logging community, but the buildings were removed many years ago, and towed to Sullivan Bay, where they burned in 1984. Anchorage, well protected, is possible in the little cove in front of the former settlement, or in the inner harbor in four to five fathoms. The bottom in the inner harbor is black, silty mud, hard to remove from an anchor rode.

Skull Cove, on the south side of Bramham Island, is one and a half miles north-northwest of the City Point Beacon, which is in the entrance to Allison Harbour. Metric Chart #3921, scale 1:20,000 is the best chart for both Allison Harbour and Skull Cove. Approaches are either through the Delorian Islands, from City Point, or along the south shore of Bramham

Island. Entry is to the east of the island that lies in the mouth of Skull Cove, don't try to pass on the west side. There are well protected anchorages in four to five fathoms, soft bottom. Anchorage is possible in the center of the first basin. If going to the back cove, keep to the west side to avoid the two drying rocks shown on the charts.

Schooner Channel leads off to the north from this area, towards Nakwakto Rapids and Seymour Inlet. We will return to these areas later in Chapter 9.

Miles Inlet is the last shelter south of Cape Caution, ten miles away. It is on the west side of Bramham Island, just east of McEwan Rock, which is about five miles northwest of Harris Island. The entrance is narrow, and very difficult to see, but depths in the entrance are adequate. The best method to locate the entrance is to take a compass heading from McEwan Rock to the entrance, which should become obvious as you near it. Use Chart #3550. The best spot to anchor is in the cross of the "T"-shaped inlet in three fathoms with a soft bottom. It is possible to explore the inlet to the south in a dinghy, but the lagoon to the north can only be entered or exited at or near high tide.

Continuing north, it is nine miles to Cape Caution from McEwan Rock. One and a half miles north of McEwan Rock, you will pass the entrance to Slingsby Channel, which leads to Nakwakto Rapids, six miles to the east, and which will be covered in Chapter 9.

When rounding Cape Caution, it is a good idea to stay at least a mile off shore, because the rapidly sloping bottom accentuates any swells coming in from the Pacific Ocean to the west. Even though we have passed Cape Caution many times, we have always had feelings of relief when it was behind us.

Egg Island Vicinity

Egg Island, and its lighthouse, are five and a half miles north of Cape Caution. Don't cut in too close to Egg Island when approaching; beware of the rock southwest of the island, shown on the chart. It is usually marked with kelp.

The light at Egg Island is on an 85 foot tower. The original Egg Island Lighthouse was constructed in 1898 to handle the sudden increase in traffic caused by the Klondike gold rush in the Yukon Territory. It was needed to show ships the proper course, and to help them avoid rocky hazards about 15 miles west and northwest. It is one of the most remote and hazardous of all the coastal lighthouses. Seas smashed into the basement of the dwelling the first winter, and continued to create havoc over the years. On November 2, 1948, a tremendous storm washed away the light tower and all of the buildings. The light keeper, his wife and ten year old son escaped to the main island on a bridge, which was soon destroyed. They spent five days, clothed only in their nightclothes, before they were rescued. The light and buildings were re-built on higher ground. One light keeper and his assistant disappeared and were never found, and another manning the station by himself, committed suicide.

Much more information on Egg Island Lighthouse, and all of the lighthouses on the British Columbia Coast, can be found in the book, *Lights of the Inside Passage*, by Donald Graham, a lightkeeper himself. (See bibliography at end of this book.)

If you are looking for shelter in this area, Smith Sound lies to the east of Egg Island, and can be entered through Alexandra Passage, between Egg Rock to the north and North Iron Rock to the south. Jones Cove, on the south side of the sound, gives some shelter in three to four fathoms, but is not a good overnight anchorage. Millbrook Cove, on the north side of the sound, is an excellent, well protected anchorage in four to five fathoms, mud bottom, north of the island marked "30" on the 1992 Metric Chart #3934, or "100" on the old charts. This island can be passed on either side. The entrance to the cove is marked by a red spar buoy "E-6", which has a radar reflector atop it. Net floats for gillnetters are sometimes moored in the inner cove, or just outside, and may, if not in use, be used for overnight moorage.

We have enjoyed good fishing for pink and coho salmon in September, just off the reefs on the east side of Shield Island, near the entrance to Millbrook Cove.

Smith Sound and Smith and Boswell Inlets are covered in Chapter 9.

Dugout Rocks, seven miles north of Egg Island, mark the entrance to Rivers Inlet, famous for its big salmon. Rivers Inlet is also covered in Chapter 9 in detail. If you need water, supplies, or moorage, Dawsons Landing is on the west side of Rivers Inlet, 16 miles northeast of Dugout Rocks, and Duncanby Landing is in Goose Bay. Each have fuel, propane, moorage, water, supplies, showers and laundromats.

Fitzhugh Sound

Clark Point Light is on the south end of Calvert Island, 11 miles north of Dugout Rocks, and 17 miles north of Cape Caution. Here you enter Fitzhugh Sound, which runs north for 30 miles to Walker Point. Unless the wind is from the south, you should begin to get some protection from seas coming off the Pacific. Safety Cove, on Calvert Island, is six miles north of Clark Point, and offers anchorage in 8 to 15 fathoms, mud bottom, protected from all but east winds. Safety Cove is 53 miles north of Port Hardy.

Addenbroke Island Lighthouse, four miles north of Safety Cove, is a weather reporting station. You should now be getting reports on WX-2, from the repeater on a mountain on Calvert Island, broadcasting reports from Comox. Three miles farther north is the entrance to Kwakshua Channel, which runs six miles west, to Pruth Bay, a favorite anchorage for boaters for many years. Anchor in or near mid-channel at the head, in six to eight fathoms, mud and sand bottom. Pruth Bay's pristine beauty was damaged in 1993 when a large sports fishing complex, the Hakai Beach Resort, was built on the shore. Further plans, which are on hold at the time of publication, are to build a large hotel on the beach on the west side of Calvert Island, one-fourth mile to the west. These developments have aroused much opposition from both residents of, and visitors to, British Columbia. We visited the Hakai Beach Resort in August, 1994, and, contrary to comments that we had heard from some boaters, found the management to be very pleasant and accommodating. Visitors' skiffs are to be moored on the small wooden float located on the south end of the big concrete floats. The trail to the West Beach has been replaced by a rough boggy road, and visitors are welcome to use it and visit the West Beach. The mask carved into a tree is still there, right behind the new gift shop. The new facilities are very impressive, and are open to visitors, including the dining facilities and rooms. Use Chart #3784, scale 1:36,760.

At this point we will digress from further progress north, up the British Columbia Coast, and go back to the Broken Islands in Johnstone Strait to cover numerous inlets and islands along the "inside" route from that point to Addenbroke Island.

Note: The next three chapters, 7, 8, and 9, cover the inlets and inside passages from Johnstone Strait to Fitzhugh Sound in detail. Coverage of the waters north of Addenbroke Island continues in Chapter 10.

Miles Inlet

Mamalilaculla

Karlukwees

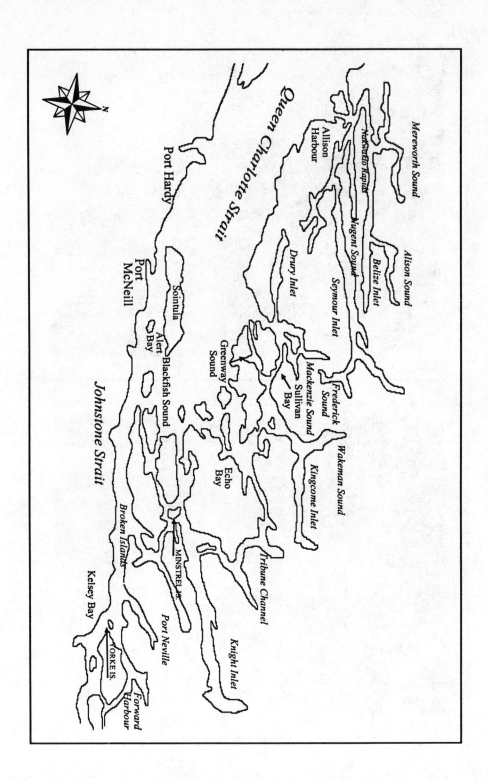

Chapter 7: Knight Inlet Area

This area was bypassed in the description of Johnstone Strait in Chapter 4. These waters, and those just to the north, the Kingcome Inlet area, comprise some of the most attractive and sheltered cruising waterways on the British Columbia Coast, all the way to Wells Passage 30 miles straight northwest. They should not be overlooked. There are inlets, both large and small, dozens of beautiful islands, with twisting channels between them, and half-a-dozen resort/marinas with facilities for boaters. As we have become more experienced and adventuresome, the lure of Alaska and British Columbia's north coast has drawn us farther north each year, but we come back for a week or two, once or twice each year to these familiar waters.

Since 1981, the pleasure boat traffic has increased dramatically, and facilities have expanded to meet the demand. The area is so large, however, that it is still possible to find many secluded anchorages where yours will be the only boat. As I mentioned previously, these are relatively protected waters, usually free from the wind and with less fog than is often present out in Queen Charlotte Strait. There is good fishing for all species of salmon, as well as bottom fish such as halibut, ling cod, greenling and several species of rockfish. Tall mountains, islands and inlets make for truly beautiful scenery. This has become one of the most popular cruising destinations on the coast, next to Desolation Sound.

Havannah Channel

Use Metric Chart #3545, scale l:40,000, or even better, Metric Chart #3564, scale 1:20,000. To enter these waters, turn north at the Broken Islands light in Johnstone Strait, nine miles west of Port Neville. One mile north of the light, Havannah Channel opens to the east. Port Harvey is straight ahead to the north, and was covered in detail in Chapter 5. In Havannah Channel, the course is north of the beacon on Lily Islet, and then on either side of the Bocket Islets. Turning north, you can pass on either side of Mistake and Hull Islands. Boughey Bay, to the south, is too open, not only to the north, but to wind coming in over low land to the south and east, to provide a desirable anchorage.

The site of the abandoned Indian village of Matilpi is off the channel on the east side of Hull Island, on the east side of the Indian Islands. There is an anchorage in eight to ten fathoms between the Indian Islands and the white shell midden marking the former village. The approach to this anchorage is from the north.

Burial Cove, on the shore of East Cracroft Island, has a well sheltered anchorage in four to six fathoms, on a mud bottom. There are some large aquaculture (fish farming) operations along the sides of Havannah Channel. Boats that create a heavy wake should slow down when passing these facilities to reduce the possibility of damage to them.

At Root Point on East Cracroft Island, the course turns into Chatham Channel to the west. Ten-mile long, steep sided, Call Inlet lies to the east. Most of this inlet is too deep for satisfactory anchorages, though some temporary anchorage is possible in the channel between the Warren Islands and the mainland shore. Winds often funnel down this inlet.

Chatham Channel

Five-mile-long Chatham Channel can be navigated at all states of the tide. The tides flood to the east and can reach a maximum rate of five knots at spring tides (maximum changes). The first mile is marked by two sets of range markers, one at each end of this section of the channel. Least depths of ten feet are in the first section, and kelp often grows across the channel. Be sure that you keep the range markers lined up, and plow through the kelp if necessary. Use inset on Metric Chart #3564.

Minstrel Island, and the community with the same name, are at the northwest end of Chatham Channel, where it joins Knight Inlet. When the Union steamships, small coastal freight and passenger ships, used to call here before they quit serving the coast, Minstrel Island was the main supply and entertainment center for this area. The community is said to have received its name because travelling minstrel shows stopped here in the past. Such names as Negro Rock, Bones Bay and Sambo Point on local charts give credence to this theory. The old hotel was dismantled in the late 1980's, and the boards and timbers were used to build a new house in Burial Cove. The Minstrel Island Resort was enlarged when the new owners, Sylvia and Grant Douglas, took over in 1990. They have added a pub, restaurant and 22 double rooms. They cater to fly-in sports fishermen, as well as pleasure boaters. Facilities include fuels, propane, water, moorage, garbage drop, showers, laundry, grocery store and a liquor store.

Cutter Cove, just east of Minstrel Island, is a good well protected anchorage in three to five fathoms, mud bottom. Anchor along the north shore during west winds and the south shore during east winds. Crabbing is usually good in Cutter Cove.

The Blow Hole, on the south side of Minstrel Island, is a shallow passage leading to **Lagoon Cove**, one mile to the southwest. It is passable at all states of the tide, using Chart #3564. Currents are negligible. Anchorages are in Lagoon Cove, and behind Dorman and Farquharson Islands in the channel separating these islands from West Cracroft Island. Lagoon Cove Marina, on the East Cracroft Island shore, was taken over by new owners in 1993, Bill and Jean Barber from Portland, Oregon. They are busy making improvements, and continue to provide moorage with water and power, and fuels, including propane.

These waters around Minstrel Island have long been known for good fishing for salmon and bottom fish, and you will no doubt encounter many sports fishermen.

Clio Channel

Before getting to Knight Inlet waters, we should first look at the channels leading west 15 miles to Cracroft Point and Blackfish Sound. Clio Channel runs west 7-½ miles from Minstrel Island, and is wide and deep; the few hazards are clearly shown on Metric Chart #3545. Bones Bay, on the south side of the channel, is the site of an abandoned fish cannery. A sports fishing lodge is now located there. Tides flood to the west at one knot. The best and most popular anchorages are in and around Potts Lagoon, on the north shore of West Cracroft Island, at the west end of Clio Channel. The easiest anchorage is in the cove on the east side, near the entrance. Crab pots are often present and care is necessary to avoid them when anchoring, but you have as much right to anchor as the crabber has to set his traps, just respect them. There is a good protected anchorage in three to four fathoms, mud bottom. Another possible anchorage is in the cove on the north side of the entrance. The channel to the inner harbor is to starboard of the island that is connected to the shore by a drying ledge. In the inner harbor the anchorage is opposite the ruins of a pier in four to five fathoms, at high tide, on mud. There is a logging camp on shore. Be sure that you will have sufficient depth at low tide when anchoring here.

Baronet Passage

Baronet Passage lies along the West Cracroft Island shore, leading to Blackfish Sound, and is often used by boaters heading to or from Alert Bay or Port McNeill. Wilson Passage joins Clio Channel and Baronet Passage. Tidal currents flood to the west and can reach three knots. Caution should be exercised in the area around Walden Island, passage may be made on either side. Fishing is usually good around Cracroft Point, at the west end of Baronet Passage, and you will probably see boats fishing in that area.

Beware Passage

This well-named waterway lies to the northwest at the west end of

Clio Channel, between Harbledown and Turnour Islands. There are many hazards, but we have used it several times without encountering problems. Entering from the south is more difficult because it is not easy to locate the proper passage. The correct passage is to the west along the Harbledown Island shore. It is best to traverse it at a lower, rising tide to see the hazards, and to keep from getting left high and dry if you should stray from the correct route. The tide floods east and ebbs west. The abandoned native village of Karlukwees is on the east side of Beware Passage, at its southern end. A wharf and public float can be seen, but they are not in a good condition. Heading northwest, Beware Rock and Care Rock are mid-channel hazards to be avoided. Caution Cove, on Turnour Island, offers anchorage in seven to eight fathoms. Caution Rock dries four feet, and marks the entrance. Another Turnour Island anchorage is Beware Cove which has a mud bottom, and has better protection in a northwest wind. Depths are from two to five fathoms.

At the northwest end of Beware Passage you enter Indian Channel which runs west five miles to Blackfish Sound. Use Metric Chart #3546. Farewell Harbour, on the west side of Berry Island, is a popular, well protected anchorage. The best location is on the south side of the island that lies off the northwest corner of Berry Island, in six fathoms on a soft bottom. The buildings on Berry Island are those of a private sports fishing lodge, and are not open to non-paying guests. Departing Farewell Harbour, you can pass Compton Island on either its north or south sides to enter Blackfish Sound, or you can go north through Swanson Passage into the entrance of Knight Inlet.

Blackfish Sound

Because of excellent fishing during the last few years, this sound has become very popular with pleasure boaters. It connects Queen Charlotte Strait with Blackney Passage and Johnstone Strait. When there is an open season for commercial fishermen, you will see a lot of their boats working these waters. If you are looking for moorage or anchorage in this area, they can both be found on the north side of Hanson Island. Double Bay Resort offers protected moorage, rooms, a restaurant and showers. The sign on a rock at the entrance to Double Bay indicates the location of this resort. Anchorage is also possible in parts of Double Bay. The next bay east of Double Bay has anchorages in several spots, though some are open to wakes of passing ships. The best protection is just south of Spout Island.

Knight Inlet

Use Metric Chart #3515, scale 1:80,000. Over 70 miles in length, this narrow, steep-sided inlet is one of the longest on the British Columbia Coast. Once you get beyond Minstrel Island, 15 miles from the entrance, anchorages are few and far between. Winds are frequently strong, as in most long inlets, funneling up or down the inlet. The logging camps and sports fishing lodges in the inlet do not welcome pleasure boaters, except in emergencies. The scenery is beautiful, mountains rise to over 7,000 feet on both sides, and there are numerous waterfalls. The fishing is good, but these are not friendly waters for pleasure boaters for the reasons mentioned. The winds are not only very strong, but are unpredictable and can rise very quickly. Some of the anchorages are niches in the steep shore line with hard, rocky bottoms. To keep your anchor from releasing from a rocky hold, it would probably be necessary to tie to shore. This is certainly not a good position to be in if the wind rises and suddenly hits you on the beam, when your boat is no longer free to turn into the wind to reduce the force of the wind on it.

In the upper part of the inlet, the water is murky from the glacial silt dumped into it by the Franklin and Klinaklini Rivers, making it impossible to see more than a few inches into the depths. Possible anchorages beyond Minstrel Island are Tsakonu Cove, hard bottom and some protection from the west, but none from east winds; Hoeya Sound, anchorage at the head, in 20 fathoms; and Siwash Bay, along the east side. Probably the best anchorage in this section of Knight Inlet is near the head of Glendale Cove; there is a sports fishing lodge here. Ahnuhat Point has limited anchorage in a niche at the valley next to the point. Wahshihlas Bay has limited anchorage, and logging operations. Anchorage at the head of the inlet, could be risky because the bottom rises so steeply at the flats, with near zero visibility in the water, and no shelter from up and down inlet winds. We have been sorely tempted to go to the head of Knight, but, we have heeded the advice of many people and have never tried it. The British Columbia Coast abounds with other desirable and safer waters.

Lower Knight Inlet, however, is another story. The winds may blow, though probably not as hard because they are not constricted in a narrow passage, and good shelter is never far away. Near the entrance, previously mentioned Farewell Harbour is down Swanson Passage. About three miles farther west, on the west side of Village Island, is the site of the abandoned native village of Mamalilaculla. There is a good, small anchorage in the bay near the ruined wharf, behind the rock islets in 25 feet, soft bottom. This was a large village, with a girls' boarding school and a tuberculosis hospital. The inhabitants moved to Alert Bay when the village was abandoned. In 1993, natives began guided tours from Alert Bay to Mamalilaculla and conducted tours through the ruins of the old village. In her book, *Curve of Time*, M. Wylie Blanchet devoted a chapter to Mamalilaculla. Canoe Passage, south of Village Islands, dries, and is not navigable on any tide.

Spring Passage, on the north side of Knight Inlet across from Mamalilaculla, leads northwest to Retreat Passage. These are described later.

Port Elizabeth, on the north side of Knight Inlet, is behind the Lady Islands, which lie in its entrance. Anchorages are in Maple Cove and Duck Cove. The Maple Cove anchorage is in five to ten fathoms, soft bottom, and protected from all but southwest winds. In Duck Cove, the best anchorage is next to an islet on the north side of the cove in two to three fathoms, soft bottom. In recent years, an aquaculture operation has been established on the south side of Port Elizabeth. Use Charts #3515 and #3545.

Tribune Channel

Tribune Channel lies on the north side of Knight Inlet, about four miles west of Minstrel Island. It runs along the east and north shores of Gilford Island, and joins Fife Sound near Broughton Island. It is an alternate route to Echo Bay and the Kingcome Inlet area. Tribune Channel is entered via Clapp Passage or Nickell Passage on the west side of Viscount Island or through Sargeaunt Passage on the east side of the island. Sargeaunt Passage has a least depth of 23 feet in its narrows, and offers good anchorages either north or south of the narrows. The best spots are on the east side of the passage. Wakes from passing boats may be a problem in these anchorages. Currents in Tribune Channel are usually less than two knots. Thompson Sound on the east side of Tribune Channel does not offer good anchorages, nor does Bond Sound to the north, which has no shelter.

In addition to being the easiest route to the Fife Sound, Kingcome Inlet area, Tribune Channel has some beautiful mountain scenery on both sides and several nice anchorages. The mountain views are especially good when looking up Thompson Sound and Bond Sound.

Watson Cove, Wahkana Bay and Kwatsi Bay all have anchorages in them. Use Metric Chart #3515, scale 1:80,000. Old Chart 3525, non-metric, scale 1:37,500 shows more detail but is no longer published. Watson Cove, on the north side of Tribune Channel, has anchorages in five to ten fathoms, protected from all but west winds. A rock is on the starboard side of the entrance. A large aquaculture operation is located just west of the entrance to Watson Cove. Wahkana Bay, on the north shore of Gilford Island, has well protected anchorages in its inner bay on soft bottoms. Depths are 16 to 17 fathoms in the center of this bay. The cove on the west side has lesser depths, 13 to 14 fathoms. Just south of the peninsula enclosing the inner cove, anchorage is possible in ten to eleven fathoms. This is a particularly nice, scenic anchorage, though it may be a bit deep for some tastes. Kwatsi Bay on the north side of Tribune Channel has deep anchorages in 15 to 18 fathoms in its inner cove. The best protected anchorage is just north of the islet on the west end of the cove.   Tribune Channel continues west, along the north shore of Gilford Island until it meets Fife Sound, southeast of Broughton Island.

Simoom Sound lies to the north at the west end of Tribune Channel and has several very good, well protected anchorages. Use the inset on Metric Chart #3515. It is entered just west of Deep Sea Bluff. Simoom Sound was named for HMS Simoom. Vancouver was anchored in this sound with the ships Discovery and Chatham from July 29 to August 5, 1792, while exploring the surrounding area in his small boats. The name was given to the sound 70 years later, when the Simoom visited. Anchorages in McIntosh Bay are in either of the two coves at its north end, mud bottoms, and very well protected. The easternmost cove has anchorage in eight to twelve fathoms, while the smaller, westernmost has an anchorage in four to five fathoms. One half mile to the east the cove north of Hannant Point has an anchorage in four to five fathoms; be aware of the drying reef on the south side of the entrance. O'Brien Bay, at the west end of Simoom Sound, has anchorages in eight to twelve fathoms throughout its west end. The best protected anchorage is in the northernmost cove in depths of only two to three fathoms.

The small settlement of **Echo Bay** is four miles south of Deep Sea Bluff, on the northwest side of Gilford Island. There are two facilities for pleasure boaters, Echo Bay Resort and Windsong Sea Village Resort. Echo Bay Marine Park has a small public float which is now restricted to vessels of less than seven meters (21 feet) in length, because its supporting pilings have become unstable.

Echo Bay Resort, owned and operated by Bob and Nancy Richter, is a popular place with visiting boaters. They have sheltered moorage with power and water, and a fuel float with diesel, gasoline and propane. There is also a 12,000 pound capacity dry dock. The very well stocked store, housing the Simoom Sound post office, sits on a big concrete float that was formerly part of the Lake Washington Bridge in Seattle. The store also carries packaged beer. A laundry and showers are available on the floats. On shore are modern housekeeping units with full kitchens. These accommodations are very popular with trailer boaters, who launch their boats at Telegraph Cove or Port McNeill on Vancouver Island, cruise over, and stay here while fishing and exploring the surrounding waters. Boat and motor rentals are available. Fishing for salmon and bottom fish, including halibut is good in this area, and Bob is very knowledgable and helpful. There is daily scheduled float plane service from Port McNeill, Seattle and

Campbell River. They also do boat sitting if you want to leave your boat for a while.

Windsong Sea Village Resort, located on the northeast side of Echo Bay, has boat, aircraft, and floathouse moorage, a floathouse for rent, and a fine arts gallery.

A one room school house is adjacent to the Echo Bay Marine Park. When the school is in session, the children are dropped off by their parents in small boats at the public float. Room must always be left for these boats to discharge their passengers. It is always interesting to watch this process, as the children go up the ramp and head for the school building. In the past, attendance has averaged about ten students, with the one teacher, who lives in the nearby mobile home.

Anchorages in the Echo Bay area are in Shoal Harbour, Viner Sound, and Laura Bay. Shoal Harbour, just south of Echo Bay, has anchorages in three to four fathoms, mud bottom and good protection. Viner Sound is three miles northeast of Echo Bay, and offers anchorage in eight to ten fathoms, well protected, on a mud bottom in the cove at its far east end. The entrance is restricted by a shoal on its south side. Laura Bay is a very attractive anchorage on the east end of Broughton Island, just north of Hayle Point. Avoid the shoal extending off Hayle Point when entering. The best anchorage is a small one, between Broughton Island and Trivett Island. Enter to port of the small islet, and anchor in five fathoms on a zero tide at Alert Bay. The anchorage has a soft bottom, and is very well protected.

Boaters approaching Echo Bay from a Vancouver Island port, or from Knight Inlet via Spring Passage, will use Fife Sound and Retreat or Arrow Passages, and Cramer Passage.

Retreat Passage

Use Metric Chart #3546. Entry is at Seabreeze Island. If approaching from Spring Passage, it is a bit shorter to pass on the east side of Henrietta and Sea Breeze Islands. The large native village of Health Bay, with its colorful houses, can be seen on the east side of the passage, on Gilford Island. One of the best and most popular anchorages in this area is in Waddington Bay on the northeast corner of Bonwick Island. Entry is from the northeast in the channel that threads through the un-named islands, just southwest of the Fox Group of islands. Depths in this attractive anchorage are in five to seven fathoms on a mud bottom, and excellent protection. We spent two nights here while 50-knot, storm force winds blew out in Queen Charlotte Strait. Strong gusts came in, but we were secure. Grebe Cove is just south of Waddington Bay and offers anchorage in five to six fathoms near its head. It is easier to approach than Waddington

Bay, but is not as secure, being open to east winds though some shelter is possible by anchoring along the starboard shore. The bottom is slimy black mud. Retreat Passage at its northeast end joins Cramer Passage, which continues northeast for three miles to Echo Bay, using Chart #3515, scale 1:80,000.

Arrow Passage

Arrow Passage, on the north side of Bonwick Island, leads from Queen Charlotte Strait to Cramer Passage, and is another way to approach Echo Bay.

Broughton Archipelago Marine Park

Embracing some 300 islands, and islets in the area, this is a "gunkholers'" delight. Park boundaries stretch from Fife Sound on the north, to Indian Channel on the south, and from Blackfish Sound on the west, to Baker Island/Bonwick Island on the east. The islands of this marine park have many possible anchorages amongst them, and various channels to explore. A few of the possible anchorages are Sunday Harbour, Monday Anchorage, Joe Cove, Cullen Harbour and Booker Lagoon, and a few un-named anchorages.

Sunday Harbour is just off Queen Charlotte Strait, between Crib Island and Angular Island. Anchorage is in four to five fathoms, soft bottom, covered with seaweed, but it will hold. At low tide this anchorage seems quite secure and comfortable, but as the tide rises, seas can come in from Queen Charlotte Strait, passing right through the anchorage, making it uncomfortable, especially if one is in a round bilged boat like the *Sea Otter*. Monday Anchorage, to the east is a more protected anchorage, especially in the bight on the north side of Mars Island. Bottom is soft and depths are from six to eight fathoms.

Joe Cove, on the south side of Eden Island, is a well protected anchorage in five to eight fathoms on mud. Use Metric Chart #3547, scale 1:40,000. The best protection is at the head of the cove. At times, several float houses have been moored in Joe Cove. Another anchorage is in the un-named cove, about one mile west of Joe Cove, on the south side of Eden Island. Anchorage is in two to three fathoms, with protection from all but east winds. There are several anchorages in the un-named bays behind Fly Island, on the northeast side of Eden Island. The thumb shaped bay to the west is the best of them. Anchorages are in two to five fathoms on a sticky mud bottom, and excellent protection from all directions. Keep to the port side when entering, to avoid the rock on the starboard side guarding the inner basin. The northwest corner of the bay has a shoal in it.

One of the rocks near Duff Islet, off the west end of Eden Island sometimes has a group of sea lions on it; you can hear them for a long distance if they are there, and you get an idea of why they are called sea lions.

Cullen Harbour is on the north side of the entrance to Fife Sound. The best anchorage is northeast of Olden Island in six fathoms, soft bottom. It is better protected than either of the coves off the east side of the entrance, where swells from Queen Charlotte Strait can enter.

Booker Lagoon lies north of Cullen Harbour, and is entered by Booker Passage, around the end of Long Island. Booker Passage is very narrow, but has a least mid-channel depth of 21 feet. Tidal streams are strong here, so it is a good idea to pass through near slack tide. Anchorage is possible in any of the four arms of the lagoon on mud bottoms. There are numerous aquaculture operations in the lagoon, and they will probably determine where you do, or do not, anchor.

Fife Sound

Fife Sound extends ten miles to the east from the Duff Island Light in its entrance to its junction with Tribune Channel, around the Burdwood Group of islands. Indian Passage on the south side of Fife Sound, south of Rees and Davies Islands is an alternate, more protected route. Old Passage, between Insect and Baker Islands is also passable, though shallow. If passing through the waters around Ragged Island, on the south side of Fife Sound, be aware of Pym Rocks, barely under the surface, and hazardous.

Cordero Channel

Chatham Channel

Float planes link facilities.

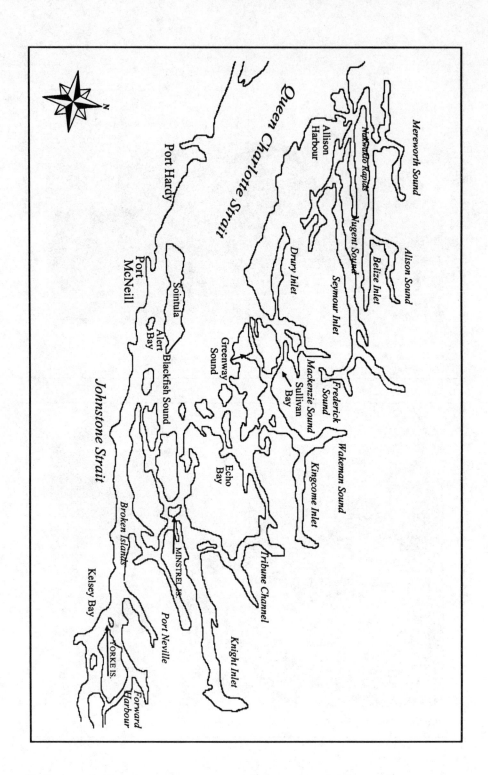

Chapter 8: Kingcome Inlet Area

The waters from Echo Bay to Wells Passage have been one of our favorite areas ever since we began cruising there in 1981. Boat traffic has increased greatly, and the marinas have enlarged available float space to meet this growth-in- demand. There are still remote, undisturbed anchorages to be found.

Penphrase Passage

Penphrase Passage, five miles long, connects Tribune Channel to the entrance to Kingcome Inlet, at Bradley Point on Gregory Island. This Inside Passage through the islands is a much more protected route to Wells Passage than cruising out in Queen Charlotte Strait. Then, at Wells Passage you go out into the Strait and face the music, if it is blowing or has been blowing outside. Use Metric Charts #3515, scale 1:80,000 and #3547, scale 1:40,000 in this area.

Sir Edmund Bay, on the south side of Penphrase Passage, has a couple of anchorages. The first is at the west end of the bay in five to eight fathoms, with good protection, and the second is in the southeast corner, behind the drying rocks shown on the charts, in four to five fathoms. There have been aquaculture operations in the bay.

Shawl Bay is on the Wishart Peninsula, on the north side of Penphrase Passage. It has been the site of a store and some float houses. In 1994, boaters were saddened by the death of Edna Brown who operated the Fanta Sea Store. Her sister, Jo, reports that plans are uncertain regarding the continued availability of moorage and supplies. In the past, the store has answered to the call sign "ATOM" on VHF Channel 73. Freshwater has been available at a float near the store. There is no fuel available. *Northwest Boat Travel* will help readers be advised of future conditions.

A shallow, narrow passage, drying on a three foot tide at Port Hardy, connects Shawl Bay with Moore Bay to the north. It is passable at high tide, and is much used by local boaters. We have used it once, but do not recommend it. It is much safer to go around Gregory Island.

Kingcome Inlet

Kingcome Inlet, 17 miles long, wide and deep, is entered at Bradley Point on Gregory Island. In the past, this was one of the best salmon fishing spots in the area, especially along the northwest shore of Gregory Island. Anchorage is possible in the cove just west of the peninsula that juts out from the north shore of Gregory Island. Depths are six to eight fathoms on a mud bottom, protection is adequate. There are great views of the mountains up Kingcome Inlet.

Moore Bay has two good anchorages. The Forest Service float which used to be anchored at the east end of the bay has been gone for several years. The site of the former float has been designated a Marine Park and the campground is still there. In Moore Bay, caution must be used to avoid Thief Rocks in the center of the bay and the rocks off the northeast corner of Gregory Island. The first anchorage is in the bight on Gregory Island, southwest of Thief Island, in four to six fathoms, with fair protection. The second anchorage is in the cove at the far southeast end of Moore Bay, behind the un-named island, in eight fathoms, soft bottom, and good protection. There are good views of 5,000 foot Mount Stevens to the northwest. At times a floating sports fishing camp has been anchored in Moore Bay. Thomas Bluff, on the east side of Kingcome Inlet, just north of Moore Bay sometimes has good salmon fishing, in close to the shore line.

At Frances Point, Kingcome Inlet turns east for 11 miles to terminate at the flats of the Kingcome River. Across the inlet from Frances Point is the huge scar on Philadelphia Point, left by an avalanche several years ago. Each year the re-growth of vegetation is noticeable as it heals the scar. Three miles east of Frances Point, the narrow entrance to Belleisle Sound is on the south side of the inlet. There are three anchorages in Belleisle Sound that we have used several times. The first two are in the coves ½-mile east of the entrance, where small streams enter, in 10 to 12 fathoms, soft bottoms. If the wind is blowing from the west, a more comfortable anchorage is in the bight three quarters of a mile south of the entrance in ten fathoms, soft bottom. The pilings to the northeast are the ruins of an old cannery. It appears that anchoring would also be possible at the west end of the sound in 10 to 15 fathoms. The steep mountains on all sides of Belleisle Sound make it very scenic.

Charles Creek, a couple of miles up the inlet from Belleisle Sound is the site of a former cannery; the ruins of the wharf are still visible. The small white cross on the north side of the inlet, past Charles Creek, commemorates the deaths of two young men from Kingcome Village. They were lost near this spot during a storm. At its head, Kingcome Inlet turns north and ends in the river flats. Tall mountains are on all sides. A small float is at the foot of the steep mountain wall on the west side, just above Petley Point. It is used by the residents of Kingcome Village, a native settlement one mile up the river, and the loggers from a camp a shorter distance up the river. Kingcome Village, and its people, are the subjects of the wonderful little book, *I Heard the Owl Call My Name*, by Margaret Craven. It is well worth reading, whether you ever visit Kingcome Inlet or not. The Anglican Church that plays such an important part in Margaret Craven's book, and her subsequent book, *The Owl Calls Again*, still stands and is in use. Kingcome Village has regular float plane service from Port McNeill and Port Hardy. The coastal supply steamer, *Tyee Princess*, makes regular calls at the float, delivering supplies. You will undoubtedly notice that the waters of the upper section of Kingcome Inlet are colored by the glacial silt from the Kingcome River, and visibility in the water is reduced to a foot or two. It is possible to go up river to the village in a dinghy, but we have never tried it because of the murky waters. We have friends who did make the trip, and enjoyed their visit. On our five or six trips up Kingcome Inlet we have always tied up to the float for lunch, but have yet to spend the night. For us, Kingcome Inlet is a special place.

Five-mile-long **Wakeman Sound**, takes off to the north at Philadelphia Point, where Kingcome turns east. The sound is very deep and there are no good anchorages. At various times, a logging camp and a sports fishing camp have operated at the head of Wakeman Sound.

The Magin Islets are on the west side of the entrance to Kingcome Inlet, across from Bradley Point. Anchorage is possible in the cove south of Reid Bay in three to five fathoms, but the bottom is rocky, and the cove is open to the southeast. At times, salmon fishing has been good around the Magin Islets, especially around the three fathom shoal to the east.

Sutlej Channel

Sutlej Channel joins Penphrase Passage at the entrance to Kingcome Inlet, and continues west for ten miles where it joins Wells Passage. Cypress Harbour, on Broughton Island, is off the south side of Sutlej Passage and has three good anchorages in it. Miller Bay is on the east side, Berry Cove on the west side. The third anchorage is south of Roffey Point, but don't go in too far. All are well protected, in reasonable depths, and have soft bottoms. Use Chart #3547, scale 1:40,000.

Greenway Sound, to the south, separates North Broughton and Broughton Islands. It is the site of a marina-resort and several anchorages. Greenway Sound Marine Resort is on the south side of Greenway Sound three miles west southwest of Walker Point. It is owned and operated by Tom and Ann Taylor. It is the newest facility in the area, starting from scratch in 1985. When approaching the resort, reduce your speed well before arriving at the floats, because the contour of the cove magnifies wakes, which can do a significant amount of damage. It is a complete service marina, except for fuel. They have 2700 feet of moorage space with water and power. Laundry, showers, garbage disposal and a beauty/barber shop are available. There is a well stocked store, an excellent licensed restaurant and take-out food service. Ice cream cones and sodas are available. There is daily air service from Seattle, Vancouver, Campbell River and Port McNeill, as well as their own *Greenway Sounder* service direct from Tacoma, Renton and Anacortes. They also do boat sitting if you want to leave your boat for some time. Tom and Ann have many years of experience in dealing with boaters, and are always glad to share their knowledge. It is a good idea to make a reservation by VHF or phone for moorage, dinner, or beauty shop service.

There are several possible anchorages in Greenway Sound. The first are around Cecil Island, the best being the one behind the small island, one fourth mile south of Cecil Island in five fathoms. Be aware of the shoal off the east end of this small island. The second anchorage is in three to ten fathoms in the cove east of Cecil Island, where the outlet from Broughton Lagoon empties into the salt water. Currents from the lagoon may make this anchorage uncomfortable at times. If travelling farther into the sound, look out for the rock in the center of the inlet just west of Greenway Point. It dries one foot. One half mile northwest of this rock, there is an anchorage in five to ten fathoms in the little cove ½-mile north of Broughton Point. At Broughton Point, it is possible to enter Carter Passage and anchor in the cove to the west in eight to 15 fathoms. Pass south of the islet in the entrance to Carter Passage. Carter Passage dries near its west end and is not recommended. There are several possible anchorages in Greenway Sound south of Broughton Point. The best is the one at the far end in six to eight fathoms, though strong winds may funnel in over the low land to the south.

Cartwright Bay, on North Broughton Island, has an anchorage in three to five fathoms, soft bottom. There is good shelter from the south and west.

Sullivan Bay, site of Sullivan Bay Marine Resort, is located near the west end of Sutlej Channel, on the shore of North Broughton Island. Pat and Lynn Finnerty are the managers. They have 4,000 feet of good moorage, a well stocked store with a liquor agency and post office, propane, fuel facilities, laundry and showers. Power and water are available on all of the floats. Everything is on floats, except for the fuel storage tanks, which are on the shore.

The original operation of Sullivan Bay Settlement began in 1945 when Bruce and Myrtle Collison moved in some floathouses and set up an aircraft refueling operation. They added a post office, marine fuels, some supplies, and Sullivan Bay took off. The Union Steamship Line vessels began making regular calls, and it became the major refueling point for float planes and seaplanes on the coast. At a peak, in 1954, they refueled 3,000 aircraft, many of them operated by Queen Charlotte Airline. When Queen Charlotte Airline sold out and was renamed Pacific Western Airline, the new owners of the airline, changed to land based aircraft, using the old RCAF base at Port Hardy, and the traffic at Sullivan Bay dropped off. Many float planes are still refueled, but nothing like the past. There is daily float plane service to Seattle, Vancouver, Campbell River, Port McNeill and Port Hardy in the summer months.

Sullivan Bay has boat sitting service available. A major fire in 1984 destroyed about half of the existing town, but a former logging camp was purchased, towed in, and operations not only continued, but greatly expanded. Privately owned floathouses have been added on new floats in recent years.

Look out for the rocks off the east end of Atkinson Island when entering from or departing to the west. Also, please reduce your speed and wake when entering or passing by Sullivan Bay.

Mackenzie Sound lies to the north of Sutlej Channel, and has some very interesting cruising waters. Use Chart #3547. It is approached via **Grappler Sound**. Hopetown Passage on the south side of Watson Island is obstructed by a drying reef, and should not be used. A native village is located in Hoy Bay, on the north side of Hopetown Passage.

There are two good anchorages on the west side of Grappler Sound. The first is in Carriden Bay, where anchorage is in four to seven fathoms in the center with protection from west and south winds. The bottom is hard mud. A better protected anchorage is available in Clayden Bay, one mile north of Carriden Bay; favor the south shore when entering to avoid the reefs. Protected anchorages are in either the north or south basins, in two to three fathoms on a mud bottom. There is a small anchorage on the south side of Woods Bay, on the west shore of Watson Island in three to four fathoms, with shelter from all but west winds. The ruins of an old saw mill are visible on Watson Point.

Kenneth Passage Vicinity

Turnbull Cove is at the west end of Kenneth Passage. Anchorage is possible in four to six fathoms anywhere in the cove, on a mud bottom, with excellent protection, though it is reported that during southeast gales, winds get in and circle the cove. This is a popular anchorage. Roaringhole Rapids, the entrance to Nepah Lagoon is one mile east of the entrance to Turnbull Cove. Entrance to Nepah Lagoon is not recommended for several reasons. Tidal currents are very swift, with over-falls, entrance is possible only at high slack, and high slack lasts for only five minutes. Least depth is only three feet and the entrance is very rocky and depths are too great for anchoring in the lagoon. A hand logger has operated in the lagoon in the past, and may still be active. A hand logger can only cut trees near the waters edge, using only a power saw and a boat to pull the downed timber into the salt water.

Kenneth Passage connects Grappler Sound to Mackenzie Sound; the inset on Chart #3547 should be used. Even though tidal currents are strong, passage is possible at any state of the tide, though it is evident that entry on a rising tide and departure on a falling tide is the easiest way to do it. The main hazards are around Jessie Point and are clearly shown on the chart. The channel has a least depth of over four fathoms, so there is always plenty of water. There are four good anchorages in Mackenzie Sound and a lot of nice scenery. Be aware of the rock off the northwest corner of Turner Island when going up the sound; it is covered at high tide.

The first anchorage in **Mackenzie Sound** is in Steamboat Bay in five fathoms, mud bottom, good protection. The second is at the head of Burly Bay in ten fathoms, good protection. The third is in Little Nimmo Bay, entry on the top half of a tide is best, as the entrance is shallow, and the spit on the north side must be avoided. Buildings on the north shore are those of a fly-in sports fishing camp, and have no facilities for pleasure boaters. Anchorage in the bay is in two to three fathoms, mud bottom, and very good protection. Anchorage is also possible just north of Nimmo Point in two to three fathoms. Entry to the inner basin of Nimmo is full of hazards. Entry would be difficult, and only feasible at high tide, but there are anchorages in five to six fathoms in this basin. Another anchorage is at the very head of Mackenzie Sound, in five to seven fathoms, soft bottom, and protection from all but west winds. Mt. Stephens, the tallest mountain in this area, rises on the north side of this anchorage. Petroglyphs are said to be up the river that comes in from Mackenzie Lake. It is too shallow for even a dinghy, and the only route is by wading in the river, unless you could locate an old logging road up the valley. Bears are around, naturally, especially in the fall when the salmon run.

Drury Inlet continues west for ten miles at the west end of Sutlej Channel. The shore lines are low all around the inlet, and to some, it is not as beautiful as other surrounding waters. There are several nice anchorages and a new marina facility. We have always enjoyed Drury Inlet on our several visits there. Entry is through Stuart Narrows, using the inset on Chart 3547. Currents can run to seven knots, so entry is best near slack water, or with the current behind you. Times of slack water are given in Volume 6 of the Canadian Tide and Current Tables. Depths are more than adequate at either low or high tide. Welde Rock on the north side of the narrows is the chief hazard to be avoided.

There is a relatively protected anchorage in Bughouse Bay in seven to ten fathoms, soft bottom. Pink salmon sometimes congregate in Bughouse Bay before ascending the stream to Bughouse Lake. There are two anchorages in Richmond Bay, across the inlet from Bughouse Bay. The most protected anchorage is in the cove at the southwest end of the bay in three to five fathoms, soft bottom. The second anchorage is in the cove on the east side of Richmond Bay in four to five fathoms, but open to the northwest. Look out for the rocks around Leche Island and in the center of the bay when entering. Tancred Bay is open to prevailing northwest winds, but there is a protected anchorage on the north side of Davis Bay in two to three fathoms. Enter south of Davis Islet.

A new marina, owned by June Schultz of Port McNeill, is being developed in Jennis Bay on the north side of the inlet. Moorage, accommodations, showers, and laundry are available. Reservations required. There is a well protected anchorage at the west end of the bay. Anchorage on a mud bottom is in four to five fathoms in front of the islet, and in one to two fathoms farther into the bay.

Sutherland Bay, at the far west end of Drury Inlet is large and shallow, with well protected anchorages in two to three fathoms on a mud bottom.

Actress Passage, on the north side of the inlet, leads to Actaeon Sound. It is rock strewn and hazardous. Passage would be best near high tide; we have never tried it. There are numerous good anchorages in Actaeon Sound, where there has been a lot of logging activity in the past.

Wells Passage

Wells Passage is five miles long and connects Sutlej Channel to Queen Charlotte Strait. The only two navigational aids in this area mark its two ends, the light on Surgeon Islets at its northeast end, and the light at James Point at its southwest end. Salmon fishing is often very good around James Point. The best protected anchorages are in Tracey Harbour, either in Napier Bay, anywhere in the bay in five to seven fathoms, or in the little cove southeast of Carter Point in similar depths. All of the bottom is mud. A very large logging camp formerly was active in Napier Bay. Other anchorages are in the cove on the northeast side of Dickson Island in five to six fathoms, with protection from the south and west, or a more exposed anchorage in six to seven fathoms off the west end of Carter Passage. There is a temporary anchorage just north of Popplewell Point, on the north side of Wells Passage in seven to eight fathoms, soft bottom, but limited protection.

Departing Wells Passage, it is about 15 miles from Boyles Point across Queen Charlotte Strait to the entrance to Hardy Bay, where Port Hardy is located and 13 miles up the coast to Blunden Harbour, discussed in Chapters 5 and 6 respectively.

If going up the coast from Boyles Point, it is a shorter distance to pass to the east and north of Lewis Rocks, after being certain that you have cleared the rocks off Boyles Point. Head straight into Lewis Cove until the passage between the point on the mainland, and the bare rock to the southeast is obvious. We have used this short cut many times, and have often seen numerous eagles on Lewis Rocks.

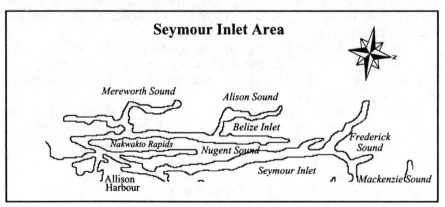

Seymour Inlet Area

Chapter 9: Seymour Inlet, Smith Sound and Inlet, and Rivers Inlet

Before proceeding farther north along the coast, there are several large inlets to explore in the Cape Caution area. The first will be the six inlets, including Seymour Inlet, that lie beyond Nakwakto Rapids.

Seymour Inlet Vicinity

Metric Chart #3552, scale 1:50,000, issued in 1987 was the first chart published for these waters, opening up a great cruising area for pleasure boaters. We have traversed Nakwakto Rapids once or twice every year since then, and never tire of exploring this locality. We have, in Septembers, been able to catch some nice coho salmon at the heads of several bays as the fish prepare to ascend the rivers or streams. We catch them from the dinghy, casting spoons or Buzz Bombs, and have a lot of sport, taking fish from eight to 15 pounds on light, fresh water spinning rods.

According to the Guiness Book of Records, **Nakwakto Rapids** are among the fastest in the world, running to 16 knots on the ebb and 14 knots on the flood. These are maximums. On most days, the currents, although much less, can still be very hazardous. The times of slack water are shown in the Canadian Tide and Current Tables Volume 6. It is best to time your passage within 15 minutes of slack water, either high or low water, as the water is deep. The preferred passage is on the west side of Turret Rock, which is festooned with signs bearing names of vessels that have passed through these narrows.

There are two routes to Nakwakto Rapids, by Schooner Channel, or by Slingsby Channel. You should use Metric Chart #3921, scale 1:20,000, for Schooner Channel, which is narrow and has several hazards, but is the best choice. Currents are moderate. The least width is 200 feet and the least depth is about two fathoms. Anchorages in Allison Harbour and Skull Cove are nearby, and are described in Chapter 6. The northern approach, via Slingsby Channel, can have extremely strong tide rips in its western entrance, especially on ebb tides, when they meet swells coming in from Queen Charlotte Strait and the Pacific Ocean. The entrance is wide and deep, but should be approached with caution, even on a moderate ebb. Use Metric Chart #3550, scale 1:40,000.

If you are waiting for a tide change at Nakwakto Rapids, anchorage is possible in Treadwell Bay in six to seven fathoms, or in the outer cove of Cougar Inlet in four to seven fathoms.

Once past Nakwakto Rapids, the six inlets in Seymour Inlet offer a variety of good cruising waters, with at least 20 good, protected anchorages available. There are no commercial facilities for boaters, but there are several active logging camps. Good radio reception is possible in most areas because you are not far from Port Hardy or Alert Bay. We have rarely encountered other pleasure boaters, but tugs and commercial prawners are usually around, plus boats running to and from the logging camps. Our three favorite areas, due to the scenery, are Alison Sound and Frederick Sound, with Salmon Arm off of it.

Because of the restriction at Nakwakto Rapids, tidal ranges in all of these inlets is only about four feet, while in the waters outside the rapids, it is 12 feet. Consequently, currents are relatively light in the inlets.

Seymour Inlet is the largest and best known. It is 38 miles long, from Mignon Point to the head of the inlet. One and a half miles east of Nakwakto Rapids, Nugent Sound lies off the north shore of Seymour Inlet. This ten-mile long inlet is very attractive. The best anchorage is three miles from the entrance, in the bay on the north side, across from Nugent Creek. Depths are eight fathoms, good holding on a sand bottom. This well protected anchorage has room for several boats. Anchorage at the head of the sound is also possible in eight to 12 fathoms, mud and sand bottom, but open to west winds up the inlet. The entrance to Schwartzenberg Lagoon at the head of Nugent Sound is less than three feet deep, with currents to five knots, and is navigable only by dinghy.

Charlotte Bay, five miles from the rapids, is on the north shore of Seymour Inlet. It is a good, sheltered anchorage in four to five fathoms, mud bottom. We have used it many times. Look out for the charted rocks in the northern part of the bay.

At Harriet Point, Seymour Inlet makes a dog-leg turn to the north. Anchorage is possible in two to three fathoms in the small bay directly across from Harriet Point, behind the 26 meter island shown on the chart. There is some kelp in this bay.

As Seymour Inlet continues to the east above Harriet Point, it becomes wider, and the shores more mountainous and scenic. On warm, clear afternoons a stiff up-inlet wind sometimes rises, creating two to three, or even four foot seas.

Frederick Bay, on the south side of Seymour Inlet, has a sheltered anchorage in the small nook at the west end of the bay in five fathoms, soft bottom. Warner Bay has some relatively protected anchorages which we have used for lunch stops. Beware of the drying rock in the center of the bay. There is a large logging camp on shore.

Proceeding east, there are two anchorages about seven miles from Warner Bay. On the north side, about one mile west of Dine Point, is an un-named cove known locally as Jesus Pocket. There is room for only one or two boats in four fathoms, with good protection. Across the inlet, on the south side, there is a good anchorage on the east side of Towry Point in ten fathoms, mud bottom, with protection from all but east winds.

Maunsell Bay, on the north side of Seymour Inlet, east of Dine Point, is too large and deep for anchorage, except for the little cove at the far eastern end. Here is an excellent, well protected anchorage in 12 fathoms, mud and gravel bottom.

Three miles east of Martin Point are Eclipse Narrows, the entrance to Frederick Sound. Seymour Inlet turns north here and continues for another eight miles to its head. There was a large logging camp on the east side of the head of the inlet in the past. Anchorage is possible at the head of the inlet, off the river flats. The bottom is steep-to and there is little shelter from up-inlet winds. The best location is on the west side, where you can get in behind a point. We have anchored here in ten fathoms, once overnight, and had no problems, but the wind was coming up as we left the anchorage.

We have made trips up the **Seymour River** three times in our dinghy. It is now necessary to have a special stamp on your license to fish there. It is possible to go about two miles before you reach a beautiful water fall, about 50 feet high. There is plenty of water all of the way, but look out for snags, or logs just under the surface. We have enjoyed good coho salmon fishing, catching fish of eight to ten pounds, fishing with spinning rods from sand bars. On one occasion, three grizzly bears appeared on the shore across from us; they were also fishing. Needless to say, we took off down the river in the dinghy. They weren't afraid of us, but stood up on their hind legs to get a better look.

Frederick Sound is entered through Eclipse Narrows, where currents run to four or five knots. Changes are about ½-hour after the tide changes at Nakwakto Rapids. The least depth in the entrance is 35 feet. Entry is possible at all states of the tide, because the narrows are very short and currents inside are very light. Frederick Sound is six miles long and has a good anchorage at its head in eight to ten fathoms, soft bottom, tall mountains make for good protection. The bottom rises very slowly, so anchorage is very easy. There are good views of Mount Stephens, the dominant peak in the area as you proceed up the inlet. In 1993, there was active logging on the east side of the inlet, about one mile from the narrows.

Salmon Arm lies off the east side of Frederick Sound, about two miles south of the narrows. There is a good anchorage at its head, 2-½ miles from the entrance, in the northeast corner in about ten fathoms. Don't go into less than ten fathoms because a drying dead head was in the cove a few years ago, and though no longer visible, is undoubtedly lurking on the bottom, waiting to foul some unsuspecting boater's anchor. Mountain views from this anchorage are beautiful, and at times, the salmon fishing for cohos and chums has been good. This is one of our favorite anchorages, and it has only one drawback; up-channel winds sometimes create a pretty good, and uncomfortable, chop. If this occurs, the head of Frederick Sound has better protection, and is only a few miles away.

Seymour Inlet also extends west of Nakwakto Rapids, but only 2-½ miles, to where it joins Belize Inlet at Mignon Point. Beware of the offshore rock when rounding Mignon Point. Lassiter Bay is two miles northwest of Mignon Point and has anchorages in 10 to 12 fathoms, mud bottom. Rowley Bay is just to the south of Lassiter Bay and also offers an anchorage in 10 fathoms, mud bottom. Both of these anchorages are open to the east, and winds coming down Belize Inlet have a long fetch, over 25 miles, but we have spent several comfortable nights in Rowley Bay.

Belize Inlet extends straight east for 25 miles from Mignon Point. The sides of the inlet are steep and mountainous, and it is too deep for anchoring. The only possible anchorage is at the very head of the inlet in 15 fathoms, but exposed to any up-inlet winds. There are, however, good anchorages in Westerman Bay and Mereworth and Alison Sounds, lying on the north side of Belize Inlet.

Westerman Bay is four miles east of Mignon Point and has a good protected anchorage in two to three fathoms in the cove at the north end of the bay.

Mereworth Sound is entered on the north side of Belize Inlet six miles east of Mignon Point. It extends 4-½ miles north before turning to the east for another 6-½ miles. It has several good anchorages. Village Cove, about two miles into the sound has a good anchorage in seven to eight fathoms in the northwest corner of the cove behind the two small islands. Strachan Bay, on the west side of Mereworth Sound, has an excellent anchorage in the cove at its southwest corner in seven fathoms, soft bottom, with good protection from every direction. Another anchorage is in the cove southwest of Rock Island, which is on the south side of the sound. There is good protection in eight to ten fathoms, mud bottom.

Alison Sound is the most scenic of all of the inlets lying beyond Nakwakto Rapids. The entrance to this sound is 18 miles east of Mignon Point. A three meter shoal is on the west side of the entrance. Obstruction Islet is 1-½ miles into the sound, at the narrows. Currents can run to five or six knots. The preferred channel is on the west side of the island and is 300 feet wide and 30 feet deep. Current changes seem to be fairly close to those at Nakwakto Rapids. Because of the short distance in these narrows, we have always traversed them whenever we arrived. The best anchorage is in very tiny Peet Bay, on the south shore of the sound, 2-½ miles past the narrows, in five to six fathoms, soft bottom, and good protection. This is a very picturesque, cozy little anchorage. Chief Nollis Bay has anchorage in 12 to 13 fathoms, and Sommers Bay has one in 12 to 15 fathoms. Both have only limited protection, but we have spent several quiet nights in Sommers Bay. Anchorage is also possible at the head of the sound, off the river flats. We have anchored here and explored the small river in our dinghy for a short distance, to a point where it becomes too shallow.

Smith Sound Region

Use Charts #3934 and 3931, both Metric on a scale of 1:40,000. The entrances to **Smith Sound** are only a few miles north of Cape Caution. Egg Island, with its lighthouse, and Table Island to the northeast, lie in its mouth. There are three ways to enter Smith Sound. The first is the southern entrance, Alexandra Passage, between Egg Rock, just south of Egg island, and North Iron Rock, which is about one mile to the southeast. North Iron Rock dries 12 feet, and is always evident because of the seas breaking over it. The second, Loran Pass, to the north of Egg Island, is the clearest of these passages, and the best choice if visibility is restricted. The third and northernmost passage has three possible entrances, Radar Passage, Irving Passage, and the innermost, between False Egg Island and Tie Island. The innermost passage is often used by commercial fishermen going from Smith Inlet to Rivers Inlet, and we have used it on several occasions. Some of the history of Egg Island Lighthouse is covered in Chapter 6.

There are several good anchorages in Smith Sound and more in Smith and Boswell Inlets to the east. If you are just coming in for shelter, the best choice is Milbrook Cove on the north shore of the inlet. The entrance would be very hard to locate if it wasn't marked by a red starboard hand spar buoy "E-6", with a radar reflector atop it. This reflector has enabled us to find Milbrook in a dense fog. We couldn't see the buoy until we were about 100 yards from it, but it showed very clearly on the radar screen. It is possible to anchor in a small cove on the port side in the outer section of Milbrook. In 1993 and 1994, a net float was there, allowing moorage when it is not being used by gill-netters. The best, most protected anchorage is in the inner cove, north of the island marked 100 feet on older charts, or 30 meters on the new chart. Passage is possible on either side of this island. We had a least depth of ten feet on a l.3 foot low tide in the western entrance. If using the wider east entrance, give the island plenty of clearance after entering the bay to avoid a big reef that is not clear on the chart.

Anchorage in this northern cove is in four to five fathoms, mud bottom, good protection. In the past, B.C. Packers stationed some net floats here, but they have been removed. We have used this little harbor several times as a welcome shelter in wind or fog. We have enjoyed good salmon fishing for pink and coho salmon in September, just off the reefs on the east side of Shield Island, just west of the entrance to Milbrook Cove.

On the south side of Smith Sound, Jones Cove is the first anchorage, but there is not much protection, and it is a temporary anchorage at best. This was especially true in 1992 when a log boom across the cove prevented you from going in far enough to get any protection from swells that are often present in this section of Smith Sound.

A better choice of anchorage on the south side of Smith Sound is Anchor Bight in Takush Harbour. The entrance to Takush is rocky, but the hazards are clearly shown on the chart. This is a roomy, well protected anchorage in ten fathoms, soft bottom.

Margaret Bay is an indentation in the peninsula that separates Smith Inlet and Boswell Inlet, at the east end of Smith Sound. There is anchorage in eight to twelve fathoms near the head of this narrow bay. If you anchor here, you can see the ruins of the old wharf that served this former settlement. Margaret Bay was a supply point for this area when the Union Steamship coastal freighters and passenger boats called here. Use Chart #3797, Plans in Queen Charlotte Sound and Fitzhugh Sound.

A new chart, Metric, #3931, published in February 1992, was the first chart for Smith Inlet and made exploration possible. Starting at **Ripon Point** on the north side, the inlet is about 18 miles long, and is very scenic. Anchorages are in McBride Bay, at the entrance to the inlet and in Anchor Cove in Quascilla Bay, five miles farther west, in eight fathoms, soft bottom, and good protection. Above these anchorages, the scenery is beautiful. Anchorage might be possible off the flats at the head of Walkum Bay, but the shoaling is very steep-to, with no protection from up-inlet winds. We made a temporary anchorage, for lunch, off the Nekite River flats in the cove on the east side of Jap Island. The island immediately south would give some protection from up-inlet winds.

We have not explored Naysash Inlet. The best anchorage may be off the Naysash River flats.

For **Boswell Inlet**, use Chart #3931. This eight-mile-long inlet is entered north of Denison Island. Finis Nook is on the south side of Boswell Inlet, 1-½ miles east of Denison Island, and offers excellent, protected anchorage in five fathoms, soft bottom. We had a least depth of 15 feet in the entrance. There are a lot of old net floats rotting in the bay, and the hull of a large sailboat is on the shore. The ruins of the former settlement of Boswell are across the inlet from Finis Nook. Security Bay is on the north side of the inlet, about two miles above Finis Nook, and appears to have good anchorage in about eight fathoms at its east end. In 1992, a very large, active logging operation was located along the north shore of this bay.

Continuing into Boswell Inlet, the narrows are wide and deep, and currents are not a problem. The cove immediately north of the narrows is a possible anchorage, but has several rocks along its shores, restricting the space for anchorage. An excellent protected anchorage is ½-mile above the narrows in the unnamed cove to the west in five fathoms, soft bottom, excellent protection, and scenic. We had a least depth of 25 feet in the entrance at high tide. Anchorage is possible at the head of Boswell Inlet in 10 to 13 fathoms, but beware of very rapid shoaling. The head of Boswell is quite beautiful.

Rivers Inlet

Use Metric Charts #3932 and #3934, scales 1:40,000 (1992). After Campbell River, this is probably the most famous sports fishing area in British Columbia. There are several large sports fishing lodges, whose customers arrive by float planes from Seattle, Vancouver and Port Hardy. Its fame is largely due to the huge chinook, or spring salmon as they are called in British Columbia, that frequent the waters. The race of spring salmon in this inlet produce some of the largest springs in the world. Coho, pink and chum salmon are also present, and there is a big run of sockeye, but few of them are taken by sports fishermen.

Rivers Inlet has been an important commercial salmon fishery since 1882. At one time 17 canneries were operating, but none have been active for some time. Some of the old canneries are now being used as sports fishing camps. Examples are at Goose Bay and Good Hope. Other canneries, such as Wadhams, are abandoned, even though the deserted buildings still remain. Most of the old canneries have just disappeared as the buildings collapsed, and bush and trees have taken over. If you look carefully, you can still see some rotting piles, all that is left of what was an old cannery wharf.

Klaquaek Channel, part of Penrose Island Marine Park, is off to the north side of Rivers Inlet, between Penrose Island to the west and Ripon and Walbran Islands to the east. There are several possible entrances from the south. The northern entrances are restricted by rocks, but entry is possible. The westernmost, next to Penrose Island, is the best choice. Darby Channel is at the north end of Klaquaek Channel. There are several good anchorages in 10 to 15 fathoms on either side of Klaquaek Channel. Frypan Bay, on Penrose Island is a good protected anchorage in seven fathoms, mud bottom. Big Frypan Bay, also on Penrose Island, has anchorages in 10 to 15 fathoms.

Goose Bay, on the south side of Rivers Inlet, has islets and drying rocks in the entrance and is the site of **Duncanby Landing**. Duncanby Landing Store and Marina has water, some power, gas, diesel and propane. Provisions, ice, laundry and showers are available. The new owners, Ken and Shelley Gillis, were busy making improvements in 1994. Goose Bay Cannery, at the head of Goose Bay, is now a fishing resort with no facilities for pleasure boaters.

Wadhams is the site of an abandoned cannery; there are no facilities. Johnston Bay, just south of the ruins of the Wadham's Cannery has a good, well protected anchorage in 10 to 12 fathoms at the head of the bay. Some old abandoned net floats are at the very end of the bay, and during July may be occupied by gill-netters, netting sockeye salmon in Rivers Inlet. It would be possible to moor to the floats when they are not in use. In August and September, Johnston Bay may have some pink salmon waiting to go up Johnston Creek. Crabbing has been good here at times.

Taylor Bay is on the east side of Walbran Island. It is a small, protected anchorage in 11 fathoms with a mud bottom.

The former Good Hope Cannery fishing resort is now operating as King Salmon Lodge, which opens for sports fishing about July 15, after the commercial season for sockeye salmon in the inlet is over. Anchorage in the cove just north of the lodge is possible in ten fathoms, mud bottom, and protection from all but south winds.

Rivers Inlet, proper, culminates in the big two-mile- wide bay ending in the Wannock River flats to the east and Kilbella Bay and it's flats on the north. The waters are always discolored, either by mud after a rain, or glacial silt at other times. Sports fishing camps are at Shotbolt Bay and McTavish Creek. At the two river flats are logging camps and native villages. Mountains as high as 4,500 to 5,000 feet rim the inlet. The only anchorage, other than those off the river flats, is a small bight behind McAlister Point, in six to eight fathoms, protected from all but east winds, good holding bottom.

Six-mile-long **Hardy Inlet** takes off to the west, from Moses Inlet, two miles north of McAlister Point. It is entered between Ralph Point and Owikeno Point, and runs straight west for six miles. Mountains as high as 2,500 feet are on both sides. There are two small anchorages at the very head of the inlet, one straight ahead, and the other to port. The first one is best, with a soft bottom in eight fathoms, and wonderful scenery, protected from all but east winds. If the wind is up the inlet, from the east, the port side bight would offer more protection in about the same depth.

Moses Inlet runs 12 miles north from McAlister Point to the drying flats at its head. Halfway up it has a dogleg to starboard, and is constricted by Nelson Narrows. The island in the narrows can be passed on either side; a day beacon marks a shoal to be avoided on the port side. Depths are adequate, and currents negligible. The currents throughout the inlet are light, and the ebb seems to predominate, due to the heavy outflows from the two rivers. The only signs of human activity are the two logging camps in the lower half of the inlet, and the four in the upper half. Some are very large and active. Mountains 3,000 to 4,000 foot high line both sides, and are tree-covered to their summits, with very little bare rock showing. This is an interesting side trip in which we have seen no pleasure boaters.

Chart #3931, scale 1:40,000, was produced in February 1992, the first chart for **Draney Inlet**. Draney is an 11 mile-long-inlet on the east side of Rivers Inlet, and is entered through Draney Narrows, shown on an inset to the chart. Since currents run to ten knots in the narrows, they are best entered at or near slack tide, which is reported in the Canadian Tide and Current Tables, Volume 6. Depths are better than five fathoms in the channel; entry may be at either high or low slack. A rock in the entrance has a least depth of 2-½ fathoms, and presents no problems at slack tide. The scenery is very good, except in Robert Arm, which has been recently logged, and another area just east of the narrows which was logged earlier.

There are several good anchorages, the first being Fishhook Bay, one mile past the narrows in two to four fathoms, with good protection. The large bay to the north after the narrows is too deep. Robert Arm has very good anchorage in about seven fathoms, mud bottom, and good protection from all but east winds.

In Draney Inlet itself, there is a very well protected anchorage in Allard Bay in six to nine fathoms, with minimum depths of three fathoms in the entrance, at high tide. There is more space than might be apparent on the chart; there is room for several boats, and a mud bottom. The head of Draney Inlet has an excellent, protected anchorage in 15 fathoms, mud bottom.

Dawsons Landing, on the west shore of Rivers Inlet just opposite the north end of Walbran Island, is one of the original communities on the British Columbia Coast that has survived. The small public float is for government fisheries vessels, not pleasure boaters. Dawsons Landing store, adjacent to the public float, has moorage for pleasure boaters, as well as fresh water, but no power on the floats. The store is a very complete, general, grocery, liquor store and post office. You won't believe how well stocked it is until you see it. Availability of fuel was much improved in 1994 with the installation of new large fuel storage tanks, making fuel available on a regular basis. Also new in 1994 were laundromat and shower facilities. Rob and Nola Bachen are doing an excellent job of managing Dawsons Landing.

Darby Channel

Darby Channel runs southwest from Dawsons Landing along the west side of Walbran Island to Fitzhugh Channel; use the inset on Chart #3943. It is easier to traverse than it may appear to be on the chart. Finn

119

Bay, on the south side of Darby Channel offers sheltered, but deep anchorage. Gill net floats are on the side of the bay and may be used for moorage if not in use. All of the floats in the bay are privately owned.

An unnamed cove on the east side of Weeolk Passage, off the north side of Darby Channel, has a good, relatively protected anchorage in eight fathoms, on a mud bottom. A rocky ridge on the north side is a hazard, and the charted rock in the entrance is best passed on the south side.

Schooner Retreat and Fury Island are two anchorages in this area that are off Fitzhugh Sound, on the southwest side of Penrose Island. Use new Metric Chart #3934. We have not used either of them. They are reported to be satisfactory, with protection from seas, but only limited protection from the winds.

Fish Egg Inlet, Chart #3921, scale 1:20,000. These interesting waters are entered to the east of Addenbroke Island, and its lighthouse. The first chart ever published for these waters was released in July 1991, so they are only now being discovered by pleasure boaters. They present excellent waters for gunkholing and have numerous good anchorages. Entry is either by Convoy Passage to the south or Patrol Passage and Fairmile Passage to the north.

A few of the anchorages are described below. Green Island Anchorage with seven fathoms, mud bottom, is well protected. The small green island covered with blackberry bushes is the usual sign of a former native village or camp. Entry is from the southeast or north entrances; the one to the southwest is too shallow. A very attractive, convenient anchorage is on the west side of Illahie Inlet. Don't try it if you don't have Chart #3921.

Illahie Inlet has an anchorage at its head in six fathoms, mud bottom, good protection. The area has recently been logged, which detracts from its scenery.

Joes Bay, at the entrance to Elizabeth Lagoon, has a protected anchorage in ten fathoms. The entrance to the lagoon has tidal rapids and many obstructions, and is best avoided.

Waterfall Inlet has a good anchorage at its head, in the northeast corner, in ten fathoms, mud bottom, good protection. An uncharted rock lies about 200 yards south of this anchorage, just off the east shore; it is clearly visible at lower tides.

Mantrap Inlet has a well protected anchorage at its southern end in ten fathoms. It is best entered on the top half of the tide, because of the very narrow, shallow, rocky entrance. Once, when we woke in the morning, the end of the bay was covered with foam from the tidal rapids that had enter on the west side. Gildersleeve Bay is open to the north. The two anchorages in the southwest corner are not very good. The northernmost is too shallow, be very careful if you look into it, and the southern one has a rocky bottom.

The passage labelled *The Narrows* on Chart #3921 leads to the eastern section of Fish Egg Inlet. The farthest eastern cove has a very nice protected anchorage in 6-½ fathoms on a mud bottom. Oyster Bay is another very good anchorage in four fathoms, mud bottom and excellent protection. Fish Trap Bay also has a possible anchorage in its very small cove.

These are only a few of the best anchorages in Fish Egg Inlet. There are so many possibilities that it would keep one occupied for quite a while poking into all of them.

Obstruction Inlet, Alison Sound

122

Chapter 10: Hakai Passage and Fitzhugh Sound to Bella Bella

Chapter 6 ended at Pruth Bay on Calvert Island. It is now time to continue north. At Pruth Bay, Kwakshua Channel turns north along the west side of Hecate Island and continues to Hakai Passage. Use Chart #3784, scale 1:36,760. There are many sports fishing lodges in this area, which is well known for its excellent salmon fishing; you will probably pass some along this section of Kwakshua Channel. At the north end of Kwakshua Channel, anchorage is possible at the north end of Choked Passage in nine to ten fathoms, soft bottom, between the north end of Calvert Island and Odlum and Starfish Islands. There is protection from the seas, but not much shelter from west and southwest winds.

Hakai Pass Recreational Area

The largest marine park on British Columbia's west coast, this area is almost 15 times larger than Desolation Sound Marine Park. Park boundaries include the north end of Calvert Island and the south end of Hunter Island, plus many islands between them, and Goose Island, in Queen Charlotte Sound. Use Charts #3784 and #3756. There are narrow passages between the islands, and numerous anchorages. Other than private fishing camps, no facilities are available.

Hakai Passage connects Queen Charlotte Sound and Fitzhugh Sound; its west end is exposed to winds and swells coming in from the Pacific Ocean. Odlum Point is a favorite salmon fishing spot, but beware of big swells and strong currents. Goldstream Harbour, at the northeast end of Calvert Island, has anchorage in seven to ten fathoms on a mud and sand bottom. It is entered off Fitzhugh Sound. A rock that dries four feet is in the center of the bay. Its location is sometimes indicated by markers placed by commercial fishermen, who often use this anchorage. Kelpie Point, on the north side of Goldstream Harbour, is a good spot for salmon fishing.

Fitzhugh Sound

Kwakume Inlet, on the east shore of Fitzhugh Sound, is across from Kelpie Point, about six miles north of Addenbroke Island Lighthouse. It has protected anchorages in seven to ten fathoms, mud bottom. It is large, with room for a number of craft. Use Chart #3784 and be cautious when entering. The small island with trees, that appears to be in the middle of the entrance, should be passed only on its north side. This entrance is 250 feet wide and has a least depth of 25 feet. Beware of the rock one-tenth of a mile west of the entrance when approaching from the north or exiting in that direction. This is the best anchorage between Addenbroke Island and Burke Channel.

The Koeye River entrance has a small cove on its south side that has an anchorage with limited protection to the west. An uncharted rock is near the entrance. There is excellent crabbing in this cove; it may be crowded with commercial fishermen at times. The river may be traversed for some distance by dinghy, and trout fishing is said to be good. The ruins of an old wharf are about one-half mile up the river.

Chart #3797 covers Namu Harbour. **Namu**, five miles north of Koeye Point, is the site of a former British Columbia Packers cannery, and was purchased in 1991 by a group, who planned to convert the operation to a sports fishing camp and a marina for pleasure boaters. In the summer of 1995, the only facilities available were the floats with moorage, water, fuel (most of the summer), and a very poorly stocked store that was opened only on demand. The future of Namu is uncertain. In 1995, new ownership took over. Some of the old houses were being improved, but some boaters reported problems with the condition of moorage floats.

An archaeological dig was in progress in July 1994, just above the bridge that crosses the river. It was led by Dr. Roy Carlson of Simon Fraser University, Vancouver. They had uncovered signs that indicated the site had been occupied as early as 9700 years ago, which made it the earliest known on the coast, inhabited shortly after the retreat of the glaciers.

Sea Otter Inlet, across Fitzhugh Sound from Namu, has two anchorages in it. There is a protected anchorage in the south arm that we have used several times. It is in ten fathoms on a soft bottom. The hull of a large boat is on the shore at the head of the inlet. The north arm, Crab Bay, has anchorage in five fathoms, soft bottom and good protection. The name is a misnomer; we have never caught any crabs here. Fishing on the reef on the north side of the entrance to the inlet is usually good, especially for bottom fish.

At Edmund Point, two miles north of Namu, Burke Channel takes off to the northeast, and continues 55 miles to the village of Bella Coola. These waters will be described in the next chapter. North of Walker Point, on the north side of the entrance to Burke Channel, Fitzhugh Sound ends, and Fisher Channel runs north for 21 miles, where it joins Dean Channel. Use Chart #3785, scale 1:40,533. Forty-five mile long, mountainous King Island lies on the east side of Fisher Channel, between Burke and Dean Channels.

Fisher Channel

Anchorages off Fisher Channel are in Codville Lagoon and Evans Inlet, both on King Island. Codville Lagoon's entrance is eight miles north of Walker Point. There are obstructions in the entrance, but they are easily avoided, and tidal currents are not a problem. Codville Lagoon has recently been named a Provincial Marine Park. Anchorage is in six to 10 fathoms, soft bottom, behind Codville Island, in the cove at the east end of the lagoon. This anchorage is protected from seas, but winds can get in over the surrounding hills, as we can attest to. In June 1988, we anchored here after hearing a forecast for hurricane force winds for the north end of Vancouver Island. The forecast was accurate. Winds reached 70 knots, well above the lower hurricane force limit of 65 knots.

We spent three nights in Codville and experienced winds that we estimated at 50 knots, with water spouts in the bay. The first day was calm. On the second day the storm hit, and lasted for two days, but we were secure.

We had been fishing off Kelpie Point on a beautiful sunny day when we heard the warning, having crossed Queen Charlotte Sound the previous day. Since we were only 60 miles from where this was supposed to happen, it behooved us to take some action. Looking over our charts the choices were obvious: moor to floats at Namu, only ten miles away; or Bella Bella or Shearwater, 35 miles distant; or find a secure anchorage. After discussing the alternatives, we decided we would rather anchor than bounce around on a float, and we chose Codville which we had used several times, because of its excellent protection, and moderate depth of ten fathoms. This would give us a 5:1 scope on our 300 foot anchor rode, on good holding bottom. To some, a 5:1 scope on the anchor rode may seem insufficient, but when we get our 33 pound Bruce anchor, and the l00 feet of three-eighths inch chain secure on the bottom, we feel certain that we are not going to drag the anchor. We have since ridden out another 50-knot blow in Alaska, where we had much less protection, and had no problems. The old float in the cove at the east end of Codville Lagoon was placed there some years ago by the Ocean Falls Yacht Club, located 25 miles to the north. We have never used it. A sign on the shore, near the float indicates the trail to Sagar Lake, one half mile away. If you are looking for a warm fresh water bath off a nice dark sand beach, this is the place. Don't let the half-mile distance fool you, however. The hike takes time because the trail is steep and rugged. Maintenance of the trail and the cooking grills at the lake are the work of the Ocean Falls Yacht Club. Wild life is plentiful in Codville Lagoon, deer, otter, geese and several types of loons may be seen.

Evans Inlet is three miles north of Codville Lagoon and has two possible anchorages. The best is at the head of this four-mile long inlet in ten to 12 fathoms. The bottom shoals rapidly, but the holding is good. Two small streams are at the head. The best spot to anchor is in the northeast corner, in ten to 12 fathoms, soft bottom. The second anchorage is in the northeast corner of Port John, in seven fathoms, soft bottom, but open to the southwest. We have used this only as a temporary anchorage, a lunch stop. We have enjoyed good Coho fishing off Exeter Point at the entrance to Port John.

If travelling from Evans Inlet to Port John via Matthew Passage, beware of Peril Rock in the center of the passage.

A glance at a chart will indicate that the New Testament was the source when names were given to the various locations in this immediate area. Matthew Island and Passage, Mark Rock, Luke Island, and Port John are all here. Port John was named by Captain Vancouver in 1793 for John Fisher, bishop at Exeter and Salisbury in England, and Captain Daniel Pender, on the Beaver, placed the other names in 1886.

Lama Passage

Directly across from the entrance to Codville Lagoon, on the west side of Fisher Channel is Pointer Island, formerly the site of the Pointer Island Lighthouse. The lighthouse, a weather reporting station, was closed in the late 1980's, and only a light remains. Pointer Island marks the east end of Lama Passage which leads, first west and then north, 13 miles to Bella Bella. It is very likely that you will encounter some cruise ships, or the ferry *Queen of the North*, in Lama Passage. We once met five large vessels on one transit. There should be no problems from their wakes, even though they pass close by, because they are required to proceed very slowly throughout the passage.

At the north end of Lama Passage there are two communities, one on each side. The larger one, on the west side of the channel is **New Bella Bella**, or by its native name, Waglisla. On the east side is old Bella Bella. B.C. Packers sold all of the facilities of the former cannery site here to the native tribe some years ago. The British Columbia Fisheries office is located here, but there are no other facilities.

New Bella Bella is primarily a native village, composed of members of the Heiltsuk Tribe. With a population of about 1400 people, it is the largest community along the "Inside Passage" between Port Hardy and Prince Rupert. The fuel facility is at the north end of the outer float, on the south side of the wharf. The fresh water supply is also here. At times it has been necessary to boil the water. Information about the water is available at either the fuel dock or the store. Some people object to the brown tint in the water, caused by the cedar roots the water runs through. We have never had any trouble with it. A garbage dump is located at the head of the ramp at the fuel facility. Part of the second, or inner float, is devoted to space for floatplanes. Be sure not to tie up in the area designated for them. The set of floats on the north side of the wharf is used mostly by the natives. We have been stopping in Bella Bella several times each year since 1984 and have always been treated courteously. This has been true in all of the native villages that we have visited throughout British Columbia and Alaska. Hours at the fuel facility, which is one of the busiest on the coast, are 8:00 a.m. to 5:00 p.m. seven days a week—closed from 12:00 p.m. to 1:00 p.m. Overnight moorage is possible on these floats, but no power is available. We have never spent a night here, but have talked to many people who have done so, without any problems. The floats are subject to wakes from frequent traffic passing in Lama Passage. These are public floats, so rafting is mandatory. Other facilities in town are the large, well-stocked general and grocery store with meat, produce and dairy products. Hours are 9:00 a.m. to 5:00 p.m., Monday, Tuesday, Wednesday, Friday, and Saturday. During summer months, June to September, the store is open seven days a week from 8:00 a.m. to 5:00 p.m., but it always closes from 12:00 p.m. to 1:00 p.m. A liquor store is adjacent and is open from 10:00 a.m. to 6:00 p.m., Tuesday through Saturday, closed noon to 1:00 p.m. The hotel has a pub, and showers are available. There is a bank office behind the store, and its hours are 12:30 p.m. to 5:00 p.m. on Tuesdays, and 8:00 a.m. to 10:00 a.m. on Wednesdays. A regional R.C.M.P. office is also located in town, as well as a hospital. Transportation is provided by B.C. Ferries that stop twice a week on their run from Port Hardy to Prince Rupert. There is a paved airstrip. Two airlines provide daily prop-jet service to and from Vancouver. WAG Air, locally based, provides floatplane transportation throughout this area. There is also taxi-cab service in town.

The Bella Bella Post Office is located in Shearwater.

There is another small set of public floats about a mile north of the Bella Bella floats. They are behind a rock breakwater, the entrance is marked by a green spar buoy. A marine repair facility is also located here.

Shearwater, site of Shearwater Marine Group, is on the east side of Denny Island, in Kliktsoatli Harbour, about two miles southeast of new Bella Bella. It is connected to new Bella Bella by water taxi service. An inset on Chart #3785 has detailed coverage of Kliktsoatli Harbour. Moorage is available. There are several large mooring buoys, and it is possible to anchor throughout the bay in ten to 12 fathoms, soft bottom, and reasonable protection. A small government float is located immediately south of the Shearwater float, but it is often crowded. Craig Widsten is president of Shearwater Marine Group. It operates a large fishing resort, as well as the most complete shipyard and marine repair facility on the north coast between Campbell River and Prince Rupert. In 1995, 1800-feet of new concrete floats were in place with water and 15-30 ampere power available at the head of the ramp. The management expects to put the water and power onto the floats in the future. The new floats were manufactured at Shearwater, in the big hangar building. Reservations are a good idea. They monitor VHF Channel 6, or the phone number is (604) 957-2305. The large lodge, that formerly provided rooms and other facilities for the sports fishing operation, was destroyed by fire in the spring of 1992. Modular units have replaced the burned facilities. The resort dining room and lounge are open only to resort patrons, but a cafe and pub are located in the building housing the marine repair facility. A good laundromat and showers were also added in 1994. A store handling marine supplies, some charts, and fishing supplies is located in the big building, as is the Bella Bella/Shearwater Post Office. Fishing licenses are available as are some grocery items.

Shearwater, during World War II, was an RCAF base. PBY's, flying boat patrol bombers, were located here. The big building housing the marine repair facilities is a former hangar. If you go around to the south side you can see the big doors that give access to the building's interior.

Kakushdish Harbour, on the east side of Kliktsoatli Harbour, one and a half miles east of Shearwater, offers protected anchorage in seven fathoms, mud bottom. There are shoals in the entrance, and on the south side near the head. An Indian Reservation, with some inhabited cabins, is at the head of the bay.

Before leaving Bella Bella/Shearwater, I should note that we consider this to be in the center of the best cruising waters on the British Columbia or Alaskan Coast. It is an ideal base when exploring the waters from Smith Sound and Rivers Inlet to the south, through Burke and Dean Channels, around King Island, and up north via Mathieson and Finlayson

Channels. This is probably the most scenic part of the entire "Inside Passage", including Alaska. It contains many inlets, bordered by high mountains. There are numerous good anchorages, though many are fairly deep by the standards of Desolation Sound, the Gulf Islands, and San Juan Islands. Pleasure boat traffic is very light, but is increasing each year as more boaters become aware of the charms of this area. The new improvements made at Shearwater make it the logical base for boaters in this area. We have been stopping two or three times a year since 1984. The transportation facilities, airlines and ferry, make Bella Bella/Shearwater an ideal place to meet or drop off visitors. We have done this five or six times.

University of British Columbia dig, Namu

Chapter 11: Burke and Dean Channels to Bella Coola

Before continuing north, we will describe the inlets and channels to the east of Bella Bella/Shearwater.

Burke Channel

As mentioned in the previous chapter, Burke Channel leads off to the northeast from Fisher Channel at Edmund Point, two miles north of Namu. It runs 46 miles to Menzies Point, where it joins North and South Bentinck Arms. The former continues east for another nine miles to the village of Bella Coola. Use Charts #3729 and #3730, both on scales of 1:75,000. Not many pleasure boaters make this side trip, but it is a most interesting diversion. High mountains, usually snow covered, and reaching as high as 5,000 feet are on both sides of the channel. It is very common for up-channel winds to rise in the afternoon, and when they oppose an ebbing tide, conditions can become very rough. Tidal currents can be strong in the lower part of the channel, especially in the first 12 miles, from Edmund Point to Restoration Bay. Because of the extreme depths anchorages are rare in these waters. Thirty five mile long King Island lies on the north side of Burke Channel, between it and Dean Channel. Mountains rise to over 4,000 feet on King Island; it is so big that you forget that it is an island.

It is possible to anchor in Fougner Bay, about one mile northwest of Edmund Point, in the outer part of the bay in seven to ten fathoms, with fair protection. The next available anchorage is in Restoration Bay, named by Captain Vancouver when he anchored here on May 29, 1793. On May 29, 1660 King Charles II was restored to the English throne, and this occasion was celebrated each year. Vancouver used this bay to overhaul his ships, which had suffered some damage in Queen Charlotte Strait. Anchorage is in nine fathoms, with a good holding bottom, but exposed to up-inlet winds from the south. We have used it twice, with no problems.

The next anchorage is at Cathedral Point, 12 miles up the inlet from Restoration Bay. There is a very small cove right on the point and anchorage is in four to five fathoms on a mud bottom, with fair protection. A strong down-channel wind can make it a little uncomfortable, but we have spent several nights here.

Kwatna Inlet is entered between Mapalaklenk Point and Cathedral Point. Salmon fishing is often good around the entrance to Kwatna Inlet. The inlet extends southwest for 12 miles and is very scenic and uncrowded. There is an excellent anchorage in ten fathoms at the head of the inlet, close by the small island on the starboard side. This beautiful anchorage is one of our favorites, especially after a rough day out in Burke Channel. Kwatna Bay is too deep and steep-to for good anchoring. In the past there has been a large logging camp in Kwatna Bay.

Three miles northeast of Cathedral Point, Gibraltar Point shoves its huge, bare, rocky bulk out into Burke Channel. It is bare rock from the waters edge to the peak, rearing 4950 feet above it. Once you have seen it you won't forget it. Past Gibraltar Point the mountain walls on the south side of the channel are a beautiful soft green when the sunlight plays on them. Rachel has said that it reminds her of some Hawaiian mountain sides.

Kwaspala Point is ten miles up the channel from Gibraltar Point. Here Burke Channel turns due east for five miles before joining North and South Bentinck Arms at Menzies Point.

South Bentinck Arm is one of the best reasons for going up Burke Channel. It is one of the best kept secrets on the entire British Columbia Coast. It is 19 miles long, with spectacular scenery on both sides. Glacier covered mountains with dark, jagged peaks rise to more than 6,000 feet on both sides. We counted over a dozen glaciers on the west side of the arm and at least half-a-dozen on the east side. Chart #3730 covers these waters. The arm is about one mile wide along its entire length, and because of the steep sides and great depths, anchorages are rare. In 1993 and 1994 there were three active logging camps in the inlet. One has been in Larso Bay, another across the inlet from the abandoned camp at Noeick River, and the last on the east side at the far end of the inlet. Anchorage in Larso Bay is in ten fathoms, protected from all but south winds. A private logging road leads from Bella Coola to Larso Bay, and if you anchor there on a weekend, you will probably have some company, people driving out or coming in small boats from Bella Coola. The logging company float in the northwest corner of Larso Bay is used by pleasure boats, when not otherwise occupied. There are beautiful views of the mountains on the west side of the arm from Larso Bay. Beware of a rock off the point when entering. In the bay at the head of the arm, an anchorage is on the southwest side in 11 fathoms, and good protection. The glacier covered mountains to the south of this anchorage are particularly beautiful at sunset and sunrise. The two narrows at the south end of South Bentinck Arm, Taleomay and Bentinck, are not difficult to traverse, just be certain to keep off the shoals. We had least depths at 12 fathoms in Taleomey and six fathoms in Bentinck Narrows. In 1993 there was a large red buoy in Bentinck Narrows, pass between it and the shore. Coming out head for the large square white board on shore, near the buoy. These are private navigational aids put there by the logging camp. Moorage is possible at a float near the abandoned Noeick River camp, but it is in a very sad state of repair. A road leads to the abandoned logging camp nearby.

Bella Coola is at the head of North Bentinck Arm which extends seven miles from Tallheo Point, at the entrance to South Bentinck Arm. Use Chart #3730. The public floats are in a sheltered small boat harbor, one and a half miles from town, a fuel float is adjacent. These floats are usually very crowded, and rafting is necessary. One float is reserved for pleasure boats, if it is crowded you may find room on another float. The harbormaster's office is at the head of the ramp. The water supply on the floats is very slow sometimes, it may be better on the fuel float. Taxi service to and from town is available.

It is impossible to get any weather reports by VHF radio in the upper reaches of any of these inlets, but in Bella Coola you can get some by calling the local airport and asking the airport manager if he (or she) can get a report for you. The automated weather reporting station at Cathedral Point would give the best local wind conditions. It is a good idea to depart Bella Coola very early in the morning to avoid strong up-inlet winds that often occur in the afternoon.

Alexander Mackenzie was the first white man to reach Bella Coola, in July 1793. He ended his trip across Canada at this point. This was the first land crossing of the North American continent north of Mexico, a truly remarkable feat, preceding Lewis and Clark's expedition by 12 years. His party totalled ten men, including him. He knew that he had reached salt water, but wanted to see the Pacific Ocean itself, about 80 miles to the west. He started down Dean Channel in a Bella Coola canoe. At a point about two miles west of Cascade Inlet he met a party of hostile Bella Bella Indians who threatened his small group. The spot is now marked by a granite monument, and is designated as a provincial park. After spending the night on shore he was prevailed upon by his Bella Coola Indian friends to return, which he did; but not before writing on the rocky face, in grease with red pigment in it, "Alexander Mackenzie, by land from Canada, July 22, 1793". Another small monument with a bronze plaque bearing this same message is on the road from town to the small boat harbor, in Bella Coola, where the road meets the water.

There was a small Hudson's Bay Company post in Bella Coola, for a while, established in 1867 and abandoned in 1882. The first permanent European settlers at Bella Coola were a group of 84 Norwegian men, women, and children from Minnesota who arrived on October 30, 1894 by coastal steamer. They settled in the community of Hagensborg, up the valley, and started farming, their previous profession in Minnesota. Currently, the area surrounding Bella Coola has a population of 2200.

Until 1953, the only connection that Bella Coola had with the rest of the world was by coastal steamer, or, in later years, seaplanes. The residents of the Bella Coola Valley had long been promised a road from Alexandria, and later from Williams Lake, both on the Fraser River, 300 miles to the east. These promises were never fulfilled, and the inhabitants decided that if it was going to be done, they would have to do it themselves. This they did, with a $50,000 grant from the provincial government. They built the road through and over the mountains of the Coast Range, about l00 miles to Anahim Lake, where it connected with a road previously built to that settlement. Rachel and I first visited Bella Coola in 1975 via this road, when it was much rougher than the Alaska Highway of those days. We understand that it has been much improved since that time. This is the only road that reaches the coast between Squamish in Howe Sound, and Kitimat. The late Cliff Kopas, a Bella Coola resident has written a fascinating book about Bella Coola's history, and the building of the road (see bibliography).

Downtown Bella Coola has an excellent Co-op food and general store, as well as a hospital, restaurants, liquor store, other shopping facilities, and, at times, a laundromat. There are several motels, but no bank, only a Credit Union, which does not have the ability to make cash disbursements on credit cards. You can get cash if you have a Canadian bank checking account, as we do for our business. There is scheduled air service to Vancouver and other points from Bella Coola.

Dean Channel

Dean Channel, on the north side of King Island, is the alternative route to Burke Channel to Bella Coola. It is connected to Burke Channel by Labouchere Channel. Use Charts 3729 and #3730, both on scales of 1:75,000. This channel is about 53 miles long, extending northeast from Rattenbury Point, in Fisher Channel, to its head at the Kimsquit River flat. Tidal currents run from one to two knots in the lower section and less in the upper part. The scenery is wonderful, especially in the upper sections, above Edward Point.

The community of **Ocean Falls** lies five miles up Cousins Inlet, which is entered between Boscowitz and Barba Points, off the south end of Dean Channel. The public floats welcome visiting boaters. The Ocean Falls Yacht Club has been instrumental in developing and maintaining these floats. Power and water are on the floats. Strong afternoon up-inlet winds are often present. This is a beautiful spot, and a good place for short walks on the paved road that runs one mile west from town out to the little settlement at Martin River Valley. The buildings of the abandoned pulp mill, and the still operating power plant are on the southeast side of the inlet at its head. Large ocean-going ships, up to 600 feet in length, used to moor at the wharf alongside the mill. The bulk of the huge dam looms above the remains of the town behind the mill and power plant buildings. When the mill was active, the population of Ocean Falls was about 2,500.

The pulp mill shut down in 1982. After 70 years in operation, it was no longer profitable. The Province of British Columbia had taken it over and operated it for several years, trying to preserve the jobs of the residents, but found that they were no more successful than the previous operators, Crown-Zellerback. When the mill shut down, the residents left town, because the mill was the only employer. With the town virtually deserted, about 50 die-hard residents remained. It was eerie to walk around town, because the buildings were still in good repair, and the numerous flower gardens in the yards were in full bloom. Every building in town was owned by the pulp mill company.

We were on the floats during the last week of August in 1985, when the town was being razed and burned. The original lease with the province provided that, before the site could be abandoned, it had to be returned to its original condition, as far as possible. The province had tried unsuccessfully to sell the town, but found no one was interested. The ruins of the bull-dozed buildings were burned to reduce future fire risks. It was difficult to sit there and watch what had been a beautiful town disappear. A few buildings were left in the center of town; the multi-storied hotel which was once the largest north of Vancouver, the old hospital, school, some of the newer dormitories, a church and a few houses and the old RCMP building, now the town hall and post office are all that remain.

The equipment in the mill was auctioned off and shipped out. The power plant continued in operation, and a few years later a power transmission line was constructed to Bella Bella and Shearwater, 24 miles southwest. You can see it on the west shore of Cousins Inlet, and throughout Gunboat Passage. This ensured that Ocean Falls would survive on some basis. The houses at Martin River Valley, one mile west of the floats, were not owned by the pulp mill company, and, since they were private property, they were not razed and burned. Many are still occupied.

Ocean Falls continues to change. Although the logging has ceased on Link Lake, behind the dam, we believe there are signs of a re-birth of the community. A federal grant has provided a double portable building to serve as the new school for the nine students in Kindergarten through Grade 7. Because the present zoning is nearly all residential, the only commercial facilities currently available are a bed and breakfast, a seasonally-operated fishing lodge, and a fish and chips shop located on the dock. As of 1995, there is no restaurant or store. See the annual edition of Northwest Boat Travel for the latest information.

The houses in Wallace Bay, in Cousins Inlet, about four miles south of Ocean Falls, were originally owned by mill employees, either as summer homes or permanent residences. None are presently occupied permanently, but some are used as summer homes. It will be very interesting to see how Ocean Falls develops. The only access is by boat or float plane.

Jenny Inlet is entered at Fosback Point, five miles up Dean Channel from Rattenbury Point. Anchorage is possible at the head of this three mile long inlet in 11 fathoms, soft bottom, protected from all but north winds. Logging has been active in recent years on the east side of the inlet. By 1994, most of the land at the head of the inlet had been clearcut. An anchorage on the west side in ten fathoms offers the most protection.

Elcho Harbour, on the northwest side of Dean Channel, is one of the best anchorages in this area. Anchorage is possible anywhere in the inlet in 16 to 19 fathoms, but the best is in 11 fathoms, on the northeast side at the head of the inlet, with very good protection. In August, bears and eagles can be seen pursuing the salmon in the river, which can be ascended a short distance by dinghy. A barge, with old buildings on it, has been stranded at the head of the inlet for years.

One mile east of Elcho Point, on the east side of the channel, is the Sir Alexander Mackenzie Monument and Provincial Park. There are no facilities at the park, and it is not feasible to go ashore, because it is much too deep for anchoring. Mackenzie's feat in crossing the continent was mentioned earlier in this chapter.

Cascade Inlet, 13 miles long, is entered about two miles northeast of the Mackenzie monument. It was named by Captain Vancouver who was here only a few weeks before Mackenzie's arrival. Although they both were representatives of Great Britain, neither man knew that the other existed. If you like waterfalls, this is the place. Cascade Inlet is truly spectacular after a few days of rain. Steep mountain sides, rising to over 4,000 feet on both sides, are adorned with innumerable falls, from small trickles to huge outpourings. That was the way we saw it on our first visit in 1984. Vancouver must have been here on such an occasion, because he stated these cascades were the largest and best that they had ever seen. There are plenty of waterfalls, even on a sunny day, and then you have the beautiful snowcapped mountains to enjoy also. The inlet is very deep right up to its head, with anchorage possible on the northeast side at the head, in ten fathoms, soft bottom, even though the flats are fairly steep-to. There is a small cabin on the northwest side of the inlet.

Eucott Bay, four miles northeast of Cascade Inlet, is an interesting little anchorage, if you can get used to a depth of only two fathoms. You may have only a fathom in the entrance if you enter or depart at low tide. It is completely protected from all winds. The deepest spot is on the east side of the bay. It is a beautiful place. The logging camp that was reported to be active in the bay in 1993 was no longer there in 1994. Except for the clear cut scar on the southwest shore, it is restored to its old beauty surrounded on three sides by tall mountains. Some hot springs are located on the east side of the bay, Chart #3729 shows the location. We have not visited them because they were reported to be in a sad state of repair. We have seen bears and other wild life on the shores. It is possible to anchor in the entrance to the bay, just before it shoals.

At Edward Point, Dean Channel turns north and continues north for 30 miles to its head at the Kimsquit River flats. Use Chart #3730, scale 1:75,000, for this section of Dean Channel. The scenery in Dean Channel north of Edward Point is spectacular, with mountains between 6,000 and 7,000 feet high on both sides. The inlet is a little over a mile wide and very deep, between 200 and 250 fathoms in most places. Just north of Edward Point, the depths reach 300 fathoms. The only anchorages are in Nascall Bay, Skowquiltz Bay, Carlson Inlet, and near the head of Dean Channel. Nascall Bay has some hot springs, used by commercial fishermen, and an anchorage exposed to southeast winds.

The anchorage in Carlson Inlet is deep, 20 fathoms at the very head, but well sheltered. The current from the stream entering the inlet will probably keep a boat headed towards it at all times. Skowquiltz Bay has an anchorage in 12 fathoms in its northeast corner.

At the head of Dean Channel there are several possibilities for anchorage or moorage. In the past there was a private float in Kimsquit Bay, it might be possible to moor there. A somewhat protected anchorage is possible on the west side of the inlet, just north of Kimsquit Narrows, near the old ruins in about 20 fathoms. A third possibility is off the Kimsquit River flats, very steep-to, and no protection from up-inlet or down-inlet winds. On our only visit here, we made the trip in one day, so cannot vouch for the anchorages.

Labouchere Channel

Seven-mile-long Labouchere Channel connects Dean and Burke Channels, running north from Mesachie Nose to Edward Point. The only anchorage is in the little un-named cove, one mile southeast of Ram Bluff in three fathoms with good protection. Seven foot depths are in the entrance. Tidal currents are light.

Roscoe Inlet

Before leaving this beautiful area, there is one more inlet that I must describe. It is Roscoe Inlet, northeast of Bella Bella. Its entrance is only about ten miles from Bella Bella/Shearwater at the junction of Johnson and Return Passages. It extends north and east for 21 miles, and is very narrow and crooked. Chart #3729, scale 1:75,000 covers the inlet. Depths are more than adequate, the few hazards are shown on the chart. About a mile south of Hansen Point a sheer cliff rises 1200 feet from the water, very spectacular. Good anchorages in ten to 15 fathoms are in Clatse Bay, Boukind Bay and at the head of the inlet. Quartcha Bay is too deep an anchorage for most boaters. On three visits here we have seen only a handful of boats. Roscoe Inlet ranks right up there with Princess Louisa and Kynoch Inlets for beautiful mountain scenery. The anchorage at the head of the inlet is an unusual one for an inlet because it is a nice tree-lined cove. This protected anchorage has depths of ten to 11 fathoms, soft bottom. The ruins of a former logging camp are about one fourth mile down the inlet.

If going from Bella Bella to Roscoe Inlet, the shortest route is via Troup Passage and Troup Narrows. The inset on Chart #3720 is essential if navigating the latter. There is a nice anchorage in the un-named bay one half mile west of the south end of Troup Narrows, in six fathoms, soft bottom, and good protection. An even more protected anchorage is in the bay to the east, on the north end of the Narrows in four to five fathoms over mud. In traversing the bay on the north end when approaching the Narrows, the best course is along the east side.

The other routes to Roscoe Inlet are Johnson Channel, which joins Fisher Channel, or Return Channel, which leads to Seaforth Channel. Both are on Chart #3720, scale 1:41,110.

Labouchere Channel Falls

Bella Coola

Ocean Falls floats

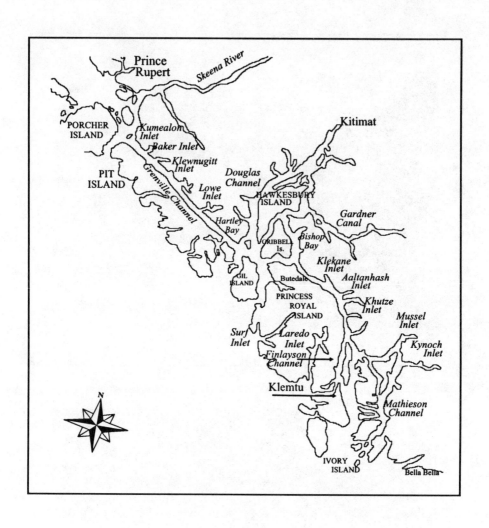

Prince
Rupert

Skeena River

PORCHER
ISLAND

Kumealon
Inlet

Baker Inlet

Klewnugitt
Inlet

PIT
ISLAND

Grenville Channel

Lowe
Inlet

Douglas
Channel

HAWKESBURY
ISLAND

Kitimat

Gardner
Canal

Hartley
Bay

GRIBBELL
Is.

Bishop
Bay

Klekane
Inlet

GIL
ISLAND

Butedale

Aaltanhash
Inlet

PRINCESS
ROYAL
ISLAND

Khutze
Inlet

Mussel
Inlet

Surf
Inlet

Laredo
Inlet

Finlayson
Channel

Kynoch
Inlet

Klemtu

Mathieson
Channel

IVORY
ISLAND

Bella Bella

N

140

Chapter 12: Bella Bella to Sarah Island

The Dryad Point Lighthouse is located at the north end of Lama Passage, one and a half miles north of Bella Bella.

Ivory Island Vicinity

Seaforth Channel leads to Ivory Island Lighthouse, 16 miles to the west where it opens into Milbanke Sound and the Pacific Ocean. Swells often enter its western end, so sea conditions can be rough. Use Chart #3720, scale 1:41,110 and Chart #3728, scale 1:76,557. You can get weather reports from Prince Rupert Coast Guard via a repeater on Swindle Island (Klemtu) WX-1. Listen for conditions at Ivory Island, because you must pass it. Reports from Dryad Point can be misleading, because it is in a relatively sheltered location. Tidal currents are weak in Seaforth Channel, flooding from the west and ebbing from the east.

A good anchorage off Seaforth Channel is in Kynumpt Harbour (known locally as Storm Bay), two and a half miles west of Dryad Point. The anchorage is in six to ten fathoms on a mud bottom at the very head of the bay, with excellent protection. A native settlement was formerly located here as evidenced by ruins of some cabins, the big area covered by blackberry bushes, and a midden, on the south shore of the bay.

On the south side of Yeo Island, 6/10ths of a mile west of Holt Rock and 7-miles west of Dryad Point Light House, is a protected anchorage on the northeast side of Wigham Cove with good holding ground. Note a rock drying at 5-feet is in the middle of the inner end of the narrow cove's entry. A 300-foot wide entry channel is west of this rock. Enter the cove staying on the west side of the channel until the two, three foot-high islets and a rock awash in the cove's middle are abeam, and then pass north of them.

Fishing is usually good in the area around Idol Point, about eight miles west of Dryad Point. We have caught Coho salmon, rockfish, and even a nice 20 pound halibut here.

Dundivan Inlet, one mile east of Idol Point has several possible anchorages. The best are in Lockhart Bay's two arms in eight to ten fathoms, soft bottoms and good protection, especially at the head of the West Arm. Use Chart #3720.

There is another good anchorage in St. John Harbour on the west side of Athlone Island, six miles south-southwest of Ivory Island. Use Chart #3781, scale 1:36,396 and Chart #3711. A red spar buoy marks reefs on the west side of the entrance. Raby Islet in the entrance can be passed on either side. Anchorage in Dyer Cove is in ten fathoms with a mud bottom. In 1993 there were two sports fishing camps located here at the southeast end, one in a building on shore, and the other in a converted British Columbia Ferry. Fishing can be very good around the entrance to St John Harbour, as you may surmise from the presence of these camps.

At Ivory Island there are two choices of routes to the north. These include picturesque Mathieson Channel along the mainland, or a more open route up Milbanke Sound and Finlayson Channel. The cruise ships, ferries, tugs and barges, commercial fishermen and most pleasure boaters go up the latter, but we prefer, and usually use, the former.

Mathieson Channel can be approached on either side of Ivory Island. Use Charts #3728 and #3710. The route on the western side enters Milbanke Sound, which is fully exposed to the Pacific Ocean to the south and west, and can therefore be rough at times. It is five miles by this route to Perceval Narrows, at the south end of Mathieson Channel, where currents run to five knots, flooding north and ebbing south. Currents in Perceval Narrows are reported in Volume 6 of the Tide and Current Tables. We have always passed through here on any state of the tide. Give Lizzie Rocks on the east side of the passage plenty of clearance, they are always visible. Strong tide rips will form just south of the narrows when an ebbing tide meets swells coming in from Milbanke Sound to the south.

Reid Passage

Returning to Ivory Island, the route that goes on its eastern side, via Reid Passage, is the one that we have used on about 90% of our 30 or more trips through this area. Chart #3710 is essential if traversing Reid Passage, as there are numerous hazards. It is four miles to Perceval Narrows by this route. All of the hazards in the southern portion can be avoided if you can see the light on Carne Rock, in the narrowest part of the channel when you are midway between the red nun buoy, "E-50" to starboard and the light to port. The light is on a reef off Ivory Island at the entrance to Reid Passage. Draw a line on your chart from this point to Carne Rock, and you will see that it misses all of the problems. Pass on the east side of Carne Rock. It is strange, but the "Sailing Directions, British Columbia Coast, North Portion", says that "tidal streams in Reid Passage generally set north on both the flood and the ebb, and can attain two knots".

Oliver Cove, a good anchorage, is on the east side of Reid Passage, about one mile north of Carne Rock. This popular cove is one of the newest Provincial Marine Parks, and has anchorage in six fathoms, a soft bottom, and with good protection. There is a charted rock in the entrance, and a ledge on the north side of the entrance, both to be avoided. No facilities are in the park.

Boat Cove, on the west side of Reid Passage across from Oliver

Cove, is another anchorage, if Oliver Cove happens to be crowded. Depths are two to three fathoms. The bottom is mud, and there is good protection.

At the north end of Reid Passage, Perceval Narrows is about one mile to the west, past Walter Island.

Mathieson Channel

Mathieson Channel runs north 35 miles from Perceval Narrows to Mathieson Narrows, where it joins Sheep Passage. It is off the regularly travelled route, and offers some beautiful scenery, especially in the Fjordland Recreational Area. Cockle Bay on the east side of Lady Douglas Island, has anchorage in 10 to 15 fathoms, soft bottom, but open to the winds from the northeast. We once watched a gray wolf romping on the beautiful sand beach while we were anchored here. It was playing with some dried kelp fronds, and finally laid down for a rest. Evidently it was not aware of our presence.

North of Stapleton Point on Lake Island, the channel widens and has no hazards all of the way to its north end 30 miles away. In the 12 miles to Jackson Passage, there are four good anchorages. Tom Bay on the east side of Mathieson Channel has a well protected anchorage in five fathoms on a mud bottom. If the hook won't hold, it is probably because of kelp on the bottom. You may have better luck in the center of the bay in ten fathoms. We have had good luck crabbing here.

Arthur Island, on the west side of Mathieson Channel, has a well protected anchorage in the easternmost of two coves on Dowager Island in ten fathoms, soft bottom. Salmon Bay, on the east side of Mathieson Channel, has a nice anchorage at its head in 10 to 12 fathoms, with a soft bottom, but open to the west. At times, eagles are present here. Use Chart #3734, scale 1:36,028.

The best anchorage in this area is in Rescue Bay at the east end of Jackson Passage, in eight to ten fathoms, soft bottom, and excellent protection and room for several boats.

Wide and deep Oscar Passage, between Dowager Island and Susan Island, is the easiest passage from Mathieson Channel to Finlayson Channel.

Jackson Passage is now the location of Jackson Narrows Marine Park. It is very picturesque, but narrow and obstructed by reefs and rocks in the east end. It should be navigated only at or near high slack tide, with Chart #3734, or better, Chart #3711. Jackson Passage leads from Mathieson Channel to Finlayson Channel.

As you proceed up Mathieson Channel you will notice several large waterfalls on the mainland side. There is usually very little traffic in

Mathieson Channel, especially the section north of Jackson Passage. We have often encountered Dall porpoises in these waters, as well as a pair of elephant seals on one occasion, and a six-gilled shark basking on the surface another time.

James Bay, which is on the west side of Mathieson Channel, offers good anchorage in eight to ten fathoms on its east side, just short of the head of the bay. The bottom is soft. Beware of shoaling on the west side at the head. There is no protection from winds to the south. We have enjoyed good crabbing and salmon fishing when they are present. Use Chart #3962, scale 1:40,000.

Fjordland Recreational Area

Fjordland Recreational Area includes Mussel and Kynoch Inlets and Pooley Island. It is one of the most spectacular of all of the province's Marine Parks and Recreational Areas.

Kynoch Inlet, eight and a half miles long, is the real jewel of this area, and is in the same class as Princess Louisa Inlet. It has the added advantage of being remote, and seldom visited, though that may not last much longer. As soon as you enter this inlet you are treated to the first spectacle, a huge waterfall on the north side of the inlet at Lessum Creek. It is safe to go in very close, close enough that you will get drenched by the spray, when the falls have a heavy runoff. Your fathometer will tell you that it is very deep, right up to the falls. The run-off from the falls will keep your boat off shore.

Farther up the inlet, big Desbrisay Bay lies on the north side. It is deep and exposed for good anchorages, but we have anchored in the northwest corner in ten fathoms for a lunch stop. It is a beautiful spot. We have often seen mountain goats on the cliffs. As Kynoch Inlet makes several turns, it becomes narrower, and the walls steeper. Careful inspection of the rock walls just above the waterline will reveal the scars left by the glaciers that carved this canyon. Note the horizontal grooves that they gouged out.

At the head of the inlet, anchorage is possible in about ten fathoms, but as is usually the case, the bottom shallows rapidly. The best spot is near the wall on the north side. Up-inlet winds can make this anchorage uncomfortable at times, but the scenery is worth it. Crabbing is usually very good. Salmon and trout can be caught in the river, which is passable by dinghy for about one half mile at high tide. If you have your dinghy on the river bank and walk along the shore, which is the best way to fish, remember that this area has big tidal ranges. We have had good luck fishing for coho and pink salmon when they are running. There are several grizzly bears in the valley, so keep an eye out for them when you are ashore. Some of these bears were transported here, and to Mussel Inlet, from Kitimat in 1991. They had been raiding trash cans and were not afraid of humans, so presented some real dangers. In June, the flats at the river's mouth are a huge bed of wild flowers. We have seen swans, hundreds of eagles, numerous seals, otter and other forms of wildlife here.

Culpepper Lagoon lies to the east at the head of Kynoch Inlet. It can be entered only at high slack tide, because the entrance is very shallow, and the currents strong. Use the inset on Chart #3962 and the tide information for Bella Bella. There is a beautiful anchorage at the very head of the lagoon in 15 fathoms. The flats, as usual, are steep-to, and very irregular; the chart is not much help. You will be anchoring at high tide, so be sure to allow for this. You will probably be surprised when you see where the flats are at low tide. If you are fortunate to be here in clear weather the scenery is spectacular. This is a better sheltered anchorage than Kynoch, although winds will also get in here at times. Crabbing is good off the river flats.

Mathieson Narrows are four and a half miles north of the entrance to Kynoch Inlet, and mark the north end of Mathieson Channel. Currents are never very strong because the flood tides in Sheep Passage and Mathieson Channel meet in the vicinity of the narrows. Mathieson Narrows is wide and deep; you could take a battleship through it. Fishing for bottom fish is always good off the little point about one half mile south of the narrows on the east side of the channel, next to Heathorn Bay. It is possible to anchor in eight fathoms in the bay, but it offers no protection to the south.

Mussel Inlet is entered just north of Mathieson Narrows, and Sheep Passage lies to the west. Mussel Inlet has several nice waterfalls. One of those in Oatswish Bay, Lizette Creek Falls, may be the most beautiful falls on the coast. There are bigger falls, but this one is special. It is wide and the rocky wall is visible through the falling water. It is hard to describe its beauty, you have to see it yourself. Oatswish Bay is deep for good anchoring, though anchorage is possible in ten fathoms near its head, on the west side, where you will have some protection from up inlet winds. We have used it as a lunch anchorage.

At Barrie Point, Mussel Inlet turns to the east. Beware of the charted rock southwest of the point. According to the "British Columbia Sailing Directions," David Bay, next to Barrie Point, is said to have an anchorage in the southwest part. We haven't been able to locate one. The only spots we found in David Bay shallow enough for anchorage were so close to the wall that there wasn't sufficient swinging room. We aren't afraid of deep anchorages; we have anchored in 20 fathoms several times, but we do like some room. Too bad, because David Bay is a pretty spot, with very good protection.

Mussel Bay, at the head of Mussel Inlet, has an anchorage in nine to ten fathoms off the river flats, which are steep to. The best spot is close to the wall on the north side. This anchorage is open to up-channel winds. We have seen mountain goats on the mountains on both sides of Mussel Bay. The river can be explored for a short distance by dinghy. Be on the alert for grizzly bears, because they are in the valley. (See information under Kynoch Inlet.)

Poison Cove lies on the south side of Mussel Bay. It is too deep for satisfactory anchorage. It was so named by Captain Vancouver because some of his crew members were poisoned from eating shellfish, mussels no doubt. All of the men except one, a sailor named Carter, survived. He was buried in Carter Bay, 20 miles to the west.

Sheep Passage

Sheep Passage joins Mathieson Channel at the narrows, and runs south and west 12 miles to Finlayson Head, where it joins Finlayson Channel. Sheep Passage is wide and deep, flooding to the east and ebbing to the west. The name probably comes from mountain goats that Vancouver mistook for sheep. There are three anchorages off Sheep Passage. The first is in Bolin Bay, on the northwest side of the channel. Mountains rise to 3,000 feet around this little bay, straight up from the water's edge. Anchorage is in 10 to 11 fathoms, on a mud bottom in the west corner of the bay, protected from all but east winds. There are drying flats at the head of the bay. Windy Bay, on the south side of Sheep Passage, has plenty of room to anchor in depths ranging from 10 to 20 fathoms, soft bottom. The best protected anchorage is behind the island at the east side of the entrance. In spite of its name we have been comfortable here.

Carter Bay lies at the junction of Sheep Passage and Finlayson Channel, about one mile east of Finlayson Head. Use Chart #3738, scale 1:35,768. The bow section of the steamer Ohio can still be seen in the northeast corner of the bay, close to shore. Her captain ran her aground here in 1909 after she struck Ohio Rock. The rock is in Finlayson Channel, just off the shore of Sarah Island, about three miles southwest of where she now lies. She hit the rock on one side of her hull, and ripped a gash the length of the ship. The captain knew she would not stay afloat for long, and Carter Bay was the nearest spot where she could be beached; all of the rest of the shoreline was solid rock walls. The rising water put her fires out, but she had enough steam left to reach the beach. In addition to numerous passengers, she was carrying a cargo of steel rails for the railroad that was being built from Skagway to Whitehorse. These were later salvaged. Two passengers died, from hitting debris in the water when they jumped from the ship. The Ohio, 335 feet in length, was a former trans-Atlantic liner.

Sometime after the grounding, the hull broke in two and the long stern section settled to the bottom. It shows on your fathometer when you cross behind the bow.

Carter Bay received its name from Captain Vancouver, who named it after Seaman Carter, who died from eating poisoned shellfish at Poison Cove in Mussel Inlet. He was buried on the shore of Carter Bay. Anchorage is possible in 12 to 15 fathoms between the wreck and the shore, but it is open to wind from the south. Another anchorage, perhaps better protected, is in the northwest corner of the bay. At high tide it is possible to go up the river by dinghy for about one half mile. Fred Roger's book, "Shipwrecks of British Columbia", has an interesting section regarding diving on this wreck.

Hiekish Narrows runs five miles north from Finlayson Head, connecting Finlayson Channel to Graham Reach of Princess Royal Channel. Currents flood from the south, reaching four knots on the flood and ebbing to the south at a maximum of four and a half knots. Use inset on Chart #3738. Times of slack water and maximum currents are given in Volume 6 of the Tide Tables. On most days the maximum rate does not exceed two and a half to three knots, we have always passed through regardless of the state of the tides, taking advantage of back waters when running against the tide. Once, we encountered a black bear swimming across the south end of the Narrows, and got some good pictures as we cruised around him at short range. The reef at Hewitt Rock is marked by a buoy that indicates passage on either side. The east side is preferred. If you arrive at or near slack tide there is good fishing around this reef and its kelp beds. We have caught nice lingcod, big black rockfish, and on one occasion Rachel caught a 35-pound chinook salmon after a 30-minute battle. She was fishing with a jig and plastic worm, fishing for bottom fish, not salmon. The light at Sarah Head, the north end of Sarah Island is about one and a half miles north of Hewitt Rock, and marks the north end of Hiekish Narrows.

Alternate Route

The alternative to the Mathieson Channel-Sheep Passage route is to go up Finlayson and Tolmie Channels. It is 23 miles north up Finlayson Channel from Ivory Island to the lighthouse at Boat Bluff on the south end of Sarah Island, and another 15 miles up Tolmie Channel to Sarah Head, at the north end of Sarah Island. Use Charts #3728, #3734, and #3738. Oscar Passage and Jackson Passage enter Finlayson Channel from Mathieson Channel to the east, and have been covered earlier in this chapter. Islands on both sides of the channel rise from 1,500 to 2,600 feet and the depths here are some of the greatest along the Inside Passage.

Tidal currents flood to the north and ebb to the south and can reach three knots in narrow sections, but only one knot in broader sections. This is the "Main Line" for traffic in the Inside Passage, and ferries, cruise ships, tugs and barges, commercial fishermen and pleasure boats will probably be seen.

Nowish Cove, on Susan Island, is one of the few anchorages in the area. It is protected by Nowish Island. Entry is north of this island, and anchorage is found in 12 to 14 fathoms on a coarse sand bottom. Currents can sweep through the cove, so you might use a little extra scope on your anchor rode. Nowish Narrows lead into Nowish Inlet, which can be explored by dinghy, but be cautious as currents can run to six knots.

Finlayson and Tolmie Channels

Tolmie Channel may be entered from Finlayson Channel by passing on either side of Jane Island, which is just south of the Boat Bluff Lighthouse, on the very southern tip of Sarah Island. The village of Klemtu is about three miles south of Boat Bluff, off Klemtu Passage on Swindle Island. When coming from the south, Bell Peak, a perfect cone on aptly named Cone Island, is a good landmark. As you might surmise, it is an extinct volcano cone. There are several more cones on this section of the British Columbia coast. Klemtu Passage offers shelter if conditions are rough in Finlayson Channel, even if you are not planning to stop at Klemtu. Chart #3711 is helpful.

Klemtu, a native settlement, is the last chance for fuel, water and supplies until you reach Prince Rupert, 140 miles to the north. Fuel was available at Butedale until 1987, and plans call for it to be available again soon. See information on Butedale in the next chapter.

Before 1984, Klemtu had a bad reputation with pleasure boaters, because some had been harassed by young natives. We have been stopping at Klemtu frequently since 1984 and have never had any problems. Around 1986, a new store, fuel facility, wharf and floats, and fish processing facility were built, greatly improving conditions for pleasure boaters. The new store is very well stocked, and the inhabitants claim that their fresh water supply, which is available at the fuel float, is the best on the coast. Although we have never spent a night here, we would not hesitate to do so. However, the floats are exposed to traffic passing in Klemtu Passage. A boardwalk connects the store to the rest of the town, which lies to the south.

Two miles north of Boat Bluff the light at Split Head, at the north end of Swindle Island, is at the junction of Tolmie Passage and Meyers Passage. Meyers Passage leads to the west side of Prince of Wales Island.

This area will be covered in a later chapter. Tolmie Channel continues north, between Sarah and Princess Royal Islands, for another 12 and a half miles to the light on Sarah Head, at the north end of Sarah Island, where it meets Princess Royal Channel.

There are two anchorages in this area, **Alexander Inlet**, off Meyers Passage, and Cougar Bay off Tolmie Channel. For Alexander Inlet, use the inset on Chart #3734. This five mile long inlet is very scenic and offers a good, well protected anchorage in the cove at its head in five fathoms, soft mud bottom. Once, while anchored, we watched two gray wolves on the shore for over an hour. They knew we were there because one wolf sat down and stared right at us for a long time. They were chasing two Sandhill Cranes along the shoreline until the cranes got tired of the game and flew away. We have never seen another boat in here.

Cougar Bay, four miles north of Split Head Light, has an anchorage in the bight on the east side of the bay around the edges of the bight in ten fathoms, soft bottom.

At Boat Bluff it is possible to continue up Finlayson Channel instead of turning into Tolmie Channel. It is 11 miles north from Boat Bluff to Finlayson Head, the north end of Finlayson Channel, where it meets Sheep Passage and Hiekish Narrows. Anchorages are in **Bottleneck Inlet**, Goat Cove, Work Bay, and Carter Bay (previously described).

Bottleneck is the best of the four anchorages, because it is better protected. Although the entrance is narrow, there are no problems. Anchorage is in six fathoms, mud bottom. When the surface of the water is calm, there are beautiful reflections. Work Bay, on the east side of Sarah Island, has a good anchorage at the northeast end of the bay in seven fathoms, protected from all but south winds.

The entrance to Goat Cove is ½-mile east of Goat Bluff. Good anchorage is found in 6½ to ten fathoms in the inner basin, east of the stream at the head. Well protected, good holding in gravel and sand.

Klemtu

Prince
Rupert

Skeena River

PORCHER
ISLAND

Kumealon
Inlet

Baker Inlet

Kitimat

Klewnugitt
Inlet

PIT
ISLAND

Grenville Channel

Douglas
Channel

Lowe
Inlet

HAWKESBURY
ISLAND

Hartley
Bay

Gardner
Canal

GRIBBELL
Is.

Bishop
Bay

Klekane
Inlet

GIL
ISLAND

Butedale

Aaltanhash
Inlet

PRINCESS
ROYAL
ISLAND

Khutze
Inlet

Mussel
Inlet

Surf
Inlet

Laredo
Inlet

Finlayson
Channel

Kynoch
Inlet

Klemtu

Mathieson
Channel

N

IVORY
ISLAND

Bella Bella

Chapter 13: Sarah Island to Prince Rupert

Princess Royal Channel

Princess Royal Channel runs northwest for 38 miles from Sarah Head to its junction with Whale Passage at Point Cumming. Use Charts #3738, scale 1:35,768, #3739, scale 1:35,574, and #3740, scale 1:35,467. It is divided into four sections, Graham Reach, Butedale and Malcolm Passages around Work Island, Fraser Reach and McKay Reach. Tidal streams flood from the south and north and meet around Aaltanhash Inlet. There are half-a-dozen anchorages in this stretch, some good and some marginal. High mountains line both sides of the deep channel, and there are several nice waterfalls along the way.

The first anchorage is in Horsefly Cove in **Green Inlet.** It is two miles north of Sarah Head. In spite of its name, we have never been bothered by these pests here, and it is one of our favorite spots. Anchorage is in 13 fathoms, on a soft bottom, just north of the gap between the small island and the mainland. Do not attempt to pass between the island and the mainland. At low tide you can see why. There is excellent protection. In early summer the eagle's nest on the island has always been occupied. There are tidal rapids at Baffle Point, four miles from the entrance to Green Inlet; these rapids are not navigable. Green Inlet was designated a Marine Park in 1992. We have enjoyed good crabbing off the flats of the stream across the inlet from Horsefly Cove, and good fishing on both sides of the entrance to Green Inlet, especially around the three fathom shoal on the north side.

Swanson Bay, on the east side of Graham Reach, is suitable as a temporary anchorage. The heavy wakes from ferries and cruise ships enter the bay making it uncomfortable for an overnight stay. Swanson Bay is the site of the first wood pulp mill on the British Columbia Coast. The red brick smoke stack that is still standing, and the rotting piles of the wharf are the only evidence that remain. The pulp mill was erected in 1909 and operated for only about 15 years. Some of the problems evidently were the lack of markets for the product and an insufficient supply of water. At one time the population of Swanson Bay was 500, but by the end of the 1920's the mill was shut down for good.

Khutze Inlet, four miles long, has two possible anchorages. The first in about 15 fathoms, soft bottom, is on the east side of Green Spit. The spit is marked by kelp beds. The protection is usually good, but we were here one night when a strong south wind out in Graham Reach, which we had come in to avoid, bounced off the mountain side on the north side of the inlet, and came right back into this anchorage. We spent the night, and the wind eventually died down. The most popular anchorages are at the head of this very scenic inlet, off the river flat. Anchoring is complicated by the extreme depth of the inlet, the steepness of the edge of the delta flats, and the charted wreck, a barge, shown on the chart. The best spot at the head, is in front of the largest waterfall on the starboard side in about 11 to 12 fathoms. The current from the stream should keep you facing the falls. If you go any closer to the flats you raise the danger of fouling your anchor on the wreck. A more difficult anchorage is off the flats in front of the river mouth in about 14 fathoms. If you don't anchor far enough out, you risk the chance of grounding if an up-channel wind comes up, or when the tide drops. Anchoring is further complicated sometimes by the presence of numerous crab traps, placed there by a commercial crabber. We have enjoyed some of the most successful crabbing of our own here.

The large river can be explored for some distance by dinghy. The high mountains with their snow fields always make this a beautiful spot. There is usually a lot of wild life to be seen: seals, otters, eagles, swans, and on the mountainside above the falls, mountain goats. In early summer wild flowers are profuse on the shore, along the river banks.

The falls of the Canoona River are on the west side of Graham Reach, across from Khutze Inlet, and have some good fishing, for bottom fish at any time, and for salmon in the fall when they can be seen jumping in front of the falls.

Aaltanhash Inlet, four miles long, is about two miles north of Khutze Inlet, and has very scenic anchorages at its head, in six to 12 fathoms. The bottom is rocky in spots, but most of it is soft. The best spot is right in front of the river on the port side in six fathoms, soft bottom. The current should keep you facing the river at all times. In the fall we have enjoyed excellent fishing for both pink and coho salmon, with spinning rods and spoons or spinners for lures. Rachel also caught a 105 pound halibut out in deeper water. It was so big that we had to tow it ashore to clean it. Aaltanhash is known as a good spot for halibut. Crabbing is usually good here.

Klekane Inlet, across from Butedale, has two possible anchorages. The first is in Scow Bay, in 12 fathoms, soft bottom, with some protection. The pilings mark the edge of the flats and must be given sufficient clearance when anchoring. Again the bottom is very steep-to. We have enjoyed good crabbing, and when they are present, good fishing for pink salmon from the dinghy. We once saw a mountain goat trot along the shoreline, crossing the valley.

There is also an anchorage at the head of Klekane Inlet, in the northwest corner in 10 to 14 fathoms, but open to up inlet winds. It is possible to take a dinghy up the river for a short distance.

Butedale is the site of a former salmon cannery, built in 1909. The ruins are still visible, along with the remains of the buildings that held the power plant, store and employees' quarters. The store was still open in the mid-1980's, but the cannery was shut down long before that. While the store was operative, fuel was available and the fresh water hose on the float ran non-stop. Later, operations, including fuel, ceased and, around 1990, the wharf collapsed. It has not been safe to go ashore for some time. Butedale's collapse was unfortunate because it was a crucial refueling point for gasoline powered boats with shorter cruising ranges. At present, because fuel is no long available at Hartley Bay, boaters must travel the 140 miles from Klemtu to Prince Rupert without refueling,

In the summer of 1994, the Oregon-based Butedale Founders Group, began restoring some of the old buildings and planned to repair the moorage and shore access. As of spring, 1995, the new owners hoped that fuel and water would be available in the summer of 1996. Boaters who are interested in the status of Butedale can call the group at 503-397-5392. *Northwest Boat Travel* will publish any new information as it becomes available.

The beautiful falls, at the west end of the bay, have always been an attraction for passing boaters, as well as for passengers on ferries and cruise ships. Anchorage is possible at the head of the bay, but it is exposed to winds from the north and the wakes from passing traffic.

Work Island lies in the channel off Butedale and can be passed on its north side, through Malcolm Passage, or on its south side by way of Butedale Passage. Fishing for bottom fish is often good along the shores of Work Island.

Fraser Reach extends northwest 12 miles from Butedale to Kingcome Point. There are several nice waterfalls along the way, but no anchorages. Use Chart #3740, scale 1:35,467. At Kingcome Point, the main route north goes west eight miles to Point Cumming on Gribbell Island, then northwest eight miles across Wright Sound to Sainty Point, at the south end of Grenville Channel. Use Chart 3742, scale 1:70,920. Rough water can be encountered in Wright Sound when winds blow up or down Douglas Channel to the north. The best anchorage in the area is in Curlew Bay, on the northeast corner of Fin Island, in eight to ten fathoms, soft bottom with good protection, though there is some exposure to north winds. Use Chart #3742.

Hartley Bay is located on the west side of Douglas Channel, northwest of Promise Island, and has moorage in a well protected small boat harbor. In earlier years, B.C. Packers had a fuel barge moored here during the summer months, but they disposed of it. In 1993, 1994, and 1995, fuel has not been available and there was no water on the floats. There is a small store in one of the houses, if you can find it open; and one of the women in the community bakes bread for sale. If you go ashore you will see a sign that states "No liquor past this point". Hartley Bay is a dry town. The population of about 200, is native Indian. We have found them to be friendly. Use Chart #3711, scale 1:18,280. Some mooring buoys are located in Stewart Narrows, and we have seen boats at anchor along the shoreline, but the area is exposed to wakes from passing traffic.

Side Trips to Kitimat and Gardner Canal
(See end of chapter.)

Grenville Channel

Grenville Channel, narrow, deep and straight, runs 45 miles from Sainty Point to Gibson Island. Use Chart 3772, scale 1:36,225. Currents run up to two knots, meeting near Evening Point. There are four good anchorages along Grenville Channel.

Lowe Inlet, the first, is the most popular. It is now a marine park, and is 15 miles north of Sainty Point. The preferred anchorage is in Nettle Basin, right in front of beautiful Verney Falls in eight to 15 fathoms. If you anchor in the stream from the falls, the current should keep you facing the falls, unless a strong west wind comes in and turns you around. The current will set you back on the anchor, but I always back down to be sure that it is well set. Because of the strong currents in the bay, it is possible to drag an anchor. You should also be aware of the big tidal ranges in this area, as much as 15 to 20 feet. When anchoring, be sure that you will still be afloat at low tide. In late summer when the salmon are jumping and trying to get up the falls, it is interesting to watch them, as well as the predators that gather, bears, seals, and eagles, not to mention humans. We have good luck catching coho salmon from our dinghy when they are present. A short trail to the left leads to the lake above the falls. Many years ago a salmon cannery was located here, some of the rotting pilings can be seen on the north shore of Nettle Basin. It is a rare occasion when there are not several boats at anchor here.

Klewnuggit Inlet, ten miles northwest of Lowe Inlet, is now a marine park, and has a good, very well protected anchorage at the north end of the East Inlet in nine fathoms on a soft bottom, and usually good crabbing. Morning Reef Light is on the south side of the entrance to Klewnuggit Inlet, and is the place where the flood tides from the northwest and southeast meet in Grenville Channel. Kxngeal Inlet, also known as East Inlet, is four miles north of the entrance to Klewnuggit Inlet, and has an anchorage in ten to 14 fathoms near its head, but it is exposed to the south. When Grenville Channel gets rough, the wind opposing the tide, it can be a very welcome shelter.

Baker Inlet is ten and a half miles north of Morning Reef Light, and would be difficult to locate if it were not for the light on the south side of the entrance to Watts Narrows. Currents are strong in the narrows and they should be entered only near slack tide, either high tide or low tide. The narrows are 200 feet wide, and you can not see the far end until you are some distance in; but it is there. Depths are more than adequate, and passage is easier than it may appear to be. Use the inset on Chart #3772. Slack tides occur at about the same time as they do at Prince Rupert. The best anchorage is at the head of the four mile long inlet. The rest of the inlet is very deep. The best spot is just south of the small island at the head, with good protection. 3,000 to 4,000 foot mountains rise right above this anchorage. We once saw a family of seven gray wolves on shore, feeding on a deer carcass, and the next morning heard them howling, not far away.

Kumealon Inlet is three miles north of Baker Inlet, and has two possible anchorages. Use Chart #3773, scale 1:36,517. The handiest anchorage is inside of Kumealon Island in six to eight fathoms, soft bottom, and good protection. Entry can be made at either end of Kumealon Island. The second anchorage is in 15 fathoms, on a mud bottom, behind the small island at the head of the inlet. This island should only be passed on its north end.

From Kumealon Inlet it is 33 miles to Prince Rupert, using Charts #3773, scale 1:36,517, #3927, scale 1:77,800, Metric #3957, scale 1:40,000, and Metric #3958, scale 1:20,000. You will pass Watson Rock, traverse Arthur Passage, pass Hanmer and Genn Islands, and Holland Rock Lighthouse. A possible anchorage, and the closest sheltered one to Prince Rupert, is in Kelp Passage, between Lewis and Porcher Islands in six fathoms, soft bottom. Entry is either from Arthur Passage, at a point just north of the light on Herbert Reefs, or via Chismore Passage to the north. Kelp Passage, to the south, is not recommended because of obstructions. When skirting the Skeena River shoals, be sure to use the navigational aids, buoys, to avoid trouble. You will pass the huge, relatively new facilities on Ridley Island that handle the loading of coal and wheat to freighters that moor there. Anchorage is possible in the Kinahan Islands, two miles northwest of Holland Rock Lighthouse, during settled weather. The anchorage is in the bay between the two islands on the southeast side, but with exposure to southeast winds.

Prince Rupert Vicinity

Prince Rupert, with a population of 16,000 is the western terminus

155

of the Canadian National Railway. It has only recently reached the expectations of its founders, and this because of the new ship loading facilities on Ridley Island completed around 1985. Because it is the closest North American port to the Orient, its founders thought that it might rival Vancouver and Seattle, but they were too optimistic. It is, however, a modern day transportation center. In addition to the railroad, it is a port for both the British Columbia and Alaska State Ferry Systems. The former has every other day service in the summer to Port Hardy, as well as twice a week to the Queen Charlotte Islands, and the latter offers service six times a week in the summer to the principal cities of Southeast Alaska. There is service four times a day to Terrace and Vancouver by jet and jet-prop aircraft. There are also daily flights to Sandspit and Masset on the Queen Charlotte Islands. Highway 16, the Yellowhead Highway, runs east to Prince George and Edmonton. Via Rail, the Canadian counter-part of Amtrack (the U.S. rail network), offers services three times a week to Vancouver, Prince George, and Jasper in Alberta, with connections to Toronto and points east. All of these facilities make Prince Rupert an excellent place for boaters to pick up, or drop off, guests.

Visiting pleasure craft have two choices for moorage, the public government floats at Rushbrooke Harbour about one and a half miles north of the center of town, or the floats at the Prince Rupert Rowing and Yacht Club, about one mile north of town. The yacht club welcomes all visiting boaters, whether members of another yacht club or not. Facilities are crowded in the summer and it is best to arrive as early in the day as possible. It may be possible to make reservations at the yacht club by calling (604) 624-4317, or on VHF Channel 72 when in range. The yacht club has water and power on the floats, and excellent showers that are included in the moorage fee. There is a public phone and garbage dump. The manager will also keep an eye on your boat if you leave it there for a short time while flying home and back. The floats, except for the outer one, have some protection from winds and wakes of passing boats. When the fishing fleet is in, moorage can be very uncomfortable, because of inconsiderate commercial fishermen refusing to obey the harbor speed limit.

The Rushbrooke Harbour floats are those public floats designated for visiting pleasure boats. The other two public floats, Fairview Harbour and Cow Bay are usually full of commercial boats. There are many commercial boats at Rushbrooke also, but certain floats are designated only for pleasure boats. No reservations are taken, it is on a first come basis, and rafting is mandatory, as it is on all public floats. Fifteen amp power and water are available. These floats are protected by a large floating breakwater. Enter around the north end. Be aware when mooring at any of the facilities in Prince Rupert of the strong tidal currents that run through them, making moorage difficult at times. The Rushbrooke manager requests that you call on VHF Channel 16, and they will then switch to Channel 9 or 10. There is good taxi service to town from either Rushbrooke or the yacht club; you can call them direct on CB Channel 4 if you have a CB. Fares have been about $4 Canadian to town. If you need some exercise, it isn't a bad walk, about 20 minutes from the yacht club, a bit longer from Rushbrooke. There are four big fuel facilities along Prince Rupert's waterfront, some of which are not open on weekends.

As you would expect, Prince Rupert has facilities of all types, many restaurants and hotels, supermarkets, a shopping mall, all open seven days a week, several banks, laundromats, and a variety of shops. There are many churches, a hospital, a good museum, a golf course and a swimming pool. With its large harbour and surrounding mountains it is a beautiful place. In early summer large numbers of eagles are to be seen in town, and once we saw a pod of killer whales go right along the waterfront.

For boaters returning from Alaska, Prince Rupert is the customs check-in point. This service is available year around, 24 hours a day, seven days a week. After mooring, only the captain is authorized to leave the vessel and call customs at 627-3003. An officer will come to the boat. If arriving between midnight to 0700, a recording will state another number to call in order to reach the on-duty officer. There has been no check-in solely by telephone, however this may change with new Canadian Customs rules. See Appendix A for more information.

Tuck Inlet lies off the north end of Prince Rupert Harbour, and is entered at Tuck Point, five miles north of Rushbrooke Harbour. Use Chart #3964, scale 1:20,000. Currents at Tuck Narrows can run to six knots. The channel is short, wide and deep, so entry can usually be made at any state of the tide. Tuck Inlet offers an alternative to one of the Prince Rupert moorages. The first anchorage is in the bight three eighths of a mile west of Tuck Point in eight to ten fathoms, mud bottom, and protected from all but down inlet winds. The other anchorage is at the head of the inlet in 16 fathoms, mud bottom. The head shoals rapidly, especially to port. There is protection from all but up-inlet winds.

Port Edward, about six miles south of Prince Rupert, is on the east side of Porpoise Harbour, between Ridley Island and the mainland. Entry is through Porpoise Channel. Greatly enlarged small boat facilities include moorage, power, water, showers, laundry, and fuel. The Harbour Manager can be reached on VHF Channel 72. The large North Pacific Cannery Museum is an attraction and a convenience store is located on the way to the museum. City bus service connects with Prince Rupert.

Side Trips to Kitimat and Gardner Canal

Ursula Channel

Going back to Kingcome Point, at the north end of Fraser Reach, Ursula Channel takes off to the north and leads to some very interesting and scenic waters. Use Chart #3743, scale 1:73,032. The first attraction is the hot spring located in Bishop Bay about six miles up Ursula Channel, and then another four miles to the head of Bishop Bay. The Kitimat Yacht Club originally developed this facility. According to the sign, it is now designated as a Forest Service Reservation Site and is user maintained. The two mooring buoys are gone, but there is anchorage in 10-15 fathoms, good holding bottom, around the head of the bay. Use of the bath house is free, and it is open to everyone. If the dock is crowded, anchor and go in by dinghy. Especially on weekends, it is often crowded with boaters visiting from Kitimat, 40 miles to the north. The usual custom is for one party to go up to the bath house at a time. Others remain on the float to await their turns. The water temperature is perfect, and the bath house is very clean. The procedure is to wash up with soap in the small square tub that is found outside, and then go into the big tub in the bath house to soak. There is an open porch on the side, with a bench and nails on which to hang clothes. Remember to be considerate, if others are waiting to use the tub.

During one June visit, we fished at the head of the bay and caught our limit of spring, or chinook, salmon in about an hour. They were immature fish, about ten pounds each, and we took them by jigging with Buzz Bombs. Since then, we have taken an occasional salmon, but that is all.

Weewanie Hot Springs are located in a cove 1/2 mile north of Weewanie Creek. This is about 2½ miles northeast of Dorothy Island Light in Devastation Channel, and about 17 miles south of M K Marina in Kitimat. These springs are not as easily accessible as Bishop Bay Hot Springs. There are two mooring buoys, and anchorage is found in eight fathoms plus. The Kitimat Yacht Club has built a metal-sided bath house, with separate areas for soaping, rinsing, and soaking. We have not used these springs; the information was given to us by another boater.

Gardner Canal

Gardner Canal is another of those "best kept secrets" on the British Columbia Coast, with snow-covered mountains over 6,000 feet high on both sides of its 45 mile length, and very few pleasure boats. It is entered at Staniforth Point where Verney Passage, Devastation Channel and Gardner Canal meet. Staniforth Point is 14 miles northeast of Riordan Point, at the entrance to Bishop Bay. The term "canal" is confusing to some, but in Vancouver's day it was used to denote long narrow saltwater passages and inlets, as well as the more common usage meaning man-made trenches. Portland Canal on the British Columbia-Alaska border, and Behm Canal around Revillagigedo Island in Alaska are two more canals named by Vancouver. Chart #3745, scale 1:73,050 should be used. At first glance it may appear that there is a dearth of good anchorages, but that is not true. The first is in Triumph Bay, about six miles southeast of Staniforth Point. The bight on the east side of the bay, about one mile south of Walkem Point has a well protected anchorage in 12 fathoms, mud bottom. The next anchorage is at the entrance to Kiltuish Inlet, 12 miles southeast of Staniforth Point, which we have used several times. The anchorage is in 12 fathoms in the bay just west of the entrance to the inlet. The inlet itself is about three miles long, with 4,000 foot to 5,000 foot peaks around it. Least depth in the entrance is six feet, but because of strong currents, passage should only be made at, or near, high slack water. We surveyed it in our dinghy before entering. There are plenty of anchorages, at reasonable depths throughout the inlet.

Kemano Bay is 18 miles northeast of Kiltuish Inlet, and 30 miles from Staniforth Point. The scenery along Europa Reach and Barrie Reach is wonderful, steep mountains sides. The canal's width is about one mile. The ALCAN (Aluminum Company of Canada) wharf and floats are located in Kemano Bay, as are the Kemano Yacht Club floats. The latter facilities are suitable only for very small craft. Some fuel may be available at the yacht club. The ALCAN floats are private, but it may be possible to use them. If not, anchorage is possible in the bay in less than 20 fathoms, but use caution, because it shoals very rapidly. The company owned town of **Kemano** is seven miles up the valley from Kemano Bay, and has a population of about 300. It was built in the 1960's when work began on the huge hydro-electric plant that is located here. The power generated here is transmitted by high-power transmission lines to ALCAN's aluminum smelter in Kitimat, 50 miles northwest. The entire generating plant is located inside a mountain, as are the company's offices. The source of water for the plant is the Nechako Reservoir on the east side of the Coast Range, and is brought to the plant by tunnels. A second tunnel and generating plant were constructed about 1990, doubling the generating capacity. The water drops 2,600 feet to reach the generators, so arrives under terrific pressure. Tours through the plant have been available for visitors in the past. If you are interested, the best way would be to call Kitimat Visitor Information, 632-6294, and see if it can be arranged. It is a very interesting place to visit. The town sits in a beautiful setting, and is complete with a school, church and hospital. Transportation to Kitimat is either by float plane, or the big aluminum ALCAN boat that runs to Kitimat several times a week. You will probably meet it if you go up the canal.

The head of Gardner Canal is at Kitlope Anchorage, 15 miles past Kemano, and has an excellent anchorage in 12 fathoms, soft bottom. It is exposed to up or down inlet winds, but we have spent several very comfortable nights there. There are beautiful mountain views, if the cloud cover allows you to see them. Very few boaters ever reach these waters, and it is one of the loveliest places on the coast. Bears may be seen along the shore, and mountain goats are on the mountain sides.

On August 16, 1994, Premier Mike Harcourt of British Columbia announced the permanent protection of 317,000 hectares (883,000 acres) of the Kitlope Valley, which has been described as the worlds largest undisturbed coastal temperate rain forest. It lies above Kitlope Anchorage. West Fraser Timber, which held the license to log this area, voluntarily gave up these cutting rights with no compensation, a very magnanimous act on their part. This means that this area will remain in its present state forever.

Chief Mathews Bay is a beautiful spot, with high glacier covered mountains at its head, and is worth a visit. It is about halfway between Kemano and Kitlope anchorage. It is said to be too deep for anchorage, but I think that it may be possible off the drying flats at the head. At any rate it is worth a visit just for the scenery.

Kitimat is located 26 miles north of Staniforth Point, up Devastation Channel and Kitimat Arm, and has a population of about 12,000. Moorage is at M.K. Marina. Built about 1990, the facility is a great improvement over the one that it replaced. Moorage, behind a breakwater, with water and power on the wide concrete floats is available, as are fuels, showers, laundry, launching and a campground. Moorage is also found across the bay at Moon Marina. Most of the boats are trailer boats that are from as far away as Prince George, 500 miles east in the interior. There is very good salmon fishing in Kitimat Arm as well as in the Kitimat River.

The town of Kitimat was created in the early 1950's when ALCAN built the big aluminum smelter here. It is seven miles away from the M.K. Marina. Taxi service is available. If you are lucky, you may be able to get a free lift at least one way. Kitimat has all of the facilities that you would expect to find in a town of its size, super market, restaurants, drug stores, hospital and churches, museum and golf course as well as varied small shops. It is served by a branch line of the Canadian National Railway, and two airlines provide jet or prop-jet service to Vancouver and Prince Rupert from the airport at Terrace, 35 miles to the north. A good paved highway runs to Terrace, where it connects to highways to Prince Rupert and Prince

George, and the rest of British Columbia. The wharves at Kitimat accommodate ocean going freighters. In recent years a large pulp and paper mill has been built here, as well as a chemical plant.

Bauxite ore, which is the source of alumina, from which aluminum is made, is not available locally, but comes in by freighter from as far away as Australia. Aluminum smelters are always located where plentiful, cheap electric power is available, and not near sources of bauxite ore, which is one of the most common minerals on earth.

Douglas Channel

Douglas Channel is the principal waterway to Kitimat, running north 43 miles from Wright Sound. Because it is wide and fairly straight, it is subject to strong up and down channel winds. The main problem is strong up-channel winds on sunny days, when the mainland heats up and sucks in cooler air from the sea. Prince Rupert Coast Guard, through a repeater on Gil Island, WX-2, gives a separate report for Douglas Channel, which is helpful. For that reason Verney Passage, between Hawkesbury Island and Gribbell Island, is sometimes a better choice, though it is a bit longer. Another advantage is the beautiful mountain scenery on Gribbell Island.

There are several anchorages between Kitimat and Hartley Bay, at the south end of Douglas Channel. The first is in Gilttoyees Inlet on the north side of Douglas Channel, 16 miles southwest of Kitimat. The best anchorage is in the small bay on the east side, two and a half miles south of the drying flats at the head of the inlet, in eight fathoms, mud bottom and good protection. The high mountains at the head of the inlet provide some spectacular scenery. Kitsaway Anchorage on the east side of Hawkesbury Island has well protected anchorages in six to 13 fathoms, on mud, and with good crabbing. Sue Channel between Hawkesbury and Loretta Islands has an anchorage in ten fathoms in the bight on the north side of Hawkesbury Island, about two miles west of Gaudin Point. The bay across Sue Channel on the south side of Loretta Island, while it is deep, is better protected. Kishkosh Inlet, south, on the west side of Douglas Channel, is not an ideal anchorage, as there is very shallow water one half mile up the inlet. If going into the inner part of the inlet, beware of the hazards.

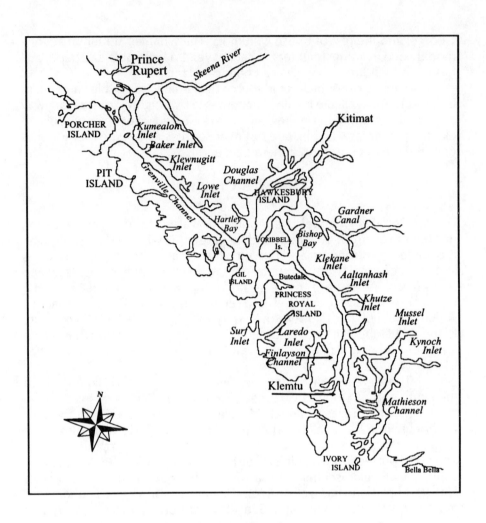

Chapter 14: West Side of Princess Royal and Pitt Islands

This chapter covers an alternate route north instead of the usual way past Butedale and Grenville Channel. The distances are about the same by either route. This is a very interesting, little traveled course, and a very welcome change from the usual one. It is not necessary to do the complete route because entry or exit may be made by either Whale Channel or Lewis Passage back to Wright Sound. This western journey, which has about 20 good anchorages available, turns south at Split Head, five miles north of Klemtu, and runs down Meyers Passage for five miles before turning west into Meyers Narrows. Chart #3734, scale 1:36,028 and Chart #3710, scales 1:37,747 and 1:12,572 are needed here.

Meyers Passage

Alexander Inlet, lying due west of Split Head is a good, attractive anchorage, and was covered in Chapter 12. If you are planning on making this cruise, I would recommend that you have detailed charts of the various harbors along the way, Charts #3719, #3721, #3753, and well as #3710 for the transit of Meyers Passage.

Passage through Meyers Narrows is recommended only at or near high tide, because there is a least depth of only three feet in the narrows. Currents can run to three knots, flooding to the east and ebbing to the west. The inset on Chart #3710 shows the recommended course through the narrows. In late summer the passage becomes choked with kelp, and it is necessary to plow through it. Be sure to stay on the course regardless of the kelp. A red spar buoy is on the south side of the channel, near a drying rock. An un-named cove on the north side of the passage, near its west end offers a possible anchorage in its north end in ten to 12 fathoms.

The west end of Meyers Passage opens into Laredo Sound, which in turn opens into Hecate Strait, so it can get rough at times. If going out into Laredo Sound, caution should be used to avoid Ellard Rock and Gaudin Rock to the west. Parsons Anchorage is five miles due south of Wingate Point, which is at the west end of Meyers Passage, and offers anchorage in six to seven fathoms, soft bottom, protected from all but northwest winds and seas.

Laredo Inlet

Laredo Inlet, 18 miles long, is the longest inlet encountered along this western route, and is entered just north of Meyers Passage. If coming from Meyers Passage, the best entry is through Thistle Passage. Chart #3737, scale 1:77,429, is an old and not very satisfactory chart, but is the only one available. A magnifying glass is helpful in reading some of the details. If coming from the north, entry to the inlet is south of the Laidlaw Islands and north of Aitken Island. The scenery is attractive in Laredo Inlet, with mountains rising from 2,000 to 3,000 feet on both sides. There are half a dozen anchorages.

The first anchorage is in Alston Cove, on the east side of the inlet in six fathoms with a mud bottom and excellent protection. The next anchorage, going up the inlet, is Weld Cove on the west side, northwest of Pocock Island. The easiest entry is between Kohl and Pocock Islands, though caution is necessary because of foul ground at the west entrance. The entrance on the west side of Kohl Island appears to be easier, but is more difficult because it is not well depicted on the chart. The passage north of the small island shown northwest of Kohl Island is extremely narrow, though we had 20 feet of water under us. Anchorage is at the north end of Weld Cove in nine to ten fathoms, and very well protected. The bottom shoals very rapidly.

The next anchorage is in the Bay of Plenty, two miles farther north. There is an excellent, well protected anchorage in nine fathoms, on the southwest shore of the bay. Two islands to the east give protection from wind or seas coming in from Laredo Inlet. This is probably the most attractive anchorage in Laredo Inlet.

Fifer Cove has anchorage on the east side of the inlet. There is an excellent, beautiful anchorage in ten fathoms, mud bottom, and good protection. A large stream enters at the head of the cove. When the salmon are running bears and eagles can sometimes be seen taking them.

Mellis Inlet, on the west side of Laredo Inlet, is the most spectacular of Laredo's inlets with its high mountains on both sides. The anchorage, at the head in 12 fathoms, on a soft bottom, is exposed to southeast winds, however, and may be uncomfortable.

The last anchorage in Laredo Inlet is at its head, on the west side of Brew Island, in ten fathoms, soft bottom, but very exposed to up-inlet winds.

Trahey Inlet, just west of the entrance to Laredo Inlet, has a good anchorage at the head of its west arm, in six to seven fathoms, well protected. Careful attention to the chart is necessary when entering. The passage on the east side of Jessop Island is easier than that on the west side.

Laredo Channel

Going along the west side of Princess Royal Island, up Laredo Channel, the first good anchorage is in Helmcken Inlet, using Chart #3719, scale 1:18,278. Entry is on the south side of Smithers Island. Anchorage is possible at the head of the inlet, but if a west wind is blowing it is much more comfortable in the little cove on the east end of Smithers Island, in nine to ten fathoms, soft bottom. We rode out a gale in this anchorage. The cove on the southwest side of Smithers Island is much too exposed if any wind is blowing.

Kent Inlet to the south of Helmcken Inlet and Commando to the north of Helmcken, have currents running six to eight knots and eight to ten knots respectively at their entrances, and should only be entered at or near slack water. Due to shallows, high slack is preferable. We have not entered Kent Inlet. However, the best anchorage is in the second basin in 11 to 14 fathoms. I imagine currents will be pretty strong in the first basin above Phillips Narrows. In Commando Inlet the best anchorage would be in the cove at the head of the inlet in five to six fathoms. Evinrude Inlet, immediately north of Commando Inlet is easy to enter. Keep to the starboard side of the channel in both of the narrows to avoid rocks and shoals. The best anchorage appears to be in the northeast corner in about ten fathoms. Chart #3719 should be used for all of these inlets on the west side of Princess Royal Island.

As you proceed through Laredo Channel you will notice that it is well marked with navigational aids, because it is used by ships going to and from the port of Kitimat.

Surf Inlet

Use (Chart #3737). This 11-mile-long inlet is the most beautiful of all of the inlets on the west sides of Princess Royal and Pitt Islands, with steep sides and a relatively narrow channel.

There are several anchorages available. The first is in Chapple Inlet on the north side just before entering Surf Inlet. Using Chart #3719, it is about one and a fourth miles north from Mallandaine Point to Doig Anchorage. The best anchorage is not the one indicated on the chart, but in the little cove just northeast of the point about one fourth mile to the south in ten fathoms, soft bottom, and protection from all but north winds. In 1992, a log boom was strung across the inner part of the cove, but it was still possible to get in far enough to be protected. Another possible anchorage is one and a quarter miles to the north, behind Chettleburgh Point in five to six fathoms. Chapple is not particularly scenic, the sides being low and logged fairly recently.

By far the best anchorage in Surf Inlet is in Penn Harbour, seven miles up the inlet. Chart #3737, with a scale of 1:77,429 or one inch to the mile, leaves a lot to be desired in anchoring, but a good magnifying glass is a great help. Anchorage in Penn Harbour is in nine to ten fathoms, soft bottom, with some nice falls at the head, and excellent protection.

The head of Surf Inlet is four miles northeast of Penn Harbour, with good mountain scenery. The dam and abandoned power house of Port Belmont, remaining from the days when the large Belmont gold mine was operating up the valley, are still visible. Anchorage is possible in eight to ten fathoms at the head. As is common at the heads of inlets, it shoals rapidly.

Other possible anchorages in Surf Inlet are in Argyle Cove, two and a half miles northeast of Bryant Point, in seven fathoms, or in the little cove just north of Penn Harbour in seven and a half fathoms, but Penn Harbour is by far the best, though reception of weather reports is not possible.

Racey Inlet lies to the south of the entrance to Surf Inlet. Hallett Rock in the entrance must be avoided, as well as several other rocks farther up the inlet. Anchorage is possible at the head, on either side of Wale Island in ten fathoms or less.

Campania Island Vicinity

When heading north from Surf Inlet, if continuing north up the west side of Pitt Island, it is possible to pass on either side of Campania Island. Passage on the east side is by Campania Sound and Squally Reach. The east side of Campania Island is steep and there are no anchorages. *Sailing Directions, British Columbia Coast (North Portion)*, states that squalls coming off the heights on Campania Island can occur in Squally Reach, we have not encountered any during summer months. The best anchorage in this area is to be found in Cameron Cove in Barnard Harbour on the north end of Princess Royal Island, using Charts #3737, #3742 or #3723. This large bay, off Whale Channel, has good anchorages in six to seven fathoms, soft bottom. The bottom slopes very gradually from 15 to six fathoms, making anchorage easy. There is good protection. In 1993 there was a very large, new looking, sports fishing camp in Barnard Harbour.

Whale Channel and Lewis Passage pass around the east and west sides, respectively, of Gil Island, and lead into Wright Sound, which is on the more commonly used route up the "Inside Passage". Use Chart #3742, scale 1:70,920. Tidal streams vary in these channels, but may reach as much as three knots in some places.

Passage along the west side of Campania Island is north via Estavan

Sound, and leads into Nepean Sound and Principe Channel. This channel continues along the west side of Pitt Island. Use Charts #3724, scale 1:71,594 and #3742. Chart #3719, scale 1:18,279 shows several inlets on the northwest side of Campania Island in detail. Possible anchorages are in McMicking Inlet, Betteridge Inlet and Weinberg Inlet. Harwood Bay and Lindsay Bay are too exposed for good anchorages.

Principe Channel

Continuing up Principe Channel, on the west side of Pitt Island, use Charts #3742, scale of 1:70,920 and #3741, scale 1:72,860. There are good anchorages in Monckton Inlet, use Chart #3721, scale 1:18,337. Entry to **Monckton Inlet** is easy because the entrance is wide and deep. The best anchorage is near the head of the large cove on the north side of the inlet, about one half mile north of Roy Island, in nine fathoms, mud bottom and good protection. Additional anchorages are in the cove northwest of Monckton Point in nine to ten fathoms, and near the head of the inlet in six to ten fathoms, both mud bottoms.

Port Stephens lies just north of Monckton Inlet, and has an excellent, protected anchorage in ten fathoms, soft bottom, in a little cove one mile northeast of Littlejohn Point. Another anchorage is in the cove to the north of the west entrance to Stephens Narrows in 11 to 12 fathoms, soft bottom, and fair protection. Stephens Narrows dries three feet in the passage on the south side of the island at the east end of the narrows, and the passage on the north side is awash at low water. Passage into the inner basin should obviously be tried only at high tide, if at all. Anchorages in the inner basin range from eight to 15 fathoms.

Buchan Inlet, was named for the author and former Governor General of Canada, John Buchan, Lord Tweedsmuir. Note Tweedsmuir Point on the south side of the entrance. The inlet is four miles northwest of Port Stephens. There is an anchorage in the cove just north of Elsfield Point in ten to 12 fathoms, soft bottom. Look out for the rock on the north side of the cove, and anchor between it and Elsfield Point. Protection is good, but the wind may come in over the low land to the south. Entry should be made to the inner bay, only after exploring it by dinghy, according to the Chart #3721, scale 1:18,303. Anchorage is possible in ten to 15 fathoms.

Patterson Inlet is five miles north of Buchan Inlet and has good, protected anchorages in either the north arm in five to six fathoms, or the south arm in seven to eight fathoms, soft bottoms and nice scenery. A stream runs into the south arm, and can be traversed for a short distance in a dinghy, even at low tide. In August, 1994, a large logging camp was located in the south arm.

Minktrap Bay is just north of Patterson Inlet, use Chart #3721 in both of them. Moolock Cove has the most protected anchorage. The cove at the south end is best, though it must be entered cautiously, as rocks abound. Anchorage depths range from seven to ten fathoms throughout this cove. The bottom is soft, but due to the low lying land around the cove, winds may be able to get in. This is an interesting place to explore, but either of the anchorages in Patterson are superior. Miller Inlet has a very protected anchorage in its inner basin in five to nine fathoms. Drying rocks are in the center of the entrance and to port on either end of the second narrows.

Ala Passage between Anger Island and Pitt Island is full of rocks, and is best avoided.

Petrel Channel

Petrel Channel is entered at Foul Point on Anger Island, and runs north and west 23 miles to Comrie Head where it meets Ogden Channel. Charts #3746, scale 1:39,100 and #3927, scale 1:77,800, should be used. Tidal currents run to three knots in Petrel Channel.

Hevenor Inlet, Newcombe Harbour and Captain Cove are anchorages off Petrel Channel. Use Chart #3753 in each of them. The entrance to Hevenor Inlet is wide and deep. There are no hazards, except for Hevenor Islet, one mile into the inlet. The best anchorage is at the very head of the inlet, in the entrance to Hevenor Lagoon, in six to eight fathoms, soft bottom. This is a very scenic, well protected anchorage. The lagoon may be explored by dinghy at all states of the tides.

Newcombe Harbour, four miles north of Hevenor Inlet, is a large, well protected, and scenic anchorage. The best anchorage is just south of the point on the northwest side of the bay in nine fathoms, mud bottom. A niche on the east side near the entrance might provide more shelter in a big blow.

Captain Cove is nine miles north of Newcombe Harbour, and four miles east of Comrie Head, at the north end of Petrel Channel. The most protected anchorage is on the south side, behind the islets, in five to eight fathoms, mud bottom. In August, 1993, and August, 1994, an active logging camp was located at the east end of the cove.

From Comrie Head it is eight miles up Ogden Channel to Gibson Island, where the route to Prince Rupert, that comes up Grenville Channel, is joined. Use Chart #3773, scale 1:36,517. It is 26 miles north to Prince Rupert. This completes the cruise along the west sides of Princess Royal and Pitt Islands.

Pacific Mariner's Memorial, Prince Rupert

Stewart, British Columbia floats

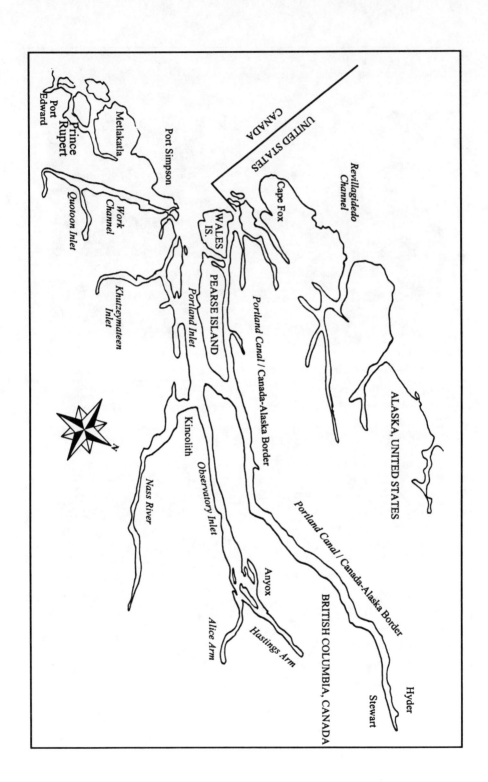

Port Edward

Prince Rupert

Metlakatla

Port Simpson

Quoioon Inlet

Work Channel

Khutzeymateen Inlet

WALES IS.

PEARSE ISLAND

Cape Fox

Revillagidedo Channel

CANADA

UNITED STATES

Portland Canal / Canada-Alaska Border

Portland Inlet

ALASKA, UNITED STATES

Kincolith

Nass River

Observatory Inlet

N

Anyox

Alice Arm

Hastings Arm

Portland Canal / Canada-Alaska Border

BRITISH COLUMBIA, CANADA

Stewart

Hyder

Chapter 15: Prince Rupert to Alaska Border

There are five large inlets lying between Prince Rupert and the Alaska border that get scant attention from pleasure boaters. This is unfortunate because they have beautiful scenery and very little traffic. The reason that most boaters neglect these waters is probably because those who have come this far have been lured here by the idea of cruising the waters of Southeast Alaska, and they just keep heading north.

The distance from Prince Rupert to Stewart, British Columbia, at the head of Portland Canal, is 113 miles, and to the head of Hastings Arm at the north end of Observatory Inlet is 95 miles. Anchorages are not plentiful, because of the great depths, and the straight, steep shorelines; but there are about 15 good ones. In addition, government floats are located at five small communities; Port Simpson, Kincolith, Alice Arm, Stewart, and Hyda, Alaska. Only Stewart has fuel available year around. Port Simpson may have fuel in the summer.

Leaving **Prince Rupert**, the shortest route north is via Venn Passage, between Digby Island and the Tsimpsean Peninsula, using Chart #3955, scale l:20,000, and Chart #3959, scale 1:40,000, both Metric. This route is narrow, crooked, and shallow; but it is about eight miles shorter than going around Digby Island. There is a least depth of seven feet in the channel, and currents can run to three knots, flooding east, and ebbing west. With the proper charts and a reliable fathometer, passage is possible at all times, except the very lowest tides, depending on how much water you draw. It is essential to stay in the well marked channel. The shallowest part is between Dundas Point and DuVernet Point.

About one mile northwest of Dundas Point you pass the native Tsimpsean Indian settlement of **Metlakatla** on the starboard side. This area has been occupied for several thousand years, the evidence is the numerous middens along the channel. It was one of the most heavily populated places on the entire coast before the arrival of the Europeans. Father William Duncan, an Anglican Church missionary, established a mission here, and built the huge wooden church which still stands. In addition to the church, the most conspicuous buildings are the school and a mission house. When Father Duncan had a falling out with Anglican Church authorities in the late 1800's, he asked the state of Alaska if they would let him settle some of his Tsimpseans in Alaska. They agreed, and he moved to Annette Island, about 15 miles southwest of Ketchikan. About half of the natives followed him, and he established another Metlakatla. He erected another big wooden church and community building there, both of which still stand.

There is a short-cut to the north about three-fourths of a mile west of Metlakatla. This is about three miles shorter than going out to Enfield

Rock to turn north. You will need Charts #3957 and #3959, both Metric on scales of 1:40,000. Both of these routes lead into Chatham Sound, and head north. Beware of the Hodgson Reefs, which are marked by a buoy on the west side. If you have taken the short cut, you can pass them on the east side. Listen to the report of sea conditions at Green Island Lighthouse, at the north end of Chatham Sound, before heading out into Chatham Sound.

The native village of **Port Simpson** is 15 miles north of Metlakatla. If using Metric Chart #3963, scale 1:40,000, which is the correct chart for these waters, you will not find the village of Port Simpson; it is now indicated by its Tsimpsean name, Lax kw'alaams. This is the oldest European settlement on the British Columbia Coast, and, at one time, was the largest European settlement on the Pacific coast between San Francisco and Sitka, Alaska. It was originally established by the Hudson's Bay Company in 1831 on the Nass River near Kincolith, as Fort Simpson, their northern fur trading post. It was moved to its present location three years later because access to the Nass River site was difficult for sailing vessels. Port Simpson may be approached by either Cunningham Passage and Dodd Passage to the south, or Inskip Passage or Rushbrook Passage to the north. Anchorage is possible in Stumaun Bay in eight to ten fathoms, protected from all but northwest winds. Moorage is also available at the government floats. Supplies are found at the general store, fuel is reported to be accessible during the summer months, and water is available.

Work Channel

Work Channel is entered at Maskelyne Point, five miles north of Port Simpson. Use Chart #3963. Fishing for both salmon and bottom fish is often good around Maskelyne Point. Work Channel is 28 miles long, and being bordered by high mountains it is quite scenic. Currents can run to three and four knots in the entrance to Work Channel, and strong tide rips can occur, but passage is possible at all times. Dudevior Passage, on the southwest side of the channel, and Paradise Passage, on the northeast side of the channel, are not recommended because they have least depths of three feet and ten feet respectively, and are very narrow. You may see commercial fishing boats going through, but we have always avoided these passages.

Anchorages are scarce in Work Channel, because of extreme depths and steep straight shorelines, but there are a few. There are two very good anchorages in Trail Bay, entered six miles south of Maskelyne Point. The first is at the head of Trail Bay in ten fathoms, sand and gravel bottom. A better protected anchorage is in Zumtela Bay, to the west, in eight fathoms, soft bottom. Good crabbing.

Another possible, but not as good an anchorage, is in Legace Bay, five miles southeast of Trail Bay, but it is deep, 15 fathoms, and not too well protected.

Quottoon Inlet, also known as the North Arm, is the most interesting section of Work Channel. It is surrounded by 3,000 to 4,000 foot mountains. Tidal currents are strong in Quottoon Narrows, but it is 450 feet wide and can be traversed on all tides. Keep to the east side of the passage when traversing the narrows. There is a good protected anchorage in 10 to 11 fathoms in the cove just north of Quottoon Narrows. It is not affected by the strong currents in nearby Quottoon Narrows. The head of the inlet has spectacular scenery with snow capped peaks and waterfalls. It is too deep for satisfactory anchorages.

Work Channel continues nine miles from Quottoon Point to Davies Bay, where there is a well protected anchorage on the east side, in eight to ten fathoms, gravel bottom. The entrance to Davies Lagoon dries nine feet, but may be entered by small craft at or near high water.

Union Inlet, just north of Work Channel, is entered at John Point about two miles northeast of Maskelyne Point. Anchorage is possible near the head of this five-mile-long inlet in 15 to 17 fathoms, mud bottom. Use Chart #3963.

Khutzeymateen Inlet has a good-sized Grizzly Bear population, and, for that reason, was designated as a wild life reserve several years ago. Restrictions on the use of the preserve have been made, but not sufficiently publicized. According to the best information available at the present time they include:

1. A ban on "disembarking from your vessel unless accompanied by a Park Ranger or approved guide."

2. "Entry into the estuary for viewing purposes is permitted only if authorized by a Park Ranger or on site guardian."

3. "Land-based viewing shall be at the discretion of the Park Ranger". He is found at the small floating Ranger Station. Call "Khutzeymateen Base" on Channel 16 VHF to register.

4. "Fishing is prohibited within the sanctuary boundaries."

5. "Firearms are allowed only by permit."

6. "Hunting is prohibited." It would be a good idea to check with the B.C. Parks Division (See footnote at end of chapter).

We saw three Grizzlies at one time on our first visit, but none on two subsequent occasions. Viewing is best when the salmon are running in the spring and fall.

The inlet is 13 miles long, and is entered between Keemein and Welgeegenk Points. The entrance is nine miles northeast of Maskelyne Point, up Steamer Passage. Neither radio nor GPS reception is possible in the upper part of the inlet.

The only anchorages are either at the head of the inlet, or in Tsamspanakuck Bay. At the head, the most protected anchorage is in the northeast corner in 15 to 17 fathoms, soft bottom. There is good crabbing, and there is a very large seal population. We have been told that on occasions Killer Whales come here to hunt for these seals. The scenery at the head of Khutzeymateen Inlet is very beautiful. On August 17, 1994, the Khutzeymateen Valley became British Columbia's newest Class A Provincial Park. Use Chart 3994, scale 1:40,000.

Continuing north in Portland Inlet, Somerville Bay, at the north end of Somerville Island, offers anchorage in 11 fathoms, clay bottom, and protection from all but northeast winds. If it is uncomfortable in the center of the bay, a more protected anchorage is on the west side, behind the point in two to three fathoms. Good anchorages are rare in these waters, because of the extreme depths, as much as 300 fathoms in Portland Inlet. The entrance to Nasoga Gulf is on the east side of Portland Inlet, about three miles northeast of the north end of Somerville Island. Anchorage is possible in 10 to 15 fathoms at the head of the bay, on a gravel bottom, but it is exposed to winds from the southwest, coming off of Portland Inlet.

At Ramsden Point, Portland Inlet ends and Portland Canal lies to port. Observatory Inlet is straight ahead. Nass Bay opens to starboard and is of historical significance, because the original Fort Simpson, the first European settlement on the British Columbia Coast, was located a few miles up the Nass River. It was established in 1831 by Aemilius Simpson, a lieutenant in the Royal Navy, and three years later it was moved to the present location of Port Simpson, because the Nass River site was difficult for sailing ships to reach.

Kincolith, a large native settlement, is located on the north side of Nass Bay. Currents can run to three knots on the ebb and two knots on the flood in the entrance to Nass Bay. Use new Metric Chart #3920, scale 1:40,000, or old chart #3790, scale 1:25,000 in Nass Bay. There are two small floats with least depths of six feet in the small boat harbor of Kincolith, behind the rock breakwater on the north side of Nass Bay. A port hand day beacon marks the entrance to this harbor. In 1993 a small float was moored outside of the breakwater. It would be suitable for temporary moorage. The tiny harbor is usually crowded with local gill-net boats. The natives on boats in the harbor were very friendly and helpful when we moored there. It is a walk of about one half mile into town, where grocery stores are located.

A cannery was once located at Arrandale, at Low Point, across Nass Bay from Kincolith; rotting pilings from the wharf can still be seen. Anchorages can be found in several places in Iceberg Bay, about three miles south of Kincolith. The front of the Nass River delta is subject to change, so it is only prudent to stay fairly close to the light on Double Islet,

174

if entering Iceberg Bay. The chart shows that anchorage is possible in five to eight fathoms throughout the entrance to the bay. Other, more protected anchorages are in Nass Harbor, east of Jacques Point, in four to five fathoms, or about one mile to the southwest in Echo Cove, in seven to eight fathoms, both on soft bottom. We have not entered Iceberg Bay, but if you do, Chart #3920, Nass Bay, scale 1:40,000 would be very helpful.

Observatory Inlet

Observatory Inlet is entered at Nass Point, just northwest of Kincolith. The inlet received its name from Captain Vancouver, when he set up his observatory on the shore of Salmon Cove to make accurate celestial observations to ascertain his correct position and to check the accuracy of his chronometers, on which instruments the accuracy of all of his observations depended. Since he was searching for the *Northwest Passage*, it was necessary to probe each of these long inlets to determine whether they were, or were not, the one that he was seeking. His two ships, the *Discovery* and the *Chatham*, were anchored in Salmon Cove from July 23 to August 17, 1793, while small boats explored as far away as Behm Canal, around Revillagigedo Island in Alaska, where Ketchikan is now located.

It is 16.5 miles up Observatory Inlet to Salmon Cove, where it might be possible to anchor in 11 to 12 fathoms on the north side but with very little protection from winds blowing up or down the inlet. Observatory Inlet is straight with 4,000 to 5,000 foot mountains on either side. Currents seldom reach as much as two knots. Use Chart #3933, scale 1:80,000. On warm summer afternoons you can expect fairly strong up inlet winds, which is true in all of the big inlets. At the light on Richards Point, about two miles north of Salmon Cove, the real beauties of Observatory Inlet open up, if you are fortunate enough to have clear weather. Instead of being restricted to a channel one mile wide, the vista suddenly opens up from Alice Mountain on the east to the peaks bordering Portland Canal on the west, and extends for another 25 miles to the head of Hastings Arm. With the various tall mountains, glaciers and valleys, and the water sprinkled with islands it is truly a sight to behold. It is one of the most beautiful areas on the entire British Columbia coast, and one of the least known. Almost invariably when we mention that we were up in Observatory Inlet the reply is, "Where is that?"

If it is cloudy, as it often is, you will have to let your imagination fill in the details, and hope for clear weather the next day. We have visited these waters four times between 1986 and 1994 and hope to be able to return again. During these four visits we saw three other boats. One was a government boat whose crew was counting salmon in the streams, and the others were pleasure boats.

One of the best anchorages in the area is in Perry Bay, about nine miles north of Richards Point. Use new Metric Chart #3920, scale 1:25,000, and give Perry Spit plenty of clearance. Depths are about two and a half fathoms in the entrance to Perry Bay, but increase once inside. The best anchorage is at the south end of the bay in eight to 12 fathoms, mud bottom, good protection, and great scenery. If you are lucky, a black bear may be patrolling the shore line. The crabbing is usually good. This is probably the best base from which to explore the surrounding waters. Good anchorages are not common.

In addition to the scenery in Observatory Inlet, there are other attractions in this area; three *ghost towns*, Anyox, Alice Arm and Kitsault are worth seeing.

The entrance to **Alice Arm** is directly north of Perry Bay, and the village of the same name lies at the head of the arm, ten miles to the northeast. There is a small public float at Alice Arm that is also used as an aircraft float, so must be cleared when a plane arrives. A small adjoining float can be used for moorage, but the only way up to the top of the wharf has been by climbing a chain ladder, not practical for senior citizens. The other option is to use a dinghy to reach the regular float. Alice Arm was a silver mining town, first settled in 1905, and at one time had 2500 residents. The Dolly Varden mine was 18 miles up the Kitsault River Valley, and a narrow gauge railway ran from saltwater to the mine. The roadbed is still passable for about six miles. It is kept this way by Vince Brown, who with his wife, Vicky, operate the Alice Arm Lodge, which can accommodate up to six guests, some of whom come from as far away as Germany. The lodge is open May 1 to September, and features coho and trout fishing in the river in the latter part of August through the last week in September, when the season closes, as well as salt water fishing in Alice Arm. There are no roads into Alice Arm, but Vince can arrange for you to get clearance to use the private road into Kitsault, across the arm. He will pick you up there, or you can fly in from Prince Rupert or Terrace by float plane. The Brown's lodge and a house in which John and Pat Wheatley, the caretakers at Kitsault, live are both new; the other buildings in town are all old. The old store building collapsed under a heavy snowfall in 1987 or 1988. It is an interesting ghost town to walk around, in a beautiful setting.

Kitsault, across Alice Arm from the village of Alice Arm, is a former molybdenum mining town. It is connected to Terrace, British Columbia, by a good road, but it is a private road, and has a locked gate on it. The Wheatleys have been the caretakers for some time. Kennecot Copper built the original mine in 1969, and operated it for four years before shutting it down. In 1983, Climax Molybdenum, later taken over by AMAX, started a new operation and spent 250 million dollars on the town site alone. The four and five story brick buildings are still very visible. The mine operated for a year and a half, and was shut down permanently, because of a world wide glut of molybdenum, which depressed the price of molybdenum to the point where this mine was no longer profitable. Molybdenum is used as an alloy in the manufacturing of steel. The mine tailings were dumped into Alice Arm by a pipe line, and environmental concerns may also have entered into the decision to shut down. The equipment has all been sold and shipped out, and the site is for sale. There are no moorage facilities at Kitsault open to the public. If you consider anchoring at the head of Alice Arm, the depths are great, and the river flats very steep-to. It is also fully exposed to up inlet winds. The area on the east side, just north of Kitsault might be the best spot. We have never spent a night at Alice Arm. We go back to Perry Bay where there is excellent shelter.

Anyox is located in Granby Bay, on the west side of Hastings Arm. Use Metric Chart #3920, scale of 1:25,000. Anyox was a huge copper mining and smelting operation. Construction of the smelter, which was the largest in the entire British Empire at the time, began in 1915. The mine and town precede that date. At one time there were as many as 3,000 residents. Since Alice Arm was still active at that time, this area, around 1920 had over 5,000 residents. Today there are only about half a dozen people living in the total area, year around. In those years there were no regulations concerning pollution, and, because the site was remote from any large centers of population, it spewed out very toxic fumes during its entire operating life. The destruction is still evident in the form of thousands of dead trees, and the stunted growth of the returning forests on the mountain sides. A huge black slag pile jutting out into Granby Bay is another result of the smelting operation. It is so large that a nine hole golf course was built on it. There was no grass on the greens or fairways, all play was on the slag surface.

In 1923, a big fire broke out in Anyox, and the inhabitants retreated to the slag pile. When the fire reached the explosive storage, it blew up, leveling the town, but the inhabitants were safe on the slag pile. Though only the foundations of buildings remained, the town was soon rebuilt, and the mine and smelter put back in operation. In 1935, during the Great Depression, world copper prices fell so low that the mine and smelter were shut down, and since there was no other employment, all of the residents departed. A salvage crew remained, dismantling the equipment and shipping it out. In 1942, two forest fires hit the abandoned town, burning it down. All that remains are the brick and stone buildings and chimneys that would not burn, such as those of the power plant. In 1993 and 1994, a watchman was on duty, and a crew was shipping out barge loads of the slag for use as aggregate in the manufacturing of concrete. It is well worth a trip into Granby Bay to see these ruins. The Summer, 1988, issue of *Beautiful British Columbia* magazine has an excellent article on Anyox, well worth reading if you are planning on visiting here.

There is a good, well protected anchorage in Granby Bay, on the east side, in the un-named cove across from Bonanza Point. Anchorage is in ten fathoms, soft bottom. We have used it several times. It is probably the most scenic anchorage in Observatory Inlet, as the low shoreline allows for good views of mountains in all directions, and they are all around. Anchorage is also possible at the head of Granby Bay in eight to ten fathoms.

There are two more anchorages in Hastings Arm. The first is at the south end of Sylvester Bay in four to six fathoms, protected from all but north winds. The second is on the west side of Doben Island, well protected, in 12 to 15 fathoms, on a gravel bottom. It may be entered from either the north or south, but the latter is easier to navigate.

Hastings Arm extends 13 miles north from Davies Point, and is bordered on both sides by tall mountains culminating in beautiful Mount Hastings, 6,500 feet high, at its head. At the head of the inlet you are about 20 miles north of Ketchikan, Alaska, 75 miles away to the southwest. Anchorage is possible at the head of the inlet, though there is no protection from up inlet winds from the south, and the flats are steep-to. There is an abandoned cabin and a buoy on the east side of the inlet at its head. On a clear day the scenery in Hastings Arm is truly spectacular.

Portland Canal

Portland Canal is entered from Portland Inlet at Ramsden Point. It stretches north for 60 miles to Stewart, British Columbia, and Hyder, Alaska at its head. If you add to this the 25 miles back down Portland Inlet to its entrance at Maskelyne Point, you get a total of 85 miles, making this the longest inlet on the British Columbia coast. Knight Inlet, the next longest, is 70 miles long. The international boundary between British Columbia and Alaska runs more or less up the center of Portland Canal, which averages a mile in width. Depths are about 100 to 150 fathoms most of the length, but an area about ten miles south of Stewart has a section of more than 200 fathoms. It is clear its entire length, except for Hattie Island, in its center 20 miles north of Ramsden Point. Use Chart #3933, scale 1:80,000. As is true in all long inlets, wind can be a problem, especially up inlet winds on clear warm afternoons, and there are only a few shelters in the whole length. For that reason we have not traversed the upper section of the canal; we turned around at Hattie Island when it started to blow. We had 40 miles to go to Stewart, not to mention coming back out. We have driven into Stewart on two occasions, and looked over their small boat harbor so we know what is available there.

Whiskey Bay, a little cove on the north end of Pearse Island, four miles northwest of Ramsden Point, has an anchorage in five to seven fathoms, soft bottom, if the wind is blowing up Pearse and Portland Canals, and you need some shelter. There is adequate protection from all but north winds.

Halibut Bay, on the Alaskan shore is 15 miles north of Ramsden Point and is probably the best anchorage in Portland Canal, though it is in Alaskan waters, and up inlet seas will come right into the anchorage, making it uncomfortable. The anchorage is in seven fathoms, good holding bottom on the west side of the bay.

The next anchorage is in Maple Bay, on the British Columbia side, eight miles north of Hattie Island. Anchorage in nine fathoms may be found off the south shore of the bay.

Fords Cove, 13 miles north of Maple Bay, has an anchorage at its south end, about halfway between Green Islets and the east shore, in 16 fathoms. It has some shelter from south winds, but none from north winds.

Stewart is 19 miles north of Fords Cove, and Hyder, Alaska, is about one mile south of Stewart. The floats of the Stewart Yacht Club, and a public float as well, are both located on the west side of the canal at its head. They are about one mile from town. The latest population figure for Stewart was 1,151, but that is subject to large fluctuations, depending on the level of mining activity. Hyder, Alaska, is also on the west side of the inlet, one mile south of the floats at Stewart. There is a very small harbor at Hyder that should be entered with extreme caution at low tides, as the entrance is very shallow. The little harbor is well protected, it is a walk of about one-quarter mile into the town of Hyder, which is small, and consists mostly of bars and a tourist information office. There is no customs service in Hyder. This creates a problem when travelling there directly from British Columbia.

Stewart has grocery stores and other shops as well as a hotel, tourist information office and museum. If you get to Stewart or Hyder, it would be well worth your time to ask at either of the tourist information offices if the bus trips to the Grand Duc mine are operating. This is a spectacular trip, above timberline, looking down on the huge Salmon Glacier. It is about 30 miles one way, on a dead end road. In 1992, we rented a car in Prince Rupert and drove this road. Another unusual attraction is Bear Glacier which faces the paved road that comes into Stewart from the north and east. It is across a small lake from the highway, at about the same altitude as the road.

Pearse Canal

Pearse Canal is on the northwest side of 16-mile-long Pearse Island, and is usually more sheltered than Portland Inlet, on the other side of Pearse Island. The International Boundary that runs down Portland Canal continues down the center of Pearse Canal for 23 miles, until it meets Tongass Passage and turns south to Dixon Entrance, where it heads due west.

There are two good anchorages in Canadian waters along Pearse Canal, and one on the Alaskan side. Whiskey Bay on the north end of Pearse Island was mentioned earlier, and does offer some shelter if it is rough in Portland Inlet and Canal, and Pearse Canal. Hidden Inlet is on the Alaskan side, seven miles southwest of Tree Point, and is not a good anchorage due to excessive depths. It can be entered only at slack tide, as currents run to eight to 10 knots in the entrance. Well preserved buildings of an abandoned cannery are in Gwent Cove, just south of the entrance to Hidden Inlet. Use Charts #3933, #3994 and Metric Chart #3960, scale 1:40,000 in Pearse Canal.

There is an excellent, very well protected anchorage in Winter Inlet, on Pearse Island, eight miles southwest of Hidden Inlet in seven fathoms, soft bottom. One mile southwest of the entrance to Winter Inlet, Wales Passage runs south for four miles to Portland Inlet. There is a temporary anchorage in Manzanita Cove, Wales Island, in the little cove just west of Swaine Point in seven fathoms, but limited protection. The best anchorage on Wales Island is in Wales Harbour, five miles southwest of Wales Passage. Anchorage is in 11 fathoms, on mud, at the head of the inlet.

Another anchorage off Pearse Canal is in Regina Cove, Alaska, on Fillmore Island, in ten fathoms, mud bottom, and good protection.

*B.C. Parks: 604-387-0082, or B.C. Government Protected Areas, 612 Government Street, Victoria, British Columbia CANADA V8V 1X4. Another contact is Hugh Markides, District Manager, Skeena District, 3790 Alfred Avenue, Bag 5000, Smithers, British Columbia CANADA V0J 2N0.

Epilogue

If the reader is one of those few fortunate people who will visit the waters that have been described in this book, I hope that you enjoy them as much as we have. Writing and proof reading this book have enabled me to make one more mental trip along our beloved British Columbia Coast.

Appendix A: Important Notices

Disclaimer & Warning: Use of this publication implies acceptance of the following: **1.** Charts and maps are included solely for artistic and general information purposes. <u>Only government approved charts should be used for navigation.</u> **2.** Hazards, navigation information, and warnings are not an exhaustive and complete listing of such items, nor are they necessarily accurate for your travels, since weather, water, tides, currents, and wind conditions can vary widely from time-to-time and the precise location of your vessel cannot be accurately predicted for such purposes. <u>Only proper instruments and government approved publications should be used for navigation.</u> **3.** Although a good faith effort has been made to provide useful and helpful information, because of the ever present possibility of human or mechanical error by ourselves, our sources of information, or others, the publishers and editors cannot guarantee the accuracy or completeness of any information contained in this publication, nor assume liability for direct, indirect, or consequential damages resulting from errors or omissions. **4.** Since conditions can change rapidly, the author recommends using a current edition of *Northwest Boat Travel Guide* as a companion for information not available at the time of publication of this book.

Canada Customs CANPASS-Private Boats: Inaugurated August 17, 1995, the CANPASS-Private Boats Program allows *pre-approved* boaters entering Canada to call ahead and receive clearance before leaving the United States. Permit holders report to a Revenue Canada customs office by calling 1-800-222-4919 at least one hour, but no more than two hours, before leaving for Canada from the U.S. After receiving clearance by telephone, boaters, who have a CANPASS, can dock at any marina in British Columbia, unless they are otherwise directed by customs officers.

Non-CANPASS participants will still have to call customs from a designated marina/moorage upon arrival in Canada (See below for locations).

How to apply for a CANPASS: The program is open to U.S. and Canadian citizens and permanent residents who have no record of criminal activities, or illegal customs or immigration activities.

Request a form by calling Revenue Canada at 1-800-222-4919. Forms can also be obtained at all Revenue Canada offices, Citizenship and Immigration offices, and at marinas in British Columbia. Return the completed version, along with photocopies of citizenship or residency documents, and a non-refundable fee of $25. Cdn. to the CANPASS Office at 28-176th St., Surrey, British Columbia V4P 1M7. The fee is collected annually.

The form will request the names of dependents and those who regularly travel with you. (If you ever have a guest who is not listed on your form, it will be necessary to check-in at a designated site.)

Permit holders will receive an authorization letter, a permit to use CANPASS-Private Boats, a non-transferable decal for the windshield of the vessel, and a small triangular flag for visual identification on the waterways.

*Because of an overlap, during which time the new program will be publicized and initiated, Revenue Canada has stated that, "boaters will be permitted to clear customs during 1996 by telephone from sites which, in previous years, have been designated as telephone customs check-in ports-of-entry". However, they also encourage all boaters to apply for a CANPASS.

*Note that these provisions are new and still evolving. For a fax of the latest information concerning both U.S. and Canadian customs requirements, call *Northwest Boat Travel's* Information Bank, at 1-800-354-2949, Ext. 520 (U.S. Customs Facts) or Ext. 521 (Canadian Customs Facts), from your fax machine and follow the instructions.

Designated Customs check-in sites for travellers without a CANPASS. Call Revenue Canada 1-800-222-4919 immediately upon arrival at one of these ports-of-entry:

Campbell River:
Discovery Chevron Dock
Discovery Harbour Marina Dock

Nanaimo:
Brechin Point Marina
Port of Nanaimo Yacht Basin

Port Alberni:
Port Alberni Government Dock

Prince Rupert:
Cow Bay Government Dock
Fairview Government Dock
Prince Rupert Yacht Club
Rushbrooke Government Dock

Powell River:
Westview Government Dock

Saanich Inlet:
Anglers Anchorage Marina

Sidney:
Canoe Cove Marina (Canoe Cove)
Port Sidney Marina
Royal Victoria Yacht Club (Tsehum Harbour)
Van Isle Marina (Tsehum Harbour)

South Pender Island:
Bedwell Harbour (May 1-September 30)

Vancouver:
Crescent Beach Marina (Boundary Bay)
False Creek
Steveston

Victoria:
Victoria Inner Harbour Customs Dock
Oak Bay Marina
Royal Victoria Yacht Club (Cadboro Bay)

Canada Customs requirements: Birth certificates or passports are required for persons bringing minors into Canada, and for the children entering Canada. This also applies to parents and their own children. In addition, persons bringing in children other than their own, also need a notarized statement from the parent having custody, authorizing them to take the child into Canada. Proof is necessary that the person signing the authorization has custody of the child. This could be in the form of a copy of a divorce decree granting custody. Lack of the proper papers could result in unnecessary delays or even being denied entrance into Canada.

Fuel that is in the vessel's tanks, wearing apparel, sporting outfits, and a supply of food appropriate to the nature, purpose, and length of stay in Canada can enter duty free. Pitted fruits, apples, pears, onions, and potatoes may not be imported. Each adult is permitted to have 40 fluid ounces of alcoholic beverages or 24 pints of beer/ale plus 50 cigars and 200 cigarettes and 2.2 pounds of tobacco for his own use. Owners of dogs or cats must have a certificate showing rabies vaccination for the pets within the last three years. Hand guns, automatic firearms, mace, and pepper spray are not permitted. Persons taking prescription drugs in the country should have them clearly labeled and carry copies of the physician's prescriptions or a from the physician describing the items and stating that they are necessary for the health of the person using them.

Customs-United States PIN Reporting System: Both Canadian and United States boaters entering, or re-entering, the United States, who been issued Personal Identification Numbers (PIN's), may use telephonic check-in prior to their departure from Canada, while en route to the U. S., or immediately upon arrival in American waters by calling **1-800-562-5943**.

If you have been issued a PIN, you may call from a cellular phone aboard your vessel, or land at any marina or port-of-call in the U.S. and use a touch tone phone ashore.

An interactive call processor will handle the call. Since reception of cellular phone signals varies with location of your vessel, you may need to keep trying the call as you get closer to the U.S. It will not work to call Roche Harbor, Friday Harbor, or other designated port. Only the 800 number above will work with your assigned PIN.

To satisfy Immigration requirements, boaters using telephonic check-in must have *completed I-68 forms for each person* (over 14 years of age) who is on board. If you would like a copy of the Immigration & Naturalization Service brochure describing the I-68 form and a list of the addresses of U.S. Immigration Offices where the forms are available, call *Northwest Boat Travel's* automated Information Bank at 1-800-354-2949 Ext. 544, from your fax machine and follow the instructions. The brochure will be faxed to you without charge. A boat without a PIN, or those requiring special documentation or inspection, must proceed to a Customs Port-of Entry. For more information about Customs Personal Identification Numbers, call 360-332-6318.

Note that the Customs Service has a random selection process to monitor telephone check-ins. If you are randomly selected, you will be directed to go to a designated port-of-entry to be checked through by Customs officials. For this reason, the Customs Service recommends that those with PIN's use telephonic check-in before or immediately upon entry, rather than after anchoring or docking in the U.S. Only the captain or designate is permitted to leave the boat until clearance is made.

United States Immigration Form I-68: Beginning in the summer of 1995, the Customs Officers at Roche and Friday Harbors have been "cross-designated" as Immigration Officers. Boats that are checked-in at a manned, designated port-of-entry are no longer required to have completed I-68 forms aboard, but boats using a PIN to check-in by telephone will be required to have the forms.

U.S. boats may be left in Canada temporarily: The owner must place the

Canada Customs Permit or telephone clearance number where it is visible from outside the vessel, and notify the marina operator of his home address and telephone. If the boat owner is unable to return before the permit expires, he may call Canada Customs for an extension and also ask the marina operator to post the new permit number of the boat.

Government/public floats in Canada: The status and availability of government-operated floats in Canada is changing, and their availability is uncertain. Information from the Department of Fisheries and Oceans in September, 1995, indicates that, during the next five years, 72 "recreational harbours" in British Columbia will gradually be offered for sale to municipalities, communities, private groups, and individuals. If not purchased and administered by another source, the docks and ramps will be closed to the public or dismantled. A "recreational harbour" facility is either a breakwater, ramp, wharf, or floats. See the annual copy of *Northwest Boat Travel* for the latest information.

Insurance coverage: Many United States boat policies designate Malcolm Island, or latitude 52, as the northernmost geographical limit. Generally, a telephone call to the broker or company will result in an endorsement for extended cruising. There is sometimes a nominal charge.

Canadian Coast Guard towing policy: The Coast Guard will tow boats only when commercial towing is not available, or when waiting for a tow could be dangerous. The tow would be to the nearest safe haven, where the owner can either arrange for repairs or a further tow. The boater requesting a Coast Guard tow must agree to waive all claims for damage, injury, or loss against the Coast Guard and its employees.

Canadian Coast Guard request regarding VHF use: All boats calling marinas must use VHF Channel 68 when south of Campbell river and VHF Channel 73 when north of Campbell River. Channel 16 use is ship-to-ship and ship-to Coast Guard only.

Seasonal Changes: Many resorts are seasonal or have seasonal hours. Memorial Day to Labor Day is high season. When travelling at other times, it is wise to call ahead to check on availability of fuel, provisions, and other services.

Environment Canada-Talk to a Weather Forecaster: The following services, using a touch-tone phone, are being promoted by Environment

Canada:

The WeatherSource: Talk to a meteorologist for $3.95 for the first three minutes and $1.50 for each additional minute. 1-900-451-7004.

The WeatherSource FAX: Dial in and ask for document 2000. Cost is $2.95 for the first two minutes and $1.50 for each additional minute. 1-900-451-3007.

The Weather Phone & Fish Hotline: Receive a recorded message of the latest forecast, weather reports, tides, and fishing info for $1.99 per minute. 1-900-451-6611.

Marine Weather Hazards Guide: This publication describes the general weather conditions of the three southern inner waters, Strait of Juan de Fuca, Strait of Georgia, and Howe Sound. It outlines how the topography affects local waters and how the warmer temperatures of summer affect the local wind patterns. To obtain a copy, contact the Pacific Weather Centre at 200-1200 West 73rd Avenue, Vancouver, British Columbia V6P 6H9. Request the Hazards Manual.

Weather Reporting Program- CPS MAREP: Participants in this rapidly growing weather reporting system are encouraging other boaters to become involved. Jointly sponsored by Environment Canada, Canadian Coast Guard Radio, and Canadian Power and Sail Squadrons, the program is interesting as well as educational, and most importantly, contributes to safe boating. Participants contact the Coast Guard and report their ships' names, position, sky condition, present weather condition visibility, wind direction, wind speed, and wave height. A MAREP weather participant must hold a Restricted Radiotelephone Operators Certificate (available through Canadian Squadron VHF courses), and have a licensed VHF radio. To become a participant, contact Environment Canada, Environmental Services Branch 200-1200 West 73rd Avenue, Vancouver, British Columbia. 604-664-9093.

RCMP Coastal Watch: Boaters are requested to help turn the tide against drug smuggling. To report any suspicious activity, or for more information, call: Comox area: 604-338-7241, Prince Rupert area: 604-624-3155, Victoria area: 604-380-6222.

Appendix B: Distance Chart Olympia to Prince Rupert

	Distance	Total
Vancouver (Brockton Point)	0	0
Pender Harbour	16	16
Westview	22	38
Lund	11	49
Squirrel Cove	10	59
Stuart Island	18	77
Green Point Rapids	18	95
Forward Harbour	13	108
Port Neville	12	120
Broken Islands	9	129
Cracroft Point	15	144
Alert Bay	10	154
Port McNeill	6	160
Port Hardy	20	180
Miles Inlet	22	202
Cape Caution	10	232
Egg Island (Entrance to Smith Sound)	5.5	237½
Dugout Rocks (Entrance to Rivers Inlet)	7.5	245
Safety Cove	10	255
Namu	20	275
Bella Bella	24	299
Rescue Bay	33	332
Klemtu	14	346
Butedale	40	386
Sainty Point	29	415
Lowe Inlet	15	430
Kumealon Inlet	23	453
Prince Rupert	33	486
Port Simpson	28	514
Kincolith	33	547
Stewart (Head of Portland Canal)	75	622

Appendix C: Non-commercial Radio Stations

CBC - Canadian Broadcasting Company

Location	AM Radio	FM Radio	Short Wave Radio
Vancouver	690	105.7	6160 KH2
Victoria		92.1	
Campbell River		104.5	
Sayward	630		
Port McNeill		92.7	
Alert Bay		105.1	
Port Hardy	630		
Bella Bella		about 90.0	
Prince Rupert	860		

Appendix D: VHF Marine Operator Channels

Appendix E: Weather Stations

Puget Sound to B.C. Border   WX-1 and WX-2 - Seattle

San Juan and Gulf Islands   WX-3 - Victoria and
                               WX-2 and WX-4 (21-B) Vancouver

Georgia Stait   WX-2 and WX-4 (21-B) Vancouver
                               WX-1 Comox
                               WX-3 Bowen Island

Campbell River to Yorke Is.   WX-4 (21-B) Discovery (Sonora Is.)

Yorke Island to Bella Bella   WX-1 Alert Bay
                               WX-4 (21-B) Holberg (N. Vancouver Is.)
                               WX-2 Calvert Island

Bella Bella to Ketchikan   WX-1 Swindle Island (Klemtu)
(Prince Rupert C.G.)   WX-2 Mt. Gil (Wright Sound)
                               WX-2, WX-4 (21-B) Prince Rupert
                               WX-2 Dundas Island

Alaska   WX-1 Ketchikan
                               WX-2 Wrangell
                               WX-1 Petersburg
                               WX-1 Juneau
                               NOAA Juneau 586-3997
                               (if you can't get a weather station)
                               WX-1 Sitka

Appendix F: List Of Charts
(m) = Metric

Chpt.	Chart No.	Scale	Title
1	L/C 3463	1:80,000(m)	Strait of Georgia-Southern Portion
1	3490	1:20,000(m)	Fraser River-Sand Heads to Douglas Is.
1	3491	1:20,000(m)	Fraser River-North Arm
1	3493	1:10,000(m)	Vancouver Harbour-Western Portion
1	3494	1:10,000(m)	Vancouver Harbour-Central Portion
1	3495	1:10,000(m)	Vancouver Harbour-Eastern Portion
1	3526	1:40,000(m)	Howe Sound
1	3534	Various(m)	Plans, Howe Sound
1	3535	Various(m)	Plans, Malaspina Strait
2	L/C 3512	1:80,000(m)	Strait of Georgia-Central Portion
2	3514	1:50,000(m)	Jervis Inlet
2	L/C 3513	1:80,000(m)	Strait of Georgia-Northern Portion
3	3555	Various	Plans in Redonda Islands, Loughborough Inlet and Vicinity
3	3538	1:40,000(m)	Desolation Sound and Sutil Channel
3	3541	1:40,000(m)	Approaches to Toba Inlet
3	3543	1:40,000(m)	Cordero Channel
4	3441	1:40,000(m)	Haro Strait, Boundary Pass and Satellite Channel
4	3442	1:40,000(m)	North Pender Island to Thetis Island
4	3443	1:40,000(m)	Thetis Island to Naniamo
4	3477	Various(m)	Plans in Gulf Islands
4	3537	1:20,000(m)	Okisollo Channel
4	3539	1:40,000(m)	Discovery Passage
4	3544	1:25,000(m)	Johnstone Strait-Race Passage and Current Passage
5	3545	1:40,000(m)	Johnstone Strait-Port Neville to Robson Bight
5	3546	1:40,000(m)	Broughton Strait
5	3564	Various(m)	Plans, Johnstone Strait
6	3548	1:40,000(m)	Queen Charlotte Strait-Central Portion
6	3551	1:40,000	Jeanette Islands to Cape Caution
6	3597	1:73,000	Pulteney Point to Egg Island
6	3727	1:73,584	Cape Calvert to Goose Island, including Fitzhugh Sound
7,8	3515	1:80,000(m)	Knight Inlet
8	3547	1:40,000(m)	Queen Charlotte Strait-Eastern Portion
9	3921	1:20,000(m)	Fish Egg Inlet and Allison Harbour
9	3932	1:40,000(m)	Rivers Inlet
9	3934	1:40,000(m)	Approaches to Smith Sound and Rivers Inlet

Chpt.	Chart No.	Scale	Title
9	3931	1:40,000(m)	Smith Inlet and Boswell Inlet
9	3552	1:50,000(m)	Seymour Inlet and Belize Inlet
10	3784	1:36,760	Kwakshua Channel to Spider Island and Namu Harbour
10	3797	1:18,275	Namu Harbour, Plans in Queen Charlotte and Fitzhugh Sounds
10	3785	1:40,533	Namu Harbour to Dryad Point
11	3781	1:36,396	Dean Channel, Cousins Inlet, Ocean Falls
11	3729	1:75,000	Dean Channel, Southern Portion and Burke Channel
11	3730	1:75,000	Dean Channel, Northern Portion and N and S Bentinck Arms
12	3720	1:41,110	Idol Point to Ocean Falls
12	3728	1:76,557	Milbanke Sound and Approaches
12	3710	1:18,853	Channels East of Milbanke Sound
12	3734	1:36,028	Jorkins Point to Sarah Island
12	3962	1:40,000	Mathieson Channel-Northern Portion
13	3738	1:35,768	Sarah Island to Swanson Bay
13	3739	1:35,574	Swanson Bay to Work Island
13	3740	1:35,467	Work Island to Point Cumming
13	3742	1:70,920	Otter Passage to McKay Reach
13	3743	1:73,032	Douglas Channel
13	3745	1:73,050	Gardner Canal
13	3772	1:36,225	Grenville Channel-Sainty Point to Baker Inlet
13	3773	1:36,517	Grenville Channel-Baker Inlet to Ogden Channel
13	3957	1:40,000(m)	Approaches to Prince Rupert Harbour
13	3958	1:20,000(m)	Prince Rupert Harbour
13	3964	1:20,000	Tuck Inlet
14	3711	Various	Plans in the Vicinity of Princess Royal Island
14	3719	1:18,300	Inlets on Campania and Princess Royal Islands
14	3721	1:18,300	Harbors on West Side of Pitt Island
14	3723	Various	Harbors on East Shore of Hecate Strait
14	3724	1:71,594	Caamano Sound
14	3737	1:77429	Laredo Channel
14	3741	1:72,860	Otter Passage to Bonilla Island
14	3746	1:39,100	Petrel Channel
14	3753	Various	Plans in Vicinity of Pitt and Banks Islands
14	3747	1:12,572	Browning Entrance
14	3927	1:77,800	Bonilla Island to Edye Passage
15	3790	1:25,000	Nass Bay
15	3956	1:40,000(m)	Malacca Passage to Bell Passage

Chpt.	Chart No.	Scale (m=metric)	Title
15	3909	1:10,000(m)	Plans Chatham Sound
15	3920	1:40,000(m)	Nass Bay and Alice Arm and approaches
15	3933	1:80,000	Portland Canal and Observatory Inlet
15	3955	1:12,000(m)	Venn Passage-Plans, Prince Rupert Harbour
15	3959	1:40,000(m)	Hudson Bay Passage
15	3963	1:40,000	Work Channel
15	3992	1:40,000	Approaches to Portland Inlet
15	3993	1:80,000	Work Channel
15	3994	1:40,000	Portland Inlet, Khutzeymateen Inlet, Pearse Canal

Photo Credits

Cover: Sea Snaps, Vancouver, B.C.

Anderson Publishing
B.C. Government
B.C. Ministry of Parks
Canadian Hydrographic Service
Cheryl Johnson
Gwen Cole
Iver Johnson
Jack Schreiber
Kelly Foss
Kelly O'Neil
Linda Schreiber
Lynn Mortensen
Shutter Shack, Prince Rupert
Stephanie Satter
Tourism Vancouver
Wilma Smith

Appendix G: Useful Information

Several questions may come to mind when considering a first trip to The New Frontier, the northern coast of British Columbia:

How much experience is necessary? In my opinion, it is not necessary to have years and years of experience. I do recommend taking a boat handling and navigation course from either the Coast Guard Auxiliary or the United States Power Squadron. Of course, you should have enough boating experience to feel comfortable running, docking, and anchoring your boat under adverse conditions, such as three to four foot seas and poor visibility. Unless you are very fortunate, you will probably encounter both of these. I don't suggest that you intentionally sail into such conditions, but you should be prepared to get out of them if they arise. If you have not done much anchoring, it would be a good idea to practice until you feel comfortable with the procedure in deep water. The area covered in this book has been formed primarily by glaciers, which explains the extreme depths of some inlets, over 1000 feet in many places, and over 2000 feet deep in a few spots.

How do you keep from getting lost? The answer is very simple — you must know exactly where you are all of the time. This means knowing your course heading, speed of your boat, travel time elapsed, and estimating the effects of wind, seas, and currents on your progress. You must be able to read and use marine charts, as well as plot course lines and headings, and have some experience in "dead reckoning" navigation. If the visibility is good, you will always have land in sight, usually quite close. You should be able to look at the islands and shore lines that you see around you, and identify them on a chart.

Before I lift the anchor to start a day's cruise, I select my moorage or anchorage for that night, planning to arrive well before dark, with one or two alternates, in case time or weather change my plans. I also get out all of the charts covering the route for the day, and make certain that I have drawn course lines and headings beforehand. I also check tides and when appropriate, currents that may be encountered. These are all posted for easy reference. I always calculate the mileage to various way points and estimate times of arrival, mostly for my own amusement, but they can be helpful in case of sudden fog or bad weather.

Should you cruise with other boats? While it may be advisable to make your first trip to wilderness areas as part of a group of more experienced boaters, it is also possible to travel alone. Although many people prefer to cruise with one or more companion boats all the time, we have always travelled alone, preferring to set our own schedules. If you do travel alone, it might be advisable, before traversing the straits and other large bodies of water, to ask someone who is crossing to accompany you. Often there will be a number of boats waiting to cross such waters and arrangements can be made the night before the crossing. Generally, boaters are a friendly and helpful lot, and finding a willing guide for a short duration will not be difficult. Several times we have escorted other boats across Queen Charlotte Sound, at their request, but only for a day at a time. In regard to traversing the straits, current issues of *Northwest Boat Travel Guide* include an article on "Crossing The Straits & Other Large Bodies Of Water".

I certainly believe that a diesel engine has a big advantage over gasoline. Not only are they safer, but the longer range of the diesel fuel is very important after you leave the Port McNeil / Port Hardy area. Fuel is now available at Dawsons Landing and Duncanby Landing in Rivers Inlet, Bella Bella, Bella Coola, Klemtu, Kitimat, and Prince Rupert. Conditions at Namu are uncertain, however fuel has usually been accessible. Butedale is scheduled to have a fuel facility in 1996, however the installation is not yet complete. I would check on availability of fuel before planning to travel there. Even if you have enough gasoline to reach these marine stations, you may well lack sufficient fuel for desired side trips or for emergencies.

We meet quite a few sailboats each summer, but they are usually under power, because of the difficulties of maneuvering in some of the narrow passages and the strong currents and head winds that are often encountered. Thus, making the journey in a sailboat may be enjoyable for sailors, but it does not necessarily alleviate the problem of refueling.

The cruise can also be made with a trailerable boat. It is possible to launch in Port McNeill or Port Hardy on the north end of Vancouver Island, or drive all the way to Prince Rupert to launch.

Whatever kind of boat you have, it is important to have it in good condition and to carry a rather extensive kit of spare parts. We carry spares for almost everything on the boat, including a spare head sewage pump, fresh water pump, bilge pump, impellers for all pumps, and a propeller. Parts for a particular boat are hard to find, even in the larger cities, and flying in spare parts can be expensive. We have a mechanic go over our boat each spring for both repairs and preventive maintenance, instead of waiting for something to break down.

What equipment do you need?

Anchoring system: We have found that the Bruce anchor has the best holding power for depths, mud, and weeds that you will encounter. An alternative would be some kind of "plow" anchor. The Danforth type anchor has a tendency to ride on top of grass and weeds and, unlike the Bruce, it will not reset itself. You will need enough anchor rode to be able to anchor in 10 to 15 fathoms. Fifty percent of the anchorages that we have used in northern British Columbia fall into this range. We use a 33 pound Bruce with 100 feet of 3/8 inch chain and 200 feet of nylon line. We have anchored satisfactorily in 20 fathoms in good weather. We have survived 50 knot winds anchored in waters as deep as 10 fathoms. Many fathometers have anchor alarms which can be set at night to avoid a live anchor watch. A spare anchor with rode should also be aboard. In current issues of *Northwest Boat Travel* an article on "Basic Boat Anchoring" describes anchor types, sizes, and rodes.

When anchoring, in addition to the usual precautions of making sure that we have enough swinging room to avoid other boats and hazards, I always take a turn around the anchorage, with an eye on the fathometer, before dropping the anchor. I also check the tide charts to see how much depth we may lose overnight. I always set the anchor watch on the fathometer before turning in for the night. We never stay on watch ourselves, but instead rely on having a good anchoring system, a fathometer with a depth alarm, selecting a well protected anchorage, and setting the anchor properly, including backing slowly down on it to set it securely.

Auto Pilot: We don't have one and have never missed having one. However, many boaters use them.

Batteries: We do not have room on our boat for a generator and, they are noisy nuisances at best. We get along well without one, even though we anchor and are without shore power for over 90% of our cruising. In order to be sure that we have enough electric power for the occasions when we are anchored or moored for several days, we have a bank of six large batteries and we charge them while underway with two alternators. If necessary, we can bring the batteries up with an hour or two of running the engine at anchor. This power allows us to keep our refrigerator at 40 degrees and our freezer at five degrees below zero.

Charts, tide, & current tables: We carry about 100 Canadian charts, but you can get along with a lesser number. In current issues of *Northwest Boat Travel Guide* there is a list of needed charts at the beginning of each chapter. There is also a list of charts needed for this cruise in Appendix F of this book. You should also have a pair of dividers and parallel rulers, and know how to use them.

The Canadian charts are excellent. Since Canada is now on the metric system, all of the new charts are metric. This means depths on the new charts are no longer in fathoms, but in meters, while, on the old charts, they are in fathoms.

If your boat doesn't have a chart drawer large enough to contain all of your charts, you will have the problem of stowing and retrieving them as needed. We have solved this by purchasing several large artist's portfolios made of very heavy paper or light cardboard. Most office supply or art supply stores carry them. Except on very large boats, with adequate storage space, it will be necessary to fold the charts and stow them according to location. This will make it easier to find the correct charts for the day.

Compass: Your compass should be compensated for magnetic deviation caused by your boat, and it should have an accurate deviation table. Our Furuno radar has an extremely accurate gyro compass incorporated in it. This is a big help for navigation.

Dinghy: A seaworthy dinghy is a necessity. A small outboard for the dinghy is a handy thing to have on board.

Fathometer: This is absolutely necessary. A spare one would be a good idea.

Licenses: Everyone who fishes in salt or fresh water in Alaska or British Columbia must purchase a license, sold at sporting goods stores. Be sure to pick up a copy of the fishing regulations.

Loran: We don't have Loran and I don't believe it is a necessity. Ninety percent of your cruising will be in close proximity to the shore.

GPS: See Loran

Magnifying glass: Helpful for reading charts.

Publications: The companion publication for this book is the current issue of the annual *Northwest Boat Travel Guide*. Over 2,000 ports, facilities, services, and anchorages, between Olympia and Skagway, are described and updated each year. For information, contact 1-800-354-2949, Ext 830. *Marine Atlas*, Volumes 1 & 2, and/or *Evergreen Pacific Cruising Atlas*. While not a substitute for detailed government charts, these reference charts and magnetic courses and headings can be helpful. There are cross hatches for each nautical mile.
Sailing Directions, British Columbia Coast (South Portion).
Sailing Directions, British Columbia Coast (North Portion).

Canadian Tide and Current Tables, Pacific Coast, Volumes 5 & 6, cover the waters from Puget Sound to Dixon Entrance.

If travelling north from the Puget Sound area, it is best to obtain all charts and publications before leaving. Armchair Sailor, in Seattle, Tanners Bookstore, in Sidney, and Nanaimo Maps & Charts have extensive collections of books and charts.

Radar: I personally wouldn't go past Port Hardy without radar. In fact, I wouldn't go anywhere without it. You almost certainly will encounter periods of limited visibility and there are many hazards along the way. Your radar can be very helpful, even in clear weather, in accurately measuring distances to shore, rocks, and other important points.

Radar reflector: This is required in British Columbia waters. It is a good idea to have at all times to help other vessels know that your boat is present under poor visibility conditions.

Radio, AM/FM: In addition to the numerous commercial stations, many Canadian Broadcasting Company and Alaska Public Radio Network stations can be picked up on an AM/FM radio. A list of these stations is in Appendix C of this book. These stations have news and weather throughout the day, and CBC has many nice music programs. If you can't get any local stations, and there are many places where it is not possible, you may be able to pick up remote AM stations, after dark, from Seattle, Portland, and several California cities. If you have a shortwave receiver, you can also get good reception on it from all over the world.

Radio, VHF: This is an absolute necessity and it must be in good working condition. Weather reports are broadcast only on VHF and SSB (single side band radios, used mostly at sea on the Pacific or Atlantic oceans). VHF 16 is the distress channel for emergency calling of boats and Coast Guard. A CB is not satisfactory. It has none of the above features and the range of legal CB's is very limited. Most boats don't use CB's, thus severely limiting your ability to get help in an emergency.

Except for remote inlets, almost all of the Inside Passage is now covered by VHF marine telephone stations and repeaters, putting the entire world of telephone communications at your disposal. A list of marine operators is in Appendix D of this book. To place a call, first select the appropriate channel for your location and listen long enough to be certain that no one is using the channel. Next, depress your "talk" button for about five seconds and release it. This should ring the operator. The operator will want to know your radio call sign and home port, the number that you are calling, and how the call is to be billed (collect, credit card, or a marine identification number - MIN). In Canada you can request "privacy", which means that your transmissions will be blocked out, but the incoming message can be heard by anyone listening in. If you have trouble communicating with the operator on a channel because of static, she may ask you to try another channel.

Radio, hand-held VHF: This is useful as a back up in case your ship's radio quits working or in case of an emergency causing you to abandon ship in a remote area. In combination with your ship's radio, a hand-held set is also useful to communicate with members of your crew who may go out in the dinghy or take a walk on shore.

Rope: We take an extra line for towing or being towed and lines of a variety of lengths and thicknesses for numerous purposes.

Space heaters: We have a Webasto diesel furnace and a separate system that uses the heat from the engine cooling system to blow hot air into the cabin. We use both of them nearly every day when we get farther north. We also carry a portable electric heater for those times when we have shore power.

Survival gear: Rachel and I have two full-length survival suits, but I realize that few boaters carry them.

Umbrella: A big golf umbrella comes in very handy.

How much time should be allowed? In my estimation, one month would be the absolute minimum to make a round trip to Prince Rupert and visit the inlets along the coast. Double this, and you have my recommendation. You obviously want to do some exploring, sightseeing, and maybe fishing along the way. You must also add in a few days for layovers due to bad weather conditions. Don't set deadlines, for that can get you into trouble when poor weather intervenes and you have your deadlines to meet. The mistake that most people make is to try to make the trip in too short a time. If you try this, you will see "everything and nothing" and arrive back in your home port exhausted.

What supplies and small items should you take along? Most supplies are available along the way. It would certainly be a good idea to have some emergency provisions, such as dry or canned food in case your planned supplies run low. If you have certain favorite foods and drinks, you may not find them enroute. A few gallons of bottled water might prove valuable, if you have a minimum size water tank on board, or in case your water becomes contaminated or acquires a bad taste or odor. We have a small 100-pound freezer in addition to a small refrigerator. Both run on either 12 or 120 volts. We start out with the freezer full of frozen foods and return with it as full of salmon as the bag limits will allow, if we are lucky.

If yours is a diesel engine, consider adding, and taking along, a fuel additive designed to prevent the growth of algae in the fuel. We have done this ever since we had a problem starting out on a long trip. The algae began to plug the fuel filters and the engine began running slower and then faster, as some of the contaminated fuel was sucked in. We solved it, after locating the algae in the fuel, visible in the Racor filter and having all of the fuel pumped out, "scrubbed" by running it through a series of big filters, and then returning it to our tanks. Fortunately we were near Naniamo, so we had the Naniamo Shipyard do the job. It is an expensive process and, of course, since it was our second day out, we were full of fuel. We use Biofor and have had no more trouble with fuel. For the winter lay-up we fill the fuel tanks and put in the additive.

It is also a good idea to carry plenty of fuel filters, because it may be necessary to change them often if you run into some contaminated fuel. It isn't always possible to find the filters when you really need them.

Since fuel is somewhat cheaper in the United States than in Canada, United States boaters will want to cross the border with full tanks, as well as with enough engine oil, oil and fuel filters, other lubricants, zincs, propellers, and spare engine parts to last for the entire cruise.

When we are preparing for a crossing where some rough water may be expected, such as in Queen Charlotte Sound, I always fill the fuel and water tanks, both because we may need the liquids and because the added weight will make the boat more stable.

Another item that we have found useful, is one of the many preparations that cause rain or spray to run off the windshield. These are available at all auto supply stores. It clears the corners that the wipers miss.

Also useful is a roller sunshade that can be attached to windowpanes with suction cups and pulled down to combat objectionable sunlight or glare. These, too, are available at some auto supply stores.

Since almost everything in Canada is weighed and measured with the metric system, some kind of metric conversion chart or tool might be handy. Lacking such a device, 3.785 litres = one U.S. gallon; one meter = 39.37 inches; one pound = 453.59 grams; one ounce = 28.350 grams; 70-degrees Fahrenheit = 20½ Celsius (centigrade); 50-degrees = 10 Celsius; 90-degrees = 32 Celsius.

What clothing do you need? In addition to the clothing you usually carry for more local cruising, you should put a greater emphasis on warm clothing and rain gear, including knee-high boots for going ashore. The distance between laundry facilities should be kept in mind when packing the clothes you wear daily.

What kind of weather can you expect? Whatever month(s) you make the trip, you can expect quite a variation in weather, both from place to place and from one year to another. You will almost certainly run into some cold and wet weather. North of Desolation Sound, the weather tends to be cooler, wetter, and foggier. You can also run into hot weather, especially in the confines of your boat while at anchor on a sunny day.

Because there are fewer severe storms in the summer months, wind is less of a problem than in fall, winter, and spring. You can't avoid winds completely. In the absence of a storm, winds are usually calm or light at dawn and increase throughout the day until sundown, when they drop again. This is especially true on clear days, when the sun will warm the land masses, causing up-drafts that bring in winds from the cooler sea. You will find this more prevalent in long inlets, where a funnel effect increases the velocity of the wind. If your course for the day takes you through waters where exposure to winds is considerable, it is a good idea to get as early a start as possible.

Pay attention to the United States and Canadian Coast Guard weather forecasts on VHF. They are available along most of the Inside Passage, except in remote inlets. A list of these stations and numerous repeaters can be found in Appendix E of this book. These reports are continuous, taped summaries and forecasts. In Canada, they are up-dated every six hours for forecasts and three hours for lighthouse reports of wind velocity, visibility, and sea condition.

In the late spring and early fall months, the probability of strong winds is higher than in late June, July, August, and early September. We usually plan to cross Queen Charlotte Sound after May 21, and to be south of Cape Caution no later than the 10th of September. May and June are usually the most fog-free months; August and September the foggiest. June, July and August are the warmest; August and September the best months for salmon fishing. For a first time cruise to Prince Rupert and back, I would probably choose June and July.

Where can we pick up guests? The following is a list of good pickup points with land or air access. All areas may be reached by float plane from Seattle, Vancouver, or Vancouver Island.

Campbell River: Access by car, bus, or regularly scheduled airlines from Vancouver.

201

Desolation Sound: Westview, Lund, or Okeover Inlet. Access by car, bus or airline. Refuge Cove access by float plane.

Port McNeill or Port Hardy: Access by car, bus, or regularly scheduled airlines from Vancouver.

Johnstone Strait & Adjacent Islands: Minstrel Island, Echo Bay, Greenway Sound, or Sullivan Bay. Access by float planes from Vancouver, Seattle, Campbell River, Port McNeill, or Port Hardy.

Northern B.C. Coast: Shearwater, or Bella Bella. Access by scheduled airlines from Vancouver or by British Columbia ferries.

Prince Rupert: Access by car, bus, airlines, Alaska or British Columbia ferries.

Where can we leave our boat while making a trip home? Big Bay Resort, Campbell River (Discovery Marina), April Point Lodge, Echo Bay Resort, Greenway Sound Resort, Sullivan Bay Marine Resort, Prince Rupert Rowing and Yacht Club.

What about Coast Guard, Customs, Fisheries, and Immigration boardings and inspections? In British Columbia, the Royal Canadian Mounted Police (RCMP) perform safety, documentation, and customs clearance checks instead of the Coast Guard. You may encounter a dark hulled boat with the word POLICE on it. These vessels belong to the Marine Branch of the "Mounties". The British Columbia coast is the only part of Canada where the RCMP has marine operations. If the Mounties come aboard, at sea or in a port, they will be checking your boat papers, customs clearance, personal identity, required safety equipment, personal flotation devices, fire extinguishers, and firearms. Canada has very stringent laws prohibiting hand and automatic guns, mace, pepper spray, and other protection devices. For weapons, you should have a permit, obtained when you cleared customs and the weapon must not be loaded or have any round or piece of ammunition in the firing chamber or anywhere else in the gun. Customs clearance information is found in Appendix A of this book.

Two of the most interesting RCMP boats are the new high speed catamarans, capable of speeds in excess of 30 knots. We have seen the first one launched, the NADON, several times, and have been boarded by her crew once. We have always enjoyed meeting these young men, and talking to them.

Canada Fisheries personnel may also approach your boat and ask to see your licenses and fish, whether or not you are fishing.

What about condensation on the boat? If you cruise in damp and cold weather, one problem that you will encounter is condensation of moisture inside your boat. For your comfort and preservation of your boat's interior, you need to battle this problem. When the windows are closed for warmth, boiling water will contribute significantly to the cabin humidity. We like to use instant potatoes and rice, and canned foods during such weather. While cooking, we try to open windows, doors, and portholes to get cross ventilation, as much as we can. We also air out the boat whenever we have the opportunity and weather permits it. Cooking crab is a problem because of boiling and steaming. We use a large pot on a 140,000 BTU portable, single burner, propane stove placed outside on the deck to avoid steaming up the cabin. We use the same propane bottles to fuel a propane-fired grill on the deck for cooking fish, steak, hamburgers, and chicken. Having guests aboard can add to the moisture, because of breathing, body moisture evaporation, and running additional water. The heating system on your boat can help keep the air dry, or can contribute to the moisture problem. We use two heating systems. One is a Webasto diesel forced-air furnace. The other is a truck type heater that converts the engine's hot water into forced air for the cabin. One commercial item that has helped us with moisture under the bunk mattress is "Dry Bunk", a thin sheet of foam. Egg-carton type foam pads, placed on top of the mattress, also increase ventilation and add to comfort.

What about harvesting fish and shellfish? The waters we will be traversing are known for their good fishing. Even if you don't like to fish, they are an excellent source of fresh food.

Salmon and halibut are the most sought after fish. We use fairly light weight rods and 20-pound test line on Penn 206 reels, or 10 to 12 pound test line on spinning reels. Most salmon fishermen troll, many with down-riggers, but since our boat will slow down enough to troll only by taking it in and out of gear, we like to "drift fish", which means turning off the power and using some kind of jig. We have reasonably good luck using Buzz Bombs and Stingsildas for salmon. The same tackle can be used for all types of bottom fish, such as rockfish (often called cod, though they are not members of the cod family), lingcod (which is a ling and not a cod), greenling and halibut. The rockfish, lingcod and greenling are usually found on rocky bottoms. They are easy to find and catch.

Halibut: We use the same tackle for these, but we use large jigs. Halibut are usually found on flat, sandy bottoms. They are much harder to locate, as well as to land. You cannot use a landing net on a halibut over 15 pounds, or so, because, even if they would fit in the net, they would merely take the net out of your hands. We use a "flying gaff" which is attached to a stout line and detaches from the handle. Don't bring a halibut into your boat until you are sure that it is dead. They are incredibly strong and can do a lot of damage. Hitting them with a club is to no avail. I kill them by cutting their gills and letting them bleed to death. The blood supply flows through the gills of fish. I do this while the halibut is hanging on the outside of the boat.

Filleting is the only way to prepare bottom fish, including halibut. If you don't know how, try to get someone to show you. You will need a special fillet knife, and a solid board on which to do this job. It is not necessary to fillet salmon, but, in our opinion, it is the best way to prepare them. In British Columbia, the skin must be left on the fillets so that the species may be identified. Read the British Columbia Fishing Regulations. We store the filets in zip-lock bags in the freezer.

Crabs: Crabbing is a way to acquire some delicious food and have some fun in the process. The Dungeness is by far the most common crab, though there are some Red Rock crabs, but they have so little meat on them that they aren't worth keeping. There are two types of crab traps: the box and the ring. Be sure that you are using a type that is legal in the area where you are crabbing. Bait is the carcass of a fish that you have filleted or, better, the head of a salmon. A can of cat food that you have punched holes in is a handy substitute. I place the bait in a wire or plastic bait container, in the box type trap, or attached to a ring type trap. A float is then attached to enough line to reach the surface at changing tides, perhaps 50-feet. You must put your name on the float. I like to place the trap in 30 to 50 feet of water, in front of a stream mouth, where eel grass (a favorite crab habitat) is likely to grow. Consulting the tide table will assure that the tide will not rise enough to pull your float under water. I like to use a box type trap and I usually leave it overnight. If you use a ring type trap, you will have to check it every hour or two. In fact, that is not a bad idea no matter what kind of trap you are using. Check your catch for the legal size of 6½ inches across the carapace, from tip to tip. Only males are legal to keep. The females have a wider flap, or cover, on the bottom side. You will probably catch other creatures in your trap, including starfish. We have also caught two 10-pound halibut, several sand sharks, and, twice, sea urchins.

Shrimp or prawns: A prawn is a large shrimp. They are both caught in box type traps, with much smaller mesh. The same type of bait is used, but the trap must be placed in much deeper water, about 200-300 feet. This is why we have used our trap only once or twice. It a long and heavy job hauling up the trap.

Clams, Mussels, and Oysters: We like these shellfish, very much, but we no longer harvest them. The reason is the danger from Red Tide or PSP, Paralytic Shellfish Poisoning. The Canadian weather reports air warnings when appropriate, but we would rather not take any chances, especially when we are in some remote location.

What about commercial fishermen? Commercial fishing is an important industry throughout the Inside Passage. You are bound to see many of their boats during open fishing seasons. You will see three basic types of "fish boats", fishing for salmon:

Trollers: These are identified by the long poles, stored vertically when not fishing, and leaning overboard at about a 45 degree angle when fishing. They troll one or two lines on a side, with several lures per line, hauling them periodically. They are small 25 to 35 foot boats. Be careful not to pass too close astern of a troller.

Gill Netters: These small fishing boats deploy their up to 1200 foot nets about 30 feet deep, in a more or less straight line. The nets are supported by a string of floats or "corks", fastened to the nets and weighted down on the bottom, so that the nets hang vertically. The fish swim into the net and are trapped by their gills. The nets are hauled about every one to four hours. They are stowed on a drum that is located at either the stern or bow of the boat. A large red float marks one end of the net and the boat the other end. Sometimes the net is not fastened to the boat. In this case, there will be a red float at each end of the net. To avoid running over a net, fouling your screw and rudder and causing considerable damage to the net, for which you are responsible, you must first decide which direction the net runs from the boat. The best way to do this is to head straight for the boat. When you are close enough to see the small, usually white, floats, pass on the clear end of the boat. Gill netters often fish in large fleets. Going through such a fleet's nets can be like slalom skiing. Gill netters are the most difficult to avoid of all the commercial fish boats.

Purse Seiners: These are, by far, the largest commercial fishing boats, ranging from 40 to 100 feet in length and carrying crews of four to eight. Seiners are usually fishing for salmon, but at certain seasons they may be used for catching herring. The seines or nets are about 1200 feet long and are set 60 to 70 feet deep. In Canada, a drum is used to reel-in and store the net. This is not legal in Alaska, so there they bring the net in by using a block and tackle attached to the long boom. When a school of fish is located on the sonar, the net is set. First, one end is attached to a skiff. Then the "seiner" runs the boat in a circle, hoping to set it around the school of salmon. The net is payed out from the main fish boat until it is returned to the skiff, where the two ends are joined. In the water, the net is supported by floats and hangs vertically, because of weights at the bottom. The salmon are now "fenced in". Next, the "purse" is closed by pulling on the line which runs through metal rings on the bottom of the net. Finally, the net and the catch are hauled aboard the main fish boat.

Trawlers and Long-liners: These boats usually work off-shore, so you probably will not see them.

Shrimpers and Crabbers: If you see two large (usually red) floats, in deep water, several hundred feet apart, they probably mark a submerged line of commercial shrimp pots or traps. The pots are on the bottom, so present no hazard, as long as you avoid the floats on top of the water. In comparison, commercial crab pots are set in much shallower water than shrimp pots and usually have individual floats for each trap. Sometimes the upper part of a line may be floating on the water, near a marker float. Crab pot lines and floats can sometimes be a nuisance when you are trying to anchor in a bay that is full of them. You both have a right to be there, just be careful to anchor where you will not foul a trap or line.

Appendix H: Contact Information

AIRLINES
Washington-British Columbia
Kenmore Air: 1-800-543-9595
West Isle Air: 1-800-874-4434

British Columbia
Air Canada: 1-800-663-3721 (from U.S. 1-800-776-3000)
Canadian Air: 1-800-426-7000 (Canada & U.S.)
Coval Air: 604-287-8371
Harbour Air: 1-800-665-0212
Helicopters: 604-624-2792
Orca Air: 604-956-3339
Rainbow Air: 604-956-2020
Wag Air: 604-627-1955

CNG CYLINDERS
Campbell River: Chevron Marine 604-287-3319
False Creek ESSO: 604-733-6731
Fisherman's Cove Marina: 604-921-7333
Gibsons: Gibsons Marina 604-886-8686
Lund: Lund Hotel 604-483-3187
Northshore Marine: 604-980-2441
Port Hardy: Quarterdeck Marine 604-949-6551
Port Moody: Lee's Marine 604-931-2359
Prince Rupert: Apex Marine 604-627-7978
Richmond: River Marine 604-270-9455

COAST GUARD
Emergencies: 1-800-567-5111
VHF 16, 21-B, 22-A, 26, 71, 83, 84
Powell River: 604-485-7511
Prince Rupert: 604-624-4703
Texada Rescue: VHF 16 or CB 9
Victoria: 604-480-2600
Vancouver: 604-666-0146

FUELS
Desolation Sound:
Gorge Harbour Marina: Cortes Island. Gas, Diesel 604-935-6433

FUELS Continued
Manson's Landing: Cortes Island. Gas, Diesel 604-935-6361
Ragged Islands: Gas, Diesel 604-483-8184
Refuge Cove Store: West Redonda Island. Gas, Diesel

Discovery Islands:
Big Bay Marina: Stuart Island. Gas, Diesel 604-286-8107
Brown's Bay Petro Canada: Gas, Diesel 604-286-3135
Campbell River Chevron: Gas, Diesel 604-287-3319
Seaway ESSO: Discovery Harbour Marina: Campbell River. Gas, Diesel 604-287-3456
Heriot Bay Inn: Quadra Island. Gas, Diesel 604-285-3322
Quathiaski Cove Petro Canada: Quadra Island. Gas, Diesel 604-285-3212

Georgia Strait North:
Beachcomber Resort: Northwest Bay. Gas, Diesel 604-468-7222
Black Fin Marina: Comox Bay. Gas, Diesel 604-339-4664
Ford Cove: Hornby Island. Gas, Diesel 604-335-2169
French Creek Seafoods: Gas, Diesel 604-248-7100
Lasqueti Island Marine: Gas, Diesel 604-333-8846
Pacific Playgrounds: Oyster River. Gas, Diesel 604-337-5600
Salmon Point: Kuhushan Point: Gas 604-923-6605
Schooner Cove Resort: Gas 604-468-7691
Snaw-naw-as Marina: Nanoose Bay: Gas, Diesel 604-390-2616

Gulf Islands North:
Anchorage Marina: Nanaimo. Gas, Diesel 604-754-5585
Brechin Point: Nanaimo. Gas, Diesel 604-753-6122
Port of Nanaimo: Gas, Diesel 604-754-7828
Page's Marina: Silva Bay, Gabriola Island. Gas, Diesel 604-247-8931
Silva Bay Resort, Gabriola Island: Gas, Diesel 604-247-8662

Gulf Islands Southeast:
Active Pass Auto & Marine: Miners Bay. Gas, Diesel 604-539-5411
Bedwell Harbour Resort: South Pender Is. Gas, Diesel 604-629-3212
Saturna Point Landing: Saturna Is. Gas, Diesel 604-539-5725

Johnstone & Queen Charlotte Straits
Alert Bay Save On: Gas, Diesel 604-974-2161
Bear Cove Petro Canada: Port Hardy. Gas, Diesel 604-949-9988
Blind Channel Resort: West Thurlow Island. Gas, Diesel 604-286-8112
Echo Bay Resort: Gilford Island. Gas, Diesel 604-949-2501

FUELS Continued
Lagoon Cove Marina: East Cracroft Is. Gas, Diesel VHF Channel 73
Minstrel Island Resort: Gas, Diesel 604-286-8444
Quarterdeck Marine: Port Hardy. Gas, Diesel 604-949-6551
Seafood Products: Port Hardy. Gas, Diesel 604-949-2710
Shell Marina: Port McNeill. Gas, Diesel 604-956-3336
Sullivan Bay Marine Resort: N. Broughton Is. Gas, Diesel 604-949-2550
Telegraph Cove: Gas (Private) 604-928-3131

Northern British Columbia Coast:
Bella Bella Petro Canada: Gas, Diesel 604-957-2440
Bella Coola: Gas, Diesel
Butedale: New fuel facility under construction Spring 1995. Latest
    information call 503-397-5392
Cow Bay Petro Canada: Prince Rupert. Gas, Diesel 604-624-4106
Dawsons Landing: Rivers Inlet. Gas, Diesel N112785
Duncanby Landing: Rivers Inlet. Gas, Diesel 604-949-2101
Fairview: Prince Rupert. Gas, Diesel 604-624-6666
M K Bay Marina: Kitimat: Gas, Diesel 604-632-6401
Klemtu: Gas, Diesel 604-839-1233
Namu: Future status uncertain
Prince Rupert Chevron: Gas, Diesel 604-624-3316
Prince Rupert ESSO: Gas, Diesel 604-624-5000

Sunshine Coast:
Bathgate General Store: Egmont. Gas, Diesel 604-883-2222
Beach Gardens Resort: near Grief Pt Gas, Diesel 604-485-7734
Buccaneer Marina: Secret Cove. Gas, Diesel 604-885-7888
Egmont Marina: Gas, Diesel 1-800-626-0599
Hyak Marine: Gibsons: Gas, Diesel 604-886-9011
Irvine's Landing, Pender Harbour: Gas, Diesel 604-883-2296
John Henry's Marina, Pender Harbour: Gas, Diesel 604-883-2253
Lund Hotel: Gas, Diesel 604-483-3187
Ragged Islands Petro Canada: Gas, Diesel 604-483-8184
Secret Cove Marina: Gas, Diesel 604-885-3533
Westview/Powell River: Gas, Diesel 604-485-2867

Vancouver Island Southeast:
Anglers Anchorage Marina: Brentwood Bay 604-652-3531
Canoe Cove Marina: Gas, Diesel 604-656-5566
Cheanuh Marina: Becher Bay. Gas 604-478-4880
Goldstream Boathouse: Saanich Inlet. Gas, Diesel 604-478-4407
Mill Bay Marina: Saanich Inlet. Gas, Diesel 604-743-4112

FUELS Continued
North Saanich Marina: Tsehum Harbour. Gas, Diesel 604-656-5558
Oak Bay Marina: Gas, Diesel 604-598-3369
Ocean West: Victoria. Gas, Diesel 604-388-7224
Pedder Bay Marina: Gas, Diesel 604-478-1771
Sunny Shores: Sooke. Gas, Diesel 604-642-5731
Van Isle Marina: Tsehum Harbour. Gas, Diesel 604-656-1138

Vancouver Metropolitan Area:
Captain's Cove Marina: Ladner. Gas, Diesel 604-946-1244
Catherwood Towing: Mission. Gas, Diesel 604-462-9221
Coal Harbour Chevron: Gas, Diesel 604-681-7725
Coal Harbour ESSO: Gas, Diesel 604-681-3841
Coal Harbour Petro Canada: Gas, Diesel 604-681-6020
Crescent Beach Marina: Gas, Diesel 604-538-9666
False Creek ESSO: Gas, Diesel 604-733-6731
Fisherman's Cove: W. Vancouver. Gas, Diesel 604-921-7333
Lion's Bay Marina: Howe Sound. Gas 604-921-7510
Mosquito Creek Marina: N. Vancouver. Gas, Diesel 604-987-4113
Newman Creek Marina: Howe Sound. Gas 604-921-9636
Pitt Meadows Marina: Gas 604-465-7713
Pitt River Chevron: Gas 604-942-7371
Point Roberts Marina: Gas, Diesel 206-945-2255
Reed Point Marina: Port Moody. Gas, Diesel 604-931-2477
Richmond Chevron: Gas, Diesel 604-278-2181
Richmond/Sea Island Petro Canada: Gas, Diesel 604-276-2164
Sewell's Marina: Horseshoe Bay. Gas, Diesel 604-921-7461
Seycove Marina: Deep Cove. Gas, Diesel 604-9292-1251
Steveston Chevron: Gas, Diesel 604-277-4712
Steveston ESSO: Gas, Diesel 604-277-5211
Steveston Petro Canada: Gas, Diesel 604-277-7744
Sunset Marina: Howe Sound. Gas 921-7476
Vancouver Marina: Richmond. Gas, Diesel 604-278-3300

HOSPITALS
Alert Bay: 604-974-5585
Bella Coola: 604-799-5311
Campbell River: 604-287-7111
Chemainus: 604-246-3291
Comox: 604-339-2242
Courtenay: 604-339-2242
Cowichan District: 604-746-4141
Deep Bay: 604-339-2242
Ganges: 604-537-5545

HOSPITALS Continued
Kitimat: 604-632-2121
Port Hardy: 604-949-6161
Port McNeill: 604-956-4461
Powell River: 604-485-3211
Prince Rupert: 604-624-2171
Texada Clinic: 604-486-7525
Victoria: 604-727-4212

IMMIGRATION (U.S.) OFFICES IN B.C.
Sidney: Washington State Ferry Dock 604-656-1014
Victoria: 254 Belleville Street 604-384-1821

LAUNCH RAMPS / HAUL-OUTS
Desolation Sound:
Gorge Harbour Marina Resort: Cortes Island 604-935-6433
Lund
Okeover Arm Public Floats

Discovery Passage:
April Point Resort: Quadra Island 604-285-3621
Brown's Bay Marina: 604-286-3135
Cape Mudge Boatworks: Quadra Island 604-285-2155
Freshwater Marina: on Campbell River 604-286-0701
Ocean Pacific Marine Supply/Shipyard: Campbell River 1-800-663-
2294
Quadra Island: Quathiaski Cove, Heriot Bay, Rebecca Spit

Georgia Strait North:
Comox
Comox Bay Marina: 604-339-6153
Deep Bay
Denman Island
Fanny Bay
Ford Cove, Hornby Island
French Creek
Gillies Bay, Texada Island
Gravelly Bay, Denman Island
Little River
Miracle Beach
Schooner Cove Resort & Marina: 604-468-7691
Union Bay

LAUNCH RAMPS / HAUL-OUTS Continued
Gulf Islands Central:
Chemainus: Kin Park
Cowichan Bay
Crofton: Ferry Landing
Galiano Island: Montague Harbour Marine Park
Ganges: Boat Harbour: 604-537-5711
Ganges: Harbours End Marine 604-537-4202
Ganges: Salt Spring Marina 604-537-5810
Ladysmith: Government Floats
Ladysmith: Oyster Harbour Marine 604-245-8233
Ladysmith: Saltair
Maple Bay Marina: 604-746-8482

Gulf Islands North:
Anchorage Marina: Nanaimo 604-754-5585
Brechin Point Ramps
Degnen Bay: Gabriola Island
Gabriola Island: Silva Bay Resort 604-247-8662
Hammond Bay
Hub City Boatyard: Nanaimo 604-755-2000
Nanaimo Harbour City Marina: 604-754-2732
Nanaimo Shipyard: 604-753-1151

Gulf Islands Southeast:
Bedwell Harbour: South Pender Island
David Cove: Mayne Island
Lyall Harbour: Saturna Island
Otter Bay Marina: North Pender Island 604-629-3579
Piggot Bay: Mayne Island
Port Browning: North Pender Island
Potato Point: Mayne Island
Thieves Bay: North Pender Island
Village Bay: Mayne Island
Winter Cove Marine Park: Saturna Island

Johnstone & Queen Charlotte Straits
Alert Bay Shipyards: 604-974-5446
Bear Cove, Port Hardy
Beaver Harbour Park
Port Hardy
Port McNeill

LAUNCH RAMPS / HAUL-OUTS Continued
Northern British Columbia Coast:
M K Bay Marina: Kitimat 604-632-6401
Ocean Falls
Rushbrooke: Prince Rupert 604-624-9400
Shearwater Resort Hotel & Marina: 604-957-2305

Sunshine Coast:
Buccaneer Marina: Secret Cove 604-885-7888
Egmont Marina: 1-800-626-0599
Fisherman's Resort & Marina: Pender Harbour 604-883-2336
Four Mile Pt.: Sechelt Inlet
Gibsons
Halfmoon Bay
Hyak Marine: Gibsons 604-886-9011
Irvine's Landing: Pender Harbour 604-883-2296
John Henry's Marinas: Pender Harbour 604-883-2253
Lund
Lund Marine & Diesel: 604-483-9002
Madeira Marina: Pender Harbour 604-883-2266
Porpoise Bay: Sechelt Inlet
Roberts Creek
Saltery Bay

Vancouver Island Southeast:
Anglers Anchorage: Brentwood Bay 604-652-3531
Bazan Bay, Sidney
Boat Yard, The: Tsehum Harbour 604-655-1511
Cattle Point: Cadboro Bay
Cheanuh Marina: Becher Bay: 604-478-4880
Fleming Bay: Esquimalt
Goldstream Boathouse: Saanich Inlet 604-478-4407
Island View Beach
Mill Bay Marina: Saanich Inlet 604-743-4112
Oak Bay Marina: 604-598-3369
Pedder Bay Marina: 604-478-1771
Philbrooks Boatyard: Tsehum Harbour 604-656-1157
Roberts Bay
Shoal Harbour
Tsehum Public Wharf
Van Isle Marina: Tsehum Harbour 604-656-1138

LAUNCH RAMPS / HAUL-OUTS Continued
Vancouver Metropolitan Area:
Captain's Cove Marina: Ladner 604-946-1244
Cates Park: Burrard Inlet
Deas Harbour Marina: Ladner 604-946-1251
False Creek Yacht Club: 604-682-3292
Fort Langley: Fraser River
Kitsilano Beach: English Bay
Lion's Bay Marina: Howe Sound 604-921-7510
Lulu Island: Main Arm Fraser River
Lynnwood Marina: Second Narrows 604-985-1533
McDonald Beach: N. Arm Fraser River
Mosquito Creek Marina: N. Vancouver 604-987-4113
Newman Creek Marina: Howe Sound 604-921-9636
Pitt Meadows Marina: 604-465-7713
Pitt Polder: Pitt Lake
Port Mann Bridge: Port Coquitlam
Porteau Cove Provincial Park
Reed Point Marina: Port Moody 604-931-2477
Rocky Point Park: Port Moody
Sea Island: Middle Arm Fraser River
Seycove Marina: Deep Cove 604-929-1251
Shelter Island Marina: Richmond 604-270-6272
Skyline Marina: Richmond 604-273-3977
Squamish River
Steveston
Sunset Marina: Howe Sound 604-921-7476
Surrey
Thunderbird Marina: W. Vancouver 604-921-7434
Tsawwassen
Westham Island: Fraser River

LIQUOR STORES
Alert Bay
Bella Coola
Blind Channel Resort: West Thurlow Island
Brentwood Bay
Campbell River
Chemainus
Comox
Cortes Island: Squirrel Cove Store
Courtenay
Dawsons Landing
Duncan

LIQUOR STORES Continued

Duncanby Landing
Egmont: Bathgate General Store
Gabriola Island
Ganges
Gibsons
Gillies Bay Store
Halfmoon Bay
Heriot Bay: Island Market/Shopeasy
Kitimat
Ladysmith
Lund: Lund Hotel.
Madeira Park
Masset
Mill Bay
Miners Bay
Minstrel Island Resort
Nanaimo: Harbour Park Mall
Nanaimo: Mid-town (late closing)
New Bella Bella
Pender Harbour: John Henry's
Port Hardy
Port McNeill
Powell River/Westview
Prince Rupert
Qualicum Beach
Queen Charlotte City
Refuge Cove: Refuge Cove Store
Secret Cove: Secret Cove Marina
Sidney: Near shopping plaza
Sointula
Sturdies Bay
Sullivan Bay Marina Resort: N. Broughton Island
Vananda
Vancouver: Several locations
Victoria: Several locations

MARINAS / MOORAGE FLOATS
Desolation Sound:

Cortes Bay Public Floats
Gorge Harbour Marina Resort: Cortes Island 604-935-6433
Manson's Landing: Cortes Island
Okeover Arm: Malaspina Inlet
Penrose Bay Marina: Malaspina Inlet 604-483-2218

MARINAS / MOORAGE FLOATS Continued
Refuge Cove Store: West Redonda Island
Squirrel Cove: Cortes Island
Whaletown: Cortes Island

Discovery Passage:
April Point Resort & Marina: Quadra Island 604-285-3621
Big Bay: Public floats
Big Bay Resort: Stuart Island 604-286-8107
Brown's Bay Marina: 604-286-3135
Campbell River
Dent Island Lodge
Discovery Harbour Marina: Campbell River 604-287-2614
Discovery Marina: Campbell River 604-287-4911
Evans Bay: Read Island
Freshwater Marina: on Campbell River 604-286-0701
Heriot Bay: Public floats
Heriot Bay Inn: Quadra Island 604-285-3322
Owen Bay: Sonora Island
Quathiaski Cove
Surge Narrows Settlement: Read Island

Georgia Strait North:
Blubber Bay: Texada Island
Comox
Deep Bay
Denman Island
False Bay: Lasqueti Island
Ford Cove: Hornby Island
French Creek
Pacific Playgrounds: Oyster River 604-337-5600
Salmon Point: Kuhushan Point 604-923-6605
Schooner Cove Resort & Marina: 604-468-7691
Snaw-naw-as: Nanoose Bay. 604-390-2616
Squitty Bay: Lasqueti Island
Vananda/Sturt Bay: Texada Island

Gulf Islands Central:
Anchor Marina: Cowichan Bay 604-746-5424
Bird's Eye Cove: Maple Bay 604-748-3142
Bluenose Marina: Cowichan Bay 604-748-2222
Burgoyne Bay: Salt Spring Island
Chemainus

MARINAS / MOORAGE FLOATS Continued

Conover Cove: Wallace Island
Cowichan Bay Harbour: 604-746-5911
Crofton
Fernwood: Salt Spring Island
Fulford Harbour Marina: 604-653-4424
Fulford Harbour: Salt Spring Island
Gabriola Island: Silva Bay Resort 604-247-8662
Ganges Boat Harbour: 604-537-5711
Ganges Marina: 604-537-5242
Genoa Bay Marina: 604-746-7621
Ladysmith
Lyall Harbour: Saturna Island
Manana Lodge: Ladysmith 604-245-2312
Maple Bay
Maple Bay Marina: 604-746-8482
Montague Harbour Marina: Galiano Is 604-539-5733
Musgrave Landing: Salt Spring Island
North Galiano
Pier 66: Cowichan Bay 604-748-8444
Preedy Harbour: Thetis Island
Retreat Cove: Galiano Island
Salt Spring Marina: Ganges 604-537-5810
Sturdies Bay: Galiano Island
Telegraph Harbour Marina: Thetis Island 604-246-9511
Thetis Island Marina: Telegraph Harbour 604-246-3464
Vesuvius: Salt Spring Island
Whaler Bay: Galiano Island

Gulf Islands North:

Anchorage Marina: Nanaimo 604-754-5585
Degnen Bay: Gabriola Island
Inn of the Sea: Yellow Point 604-245-2211
Port of Nanaimo: 604-754-5053
Nanaimo Harbour City Marina: 604-754-2732
Nanaimo Shipyard Ltd: 604-753-1151
Newcastle Island Provincial Park: 604-754-7893
Pages Marina: Silva Bay 604-247-8931
Silva Bay Boatel: 604-247-9351
Silva Bay Resort: 604-247-8662
Stone's: Nanaimo 604-753-4232

MARINAS / MOORAGE FLOATS Continued
Gulf Islands Southeast:
Bedwell Harbour Resort: South Pender Island 604-629-3212
Hope Bay Store: North Pender Island 604-629-3423
Horton Bay: Mayne Island
Lyall Harbour: Saturna Point Landing 604-539-5725
Miners Bay: Mayne Island
Otter Bay Marina: North Pender Island 604-629-3579
Port Browning Harbour
Port Browning Marina: North Pender Island 604-629-3493
Port Washington: North Pender Island

Johnstone & Queen Charlotte Straits
Alert Bay
Blind Channel Resort: West Thurlow Is 604-286-8112
Camp Cordero Lodge: 604-286-8404
Double Bay Resort: Hanson Island 604-949-2500
Echo Bay Park
Echo Bay Resort: Gilford Island 604-949-2501
Forward Harbour Fishing Lodge: 604-338-6689
God's Pocket: Hurst Island 604-949-9221
Greenway Sound Marine Resort: Broughton Island 604-949-2525, 1-800-800-2080
Jennis Bay Marina, Drury Inlet 604-956-3781
Kelsey Bay
Kingcome Inlet
Lagoon Cove Marina: E. Cracroft Island VHF Channel 73
Minstrel Island
Minstrel Island Resort: 604-286-8444
Mitchell Bay: Malcolm Island
Port Hardy
Port McNeill: 604-956-3881
Port Neville
Quarterdeck Marina: Port Hardy 604-949-6551
Shoal Bay
Sointula
Sullivan Bay Marine Resort: N. Broughton Is 604-949-2550
Windsong Sea Village: Echo Bay 604-956-4005

Northern British Columbia Coast:
Alice Arm
Bella Bella
Bella Coola

MARINAS / MOORAGE FLOATS Continued

Cow Bay: Prince Rupert 604-624-9400
Dawsons Landing: Rivers Inlet N112785
Duncanby Landing: Rivers Inlet 604-949-2101
Fairview Harbour: Prince Rupert (Primarily for fishboats) 604-627-3127
Hartley Bay
Hunt Inlet
Kemano
Kincolith
Klemtu: 604-839-1233
M K Bay Marina: Kitimat 604-632-6401
Moon Marina: Kitimat 604-632-4655
Namu
New Bella Bella
Ocean Falls
Port Clements
Port Edward: 604-628-3211
Port Simpson
Prince Rupert Yacht Club: 604-624-4317
Rushbrooke: Prince Rupert 604-624-9400
Shearwater Resort Hotel & Marina: 604-957-2305

Sunshine Coast:

Bathgate General Store: Egmont 604-883-2222
Beach Gardens Resort & Marina: near Grief Point 604-485-7734
Duncan Cove Marina: Pender Harbour 604-883-2424
Egmont Village
Egmont Marina: 1-800-626-0599
Finn Bay
Fisherman's Resort & Marina: Pender Harbour 604-883-2336
Garden Bay Hotel & Marina: Pender Harbour 604-883-9919
Gibsons
Gibsons Marina: 604-886-8686
Halfmoon Bay
Hospital Bay: Pender Harbour
Irvine's Landing: Pender Harbour 604-883-2296
Lund
Lund Hotel: 604-483-3187
Madeira Park: Pender Harbour
Madeira Marina: Pender Harbour 604-883-2266
Royal Reach Marina: Porpoise Bay 604-885-7844
Princess Louisa Marine Park
Saltery Bay
Savary Island

MARINAS / MOORAGE FLOATS Continued
Secret Cove
Secret Cove Marina: 604-885-3533
Sunshine Coast Resort: Pender Harbour 604-883-9177
Tillicum Bay Marina: Sechelt Inlet 604-885-2100
Westview, Powell River

Vancouver Island Southeast:
Anglers Anchorage: Brentwood Bay 604-652-3531
Brentwood Inn Marina: Brentwood Bay 604-652-2413
Canoe Cove Marina: 604-656-5566
Cheanuh Marina: Becher Bay 604-478-4880
Fishing Fleet Docks: Victoria
Goldstream Boathouse: Saanich Inlet 604-478-4407
Inner Harbour: Victoria
Johnson Street floats: Victoria
Mill Bay Marina: Saanich Inlet 604-743-4112
North Saanich Marina: Tsehum Harbour 604-656-5558
Oak Bay Marina: 604-598-3369
Pedder Bay Marina: 604-478-1771
Piers Island
Port Sidney Marina: 604-655-3711
Rithet Basin: Victoria
Sidney Spit Marine Park
Sooke Harbour Marina: 604-642-3236
Sunny Shores Marina: Sooke 604-642-5731
Van Isle Marina: Tsehum Harbour 604-656-1138
West Bay Marina: Victoria 604-385-1831
Westport Marina: Tsehum Harbour. Limited moorage 604-656-2832

Vancouver Metropolitan Area:
Barbary Coast: Coal Harbour 604-669-0088
Bridgeport Marina: Richmond 604-273-8560
Captain's Cove Marina: Ladner 604-946-1244
Caulfeild Cove: W. Vancouver
Coal Harbour Marina: 604-682-6841
Crescent Beach
Crescent Beach Marina: 604-538-9666
Deas Harbour Marina: Ladner 604-946-1251
Delta Marina: Richmond 604-278-1241
Eastbourne: Keats Island
False Creek Yacht Club: 604-682-3292
Galbraith Bay: Bowen Island
Gambier Harbour: Howe Sound

MARINAS / MOORAGE FLOATS Continued

Halkett Bay: Gambier Island
Harbour Ferries: Coal Harbour 604-687-9558
Heather Civic Marina: False Creek 604-874-2814
Hopkins Landing: Howe Sound
Horseshoe Bay
Keats Island Settlement
Lion's Bay: Howe Sound 604-921-7510
Mission
Mosquito Creek Marina: N. Vancouver 604-987-4113
New Brighton: Gambier Island
Newman Creek Marina: Howe Sound 604-921-9636
Pelican Bay Marina: False Creek 604-682-7454
Pitt Meadows Marina: 604-465-7713
Plumper Cove Marine Park: Keats Island
Point Roberts Marina: 206-360-945-2255
Port Graves: Gambier Island
Quayside Marina: New Westminster 604-520-1776
Reed Point Marina: Port Moody 604-931-2477
Sewell's Marina: Horseshoe Bay 604-921-7461
Seycove Marina: Deep Cove 604-929-1251
Shelter Island Marina: Richmond 604-270-6272
Snug Cove: Bowen Island
Squamish
Steveston
Sunset Marina: Howe Sound 604-921-7476
Union Steamship Co. Marina: Bowen Island 604-947-0707
Vancouver Marina: Richmond 604-278-3300
West Bay: Gambier Island
Westin Bayshore Marina: Coal Harbour 604-682-3377

POISON INFORMATION

Alert Bay: 1-800-567-8911
Campbell River: 604-287-7111
Comox/Courtenay: 604-339-2242
Northern B.C. Coast: 604-624-2171
Powell River: 604-485-3211
Vancouver:604-682-5050
Victoria: 1-800-567-8911

PROPANE
Desolation Sound:

Gorge Harbour Marina Resort: Cortes Island 604-935-6433

PROPANE Continued
Refuge Cove Store: West Redonda Island
Squirrel Cove Store: Cortes Island 604-935-6327
Whaletown Store: Cortes Island 604-935-6562

Discovery Passage:
Campbell River Chevron: 604-287-3319
Heriot Bay Inn: Quadra Island: 604-285-3322
Quathiaski Cove Petro Canada: Quadra Island 604-285-3212

Georgia Strait North:
Comox Bay Marina: 604-339-6153
Gillies Bay Store: Texada Island

Gulf Islands Central:
Genoa Bay Marina: 604-746-7621
Maple Bay Marina: 604-746-8482
Thetis Island Marina: 604-246-3464

Gulf Islands North:
Brechin Point: 604-753-6122
Gabriola Island: Silva Bay Resort 604-247-8662

Gulf Islands Southeast:
Active Pass Auto & Marine: Miners Bay 604-539-5411
Bedwell Harbour Resort: South Pender Island 604-629-3212

Johnstone & Queen Charlotte Straits
Alert Bay Save On: Gas, Diesel 604-974-2161
Bear Cove Petro Canada: Port Hardy 604-949-9988
Blind Channel Resort: West Thurlow Island 604-286-8112
Echo Bay Resort: Gilford Island 604-949-2501
Lagoon Cove Marina: East Cracroft Is. VHF Channel 73
Minstrel Island Resort: 604-286-8444
Quarterdeck Marine: Port Hardy 604-949-6551
Port McNeill: Shell Marina 604-956-3336
Sointula
Sullivan Bay Marine Resort: N. Broughton Is 604-949-2550

Northern British Columbia Coast:
Klemtu: 604-839-1233
Namu (future status uncertain)

PROPANE Continued
Prince Rupert: ICG & Valley Oxygen
Shearwater Resort Hotel & Marine: 604-957-2305

Sunshine Coast:
Bathgate Store: Egmont 604-883-2222
Buccaneer Marina: Secret Cove 604-885-7888
John Henry's Marina: Pender Harbour 604-883-2253
Lund Hotel: 604-483-3187
Westview: 604-485-5232

Vancouver Island Southeast:
Canoe Cove Marina: 604-656-5566

RECOMPRESSION: 604-363-2379

RED TIDE INFO: 604-666-3169

REPAIRS / SERVICE
Desolation Sound:
April Point Resort: 604-285-3621
Boatland: Campbell River 604-286-0752
Cape Mudge Boatworks: Quadra Island 604-285-2155
Island Outboard: Campbell River 604-287-9248
Lund Auto & Outboard: 604-483-4612
Lund Marine & Diesel: 604-483-9002
Ocean Pacific Marine: Campbell River 604-286-1011

Discovery Passage:
April Point Resort: Quadra Island 604-285-3621
Boatland: Campbell River 604-286-0752
Cape Mudge Boatworks: Quadra Island 604-285-2155
Carmac Diesel: Campbell River 604-287-2171
Island Outboard: Campbell River 604-9287-9248
Ocean Pacific Marine: Campbell River 604-286-1011

Gulf Islands Central:
Harbours End Marine: Ganges 604-537-4202
Maple Bay Marina: 604-746-8482
Oyster Harbour Marine: Ladysmith 604-245-8233
Salt Spring Marina: Ganges 604-537-5810
Silva Bay Resort: Gabriola Island 604-247-8662

REPAIRS / SERVICE Continued
Telegraph Harbour Marina: Thetis Island 604-246-9511

Gulf Islands North:
Anchorage Marina: 604-754-5585
Dogwood Marine: 604-754-3261
Hub City Boatyard: 604-755-2000
Nanaimo Harbour City: 604-754-2732
Nanaimo Shipyard: 604-753-1151

Gulf Islands Southeast:
Active Pass Auto & Marine: Mayne Island 604-539-5411

Johnstone & Queen Charlotte Straits
Alert Bay Shipyards: Cormorant Island 604-974-5446
Quarterdeck Marine: Port Hardy 604-949-6551
Shell Marina: Port McNeill 604-956-3336

Northern British Columbia Coast:
Bill's: Prince Rupert 604-627-1601
Bytown Diesel: Prince Rupert 604-627-1304
Finning Tractor: Prince Rupert 604-624-3336
R G's Marine: Kitimat: 604-632-7722
Northern Tire: Prince Rupert: 604-624-9681
Shearwater Resort Hotel & Marina: 604-957-2305

Sunshine Coast:
Beach Gardens: Grief Point 604-485-7734
Buccaneer Marina: Secret Cove 604-885-7888
Lund Auto & Outboard: Mobile also 604-483-4612
Lund Marine & Diesel: 604-483-9002
Madeira Marina: Pender Harbour 604-883-2266
Tideline Marine: Mobile also Sechelt 604-885-4141

Vancouver Island Southeast:
Boatyard The: Tsehum Harbour 604-655-1511
Canoe Cove Marina: Canoe Cove 604-656-5566
Goldstream Boathouse: Saanich Inlet 604-478-4407
Philbrooks Boatyard: Tsehum Harbour 604-656-1157
Van Isle Marina: Tsehum Harbour 604-656-1138

Vancouver Metropolitan Area:
Lynnwood Marina: North Vancouver 604-985-1533

REPAIRS / SERVICE Continued
West Wind Marine: Point Roberts 206-360-945-5523

RESCUE COORDINATION
Search & Rescue: 1-800-567-5111
Marine Distress: 604-363-2333

SEWAGE DISPOSAL
False Creek Yacht Club: 604-682-3292
Nanaimo, Port of: 604-754-5053
Pelican Bay Marina, False Creek: 604-682-7454
Point Roberts Marina: 206-360-945-2255
Port Sidney Marina, Sidney
Van Isle Marina, Tsehum Harbour

VISITOR INFORMATION
Alert Bay: 604-974-5213
All Islands: 604-382-3551
British Columbia: 1-800-663-6000
Campbell River: 1-800-463-4386
Chemainus: 604-246-4701
Courtenay-Comox: 604-334-3234
Cowichan Bay: 604-746-4636
Gabriola Island: 604-247-9332
Galiano Island: 604-539-2233
Gibsons: 604-886-2325
Hornby-Denman Islands: 604-335-2321
Kitimat: 1-800-664-6554
Ladysmith: 604-245-2112
Maple Bay: 604-746-4636
Masset: 604-626-3982
Mill Bay: 604-743-3566
Nanaimo: 604-754-8474
Parksville-French Creek: 604-248-3613
Port Hardy: 604-949-7622
Port McNeill: 604-956-3131
Powell River: 604-485-4701
Prince Rupert: 1-800-667-1994
Prince Rupert: 604-624-5637
Quadra Island: 604-285-3322
Queen Charlotte City: 604-559-4742
Saanich Peninsula/Sidney: 604-656-0525
Salt Spring Island: 604-537-5252

VISITOR INFORMATION Continued
Sechelt: 604-885-3100
Sooke: 604-642-6351
Vancouver: 604-683-2000
Victoria/Oak Bay: 604-382-2127

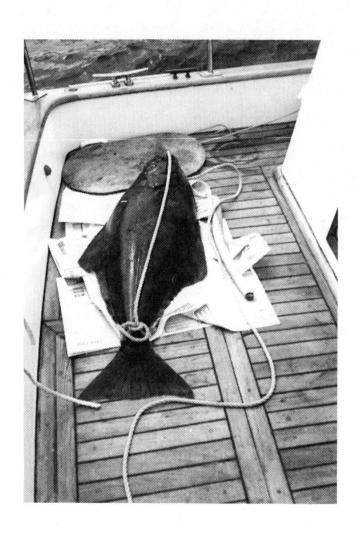

Index of Subjects, Facilities, & Places

227

Bibliography

Akrigg, G.P.V. and Helen B. *British Columbia Place Names*, Sono Nis Press, Victoria, British Columbia. 1968.

Akrigg, G.P.V. and Helen B. *British Columbia Chronicle 1778-1846*, Discovery Press, Vancouver, British Columbia. 1975.

Akrigg, G.P.V. and Helen B. *British Columbia Chronicle 1847-1871*, Discovery Press, Vancouver, British Columbia. 1977.

Anderson, Bern. *The Life and Voyages of Captain George Vancouver, Surveyor of the Sea*, University of Toronto Press. 1960.

Beautiful B.C. Vol. 30, No. 2, Summer 1988. Victoria, British Columbia.

Blanchet, M. Wylie. *The Curve of Time*, Gray's Publishing Company, Sidney, British Columbia. 1968.

Campbell, Kenneth. *North Coast Odyssey*, Sono Nis Press, Victoria, British Columbia. 1993.

Craven, Margaret. *I Heard the Owl Call My Name*, Dell Publishing Co., New York, New York. 1973.

Graham, Donald. *Lights of the Inside Passage*, Harbour Publishing Co., Madeira Park, British Columbia. 1986.

Kennedy, Liv. *Coastal Villages*, Harbour Publishing, Madeira Park, British Columbia. 1991.

Northwest Boat Travel Vol. 18, No.2. Anderson Publishing Co., Anacortes, Washington. 1995.

Ormsby, Margaret A. *British Columbia, A History*, Macmillan of Canada. 1958.

Rogers, Fred. *Shipwrecks of British Columbia*, Douglas and McIntyre, Vancouver/Toronto. 1973.

Rushton, Gerald A. *Whistle Up the Inlet*, J.J. Douglas, Ltd., Vancouver. 1974.

Sailing Directions, British Columbia Coast (South Portion), Vol. 1, 15th Edition. Department of Fisheries and Oceans, Ottawa, Canada. 1990.

Sailing Directions, British Columbia Coast (North Portion), Vol. 2, 12th Edition. Department of Fisheries and Oceans, Ottawa, Canada. 1991.

Walbran, John T. *British Columbia Coast Names*, Douglas and McIntyre, Vancouver/Toronto. 1971.

Woodcock, George. *British Columbia, A History of the Province*, Douglas and McIntyre, Vancouver/Toronto. 1990.

Log of Our Cruise & Guests

Log of Our Cruise & Guests